Herder & Herder welcomes Erin Lothes Biviano to our theological program. Dr. Lothes Biviano received her doctorate in contemporary systematic theology from Fordham University, where her research focused on the interpretation of religious symbols, and specifically, the paradoxical function of sacrifice as a model for Christian identity. This research is the focus of the present monograph. She also holds a master's degree in theology from Boston College and a bachelor's degree in English literature from Princeton University. She has served as assistant provost for academic affairs and associate director of service learning at St. John's University in New York, and is a charter member of the New Jersey Catholic Coalition for Environmental Justice. As a fellow of the Earth Institute of Columbia University, Dr. Lothes Biviano is associated with the Center for the Study of Science and Religion. Her research focuses on how religious congregations are taking leadership in environmental awareness and advocacy; results of this research will appear in a forthcoming Herder & Herder book on religious responses to the environmental crisis.

# THE PARADOX OF
# CHRISTIAN
# SACRIFICE

## THE LOSS OF SELF,
## THE GIFT OF SELF

### ERIN LOTHES BIVIANO

*A Herder & Herder Book*
The Crossroad Publishing Company
New York

The Crossroad Publishing Company
16 Penn Plaza – 481 Eighth Avenue, Suite 1550
New York, NY 10001

Printed in the United States of America on acid-free paper.

The text of this book is set in 11/15 Sabon.

**Library of Congress Cataloging-in-Publication Data**

Lothes Biviano, Erin.
      The paradox of Christian sacrifice / Erin Lothes Biviano.
            p.   cm.
      Includes bibliographical references (p.      ) and index.
      ISBN-13: 978-0-8245-2456-2 (alk. paper)
      ISBN-10: 0-8245-2456-X (alk. paper)
      1. Sacrifice – Christianity.  2. Feminist theology.  I. Title.
      BT265.3.L68 2007
      233 – dc22

                                             2007022169

1   2   3   4   5   6   7   8   9   10          12   11   10   09   08   07

*Dedicated to my mother,*
*Elspeth Anne Robinson Lothes,*
*A natural teacher*

# Contents

Acknowledgments                                                          ix

Introduction                                                              1

Chapter One
THE SACRIFICIAL NATURE OF CHRISTIAN LIFE                                  13

    I. Sacrifice and Religious Identity / 15
    II. First Christian Interpretation: Jesus Christ / 36
    III. Second Christian Interpretation: Application to the Disciple / 57

Chapter Two
THE FEMINIST CRITIQUE OF A DISTORTED IDEAL
OF SACRIFICE                                                              71

    I. A Hermeneutic Approach to Freeing the Symbol of Sacrifice / 74
    II. Critique of Atonement Theories as a Theological Justification
        of Victimization / 81
    III. Sources of Distortion in Sacrificial Discipleship / 97
    IV. A New Context for Sin and Transcendence / 109

Chapter Three
INTERPRETING SELFHOOD THROUGH GIVING
TO THE OTHER                                                             119

    I. Phenomenological Hermeneutics and the Hermeneutics of
        Self-Interpretation / 121
    II. Creation of Identity via Response to Otherness / 131
    III. An Ethics of Summons / 146

Chapter Four
SACRIFICE IN A CREATION CATECHISM                            154

    I. God the Creator / 161
    II. Concentrated Creation: Christology / 167
    III. Integrating Accepted Suffering into Christian Discipleship as
         Sacrifice / 182
    IV. Creation Faith / 199

Chapter Five
SACRIFICE IN THE IMAGE OF GOD                                207

    I. Retrospective Assessment of the Sources / 208
    II. A New Foundation for Sacrifice in Creation Faith / 215
    III. Renewing the Symbol of Sacrifice / 226

STUDY GUIDE                                                  233

NOTES                                                        237

BIBLIOGRAPHY                                                 271

INDEX                                                        283

# ACKNOWLEDGMENTS

I am indebted to many persons whose insight and support guided me during the writing of this book and made the process a fascinating and rich experience. I am especially thankful for having had the opportunity to begin this work as a doctoral dissertation under the direction of Rev. Leo D. Lefebure, who encouraged me to approach complex problems with respect for their ambiguities as well as their intellectual heritage. His scholarship taught me to value precision and depth as essential qualities of theological method, and his extraordinary generosity provided time for many valued conversations. I am also most grateful for the opportunity to learn from Elizabeth A. Johnson, CSJ; her scholarship sparked new questions that were fundamental to this work and suggested the tools with which to investigate them. The support of the Johnson Fellowship provided significant assistance and encouragement for the writing process. The insights of Daniel Speed Thompson also enriched my thinking in many important regards. In addition, I wish to thank the faculty of the Fordham University Department of Theology as a whole for presenting a model of the theological vocation as established upon both intellectual inquiry and a desire for justice.

Special thanks go to Kathryn Lilla Cox for her faithful and intelligent reading and questioning of many drafts; her companionship made this theological endeavor one both collegial and spiritual. My sisters, Katherine L. Walker and Alison E. Lothes, have been a unique source of self-understanding and humor, which contributed significantly to this work. I have also been blessed to be introduced to the love of intellectual participation in the Catholic tradition by my father, Peter B. Lothes, and my grandmother, Evelyn Brink Lothes.

I am indebted to my editor at Crossroad, John Jones, for his perspicacious guidance and gift for seeing to the heart of the matter as well as elucidating its fine distinctions.

I especially wish to thank Julia A. Upton, RSM, for her friendship and support throughout the writing of the book. This work would not have been possible without her support and that of the St. John's University community, whose values and integrity are a continual source of inspiration.

Finally, my profound admiration, thanks, and love go to my husband, Angelo, who invited me to begin the journey of theological study and whose daily life is to me, to David, and to many others a gift of sacrificial love.

# INTRODUCTION

*Then Jesus told his disciples, "If any man would come after me,
let him deny himself and take up his cross and follow me. For
whoever would save his life will lose it, and whoever loses his
life for my sake will find it."* —Matthew 16:24–25

In a short homily entitled "Whoever Loses Their Life for My Sake
Will Find It," Paul Ricoeur reflects upon the connection between the
identity of Christ and the identity of the disciple. This is the connection made in the difficult witness of Christian life. Ricoeur reads
Matthew 16:25 as a paradoxical proverb, perhaps originally from
the family of Ancient Near Eastern wisdom sayings, with the power
to reorient one's vision of human possibility in radical ways. "This invitation of the gospel to lose one's life 'for the sake of Jesus' has been
interpreted in many different ways across centuries, of course, and all
these ways are valuable to us because they constitute the treasure of
the universal Church's tradition." The spiritual interpretations of the
cited proverb, "placed under the sign of the *imitatio Christi,* all seek
in one way or another to make us participate as believers in Christ's
sufferings, through a life of sacrifice and letting go of self."[1]

The problem to which Ricoeur alludes — the fundamental relationship between sacrifice and identity for believers in Christ — is the
subject of this study. An interpretation of sacrificial symbolism for
Christian identity must acknowledge its often distorted history, but
may seek nonetheless to preserve the paradox uniting self-sacrifice
and self-realization. Aware of important critiques that question the
idealization of self-sacrifice and its potential for harm, I argue that
self-sacrifice remains a necessary part of Christian identity.

In many instances, sacrifice is instinctively affirmed as a natural expression of love. Parents sacrifice in countless ways for their children.
Ministers, teachers, and school coaches sacrifice personal time and
possibly more financially enriching careers to care for and educate
others. Women commonly sacrifice their own achievement by delay-
ing or relinquishing career plans for the good of their children, or
sacrifice personal interests to support a spouse's demanding career. A
man might give up great amounts of time and money to provide for
the comfort of a sick parent. Even more dramatically, the spouse of a
firefighter, soldier, or police officer shares the sacrifices of their service.

Then there are sacrifices that meet with nagging hints of misgiving,
perhaps shaded by understanding and regret, or marked by a stronger
unease. These draw forth an ambiguous range of emotional reactions.
By mortgaging the house, parents may sacrifice their retirement security for their children's college education. A doctor relinquishes the
free time needed for a personal life at the cost of his or her own relax-
ation and relationships. There are spouses and siblings who sacrifice
the expression of their own talents and achievements to prop up the
ego of an insecure but domineering relative. Adult children curtail
their independent choices for a demanding parent. The eldest son sacrifices his dreams for the family business. A father sacrifices his love
of performing music for a higher-paying job to support his family in
their preferred lifestyle. An intelligent woman submits to the physical
or emotional abuse of her critical husband because she does not value
or assert her independent aims as worthy of protection. In different
ways, these examples show how the claims of the other may sit in
uneasy balance with the desires of the self. Is sacrifice always holy?

The ambiguity of sacrifice contributes to its problematic nature
and status as a question for contemporary theological anthropology.
The use of sacrificial language must be clarified and justified; the
term "sacrifice" itself can have many meanings and many valuations.
Often used ambiguously in place of sacrifice are phrases that express a
changed, reduced self, even a damaged self: self-giving, self-emptying,
loss of self, self-denial, and self-abnegation. Each term seems to
have positive as well as negative connotations, for thinkers regard

them differently. The varied moral assessment applied to the vocabulary of self-loss (to choose one word among many) complicates the distinction between healthy and destructive sacrifice even more.

The idea of self-sacrifice is complex not only because it is subject to distortion, but because it involves a genuine inner paradox. The true paradox is the inner dependence between the two poles of self-sacrifice and self-realization. This is the mysterious dynamic at the heart of Christian wisdom in which outpouring love confirms genuine selfhood. However, this ideal is deceptively similar to a distorted prescription that overemphasizes sacrifice. In this prescription it is the contraction, not the outpouring, of oneself that is mislabeled as virtuous self-sacrifice. The resulting equivocal idea of sacrifice misrepresents the authentic ideal. Thus, the paradox can become equivocal in two ways, corresponding to the excess of one pole or the other. One example of such distortion is to exalt self-sacrifice to the point of denying that self-regard is a legitimate form of Christian love. At its worst, that overemphasis on sacrifice results not from an ideology of suffering or self-neglect, but from aggressive domination by another.

The Christian ideal of sacrifice originates in the radical call of the gospel to lose one's life to save it, to give up one's life for one's friends, to take up one's cross and follow Jesus. These radical and idealized exhortations exist alongside another command: to love one's neighbor as oneself. In Jesus' summary of the law and the prophets, the neighbor should receive the consideration one takes for oneself. Looked at the other way, the self deserves the same care as the neighbor. These juxtaposed sayings present paradoxical commands — to lose one's life, and to love one's self. Oliver O'Donovan observes that "the notion of self-love has never been long absent from Christian theology, and whenever it has returned it has brought its sheaves of paradox with it."[2] Two Gospel texts fundamental to Western Christian moral thinking and spiritual reflection have kept this paradox alive. The first is "you shall love your neighbor as yourself" (Mark 12:28 and parallels); the second is "whoever would save his life will lose it; and whoever loses his life for my sake and the gospel's will save it" (Mark 8:34). Both of these texts are central to my investigation, which seeks to heighten the paradox by conjoining the texts — how is the love of neighbor as oneself a way to save one's life by losing it?

## *Sacrifice as a Pervasive Theme in Christianity*

Sacrifice is a central Christian mystery with many expressions. The cross is the most fundamental and powerful symbol of sacrifice, a symbol that defines Christianity. The symbol of sacrifice in Christian theology can be understood as a complex of genres, including symbols, images, doctrines, theological reflection; the "witnesses and actions of the entire tradition."[3] The symbol of sacrifice, in this larger sense, includes the visible sign of the cross, the Passion narratives, the gospel command to take up one's cross, subsequent theological reflection on the meaning of self-gift, and the metaphorical expression of dedication and self-giving as "sacrifice." Theologically, the meaning of sacrifice poses a central question for soteriology, Christology, and Trinitarian theology. Sacrifice is also a mode of worship. Christians continue to experience sacrifice as a cultic ritual through the Eucharist. Sacrifice in its many expressions has major significance as a model for Christian life.

The idea of sacrifice is rooted in ancient cults, yet its contemporary theological meaning reaches far beyond cultic practice. The terminology of cultic practice has been radically transformed in both formal theological discourse and more general usage. The meaning of the original word has been transferred to indicate an interior dedication to the other expressed in ethical action. In this context sacrifice is an interior action, the dedication of self to God that is made incarnate through its expression in love of neighbor. Sacrifice involves a gift of self that may take many forms. At best it conveys love and esteem for the well-being of the other by a willingness to accept material or intangible losses — perhaps of time, convenience, or control. Sacrifice in this context, as a spiritual action, is what I mean by self-sacrifice. Sacrifice is an unavoidable aspect of human relationships, even those grounded in mutual love and respect.

Because of these many meanings, the study of the meaning of sacrifice requires both interpretation and limitation. Limiting the scope of the study is essential because the term itself opens out to many related concepts. This study is limited to sacrifice as the chosen and risky offering of self expressed in Christian life. As an exercise in contemporary theological anthropology, the present discussion does not treat the implications of sacrifice for Eucharist or sacraments in general; nor for Christology, soteriology, or martyrology. It does not address cultic sacrifice or sacrifice through a history of religions approach.

## Love of God, Self, and Neighbor

The rich texture of sacrificial language with its overlapping referents has long been noted. In the fifth century, St. Augustine observed that the language of sacrifice was part of religious practice that included reverence and consideration of persons, though it most properly meant that dedication owed to God alone.

> As not only the uneducated, but also the best instructed, use the word religion to express human ties, and relationships, and affinities, it would inevitably produce ambiguity to use this word in discussing the worship of God, unable as we are to say that religion is nothing else than the worship of God, without contradicting the common usage which applies this word to the observance of social relationships. . . . The common people, too, use it of works of charity, which, I suppose, arises from the circumstance that God enjoins the performance of such works, and declares that He is pleased with them instead of, or in preference to sacrifices.[4]

Religious practices, piety, and charity are described in sacrificial terms. Augustine writes that sacrifice expressed outwardly in action is the visible sacrament of the inner sacrifice. Inner sacrifice, or worship, spills over into the outward sacrifice which is love of one's neighbor. Augustine does not sever inner sacrifice from outer sacrifice, because God's presence among the human family unites individuals into one body. Because we seek to love God, we naturally seek to draw all those we love to that same source of blessedness.

> To Him we owe the service which is called in the Greek [*latreia*],
> whether we render it outwardly or inwardly; for we are all His
> temple, each of us severally and all of us together, because he
> condescends to inhabit each individually and the whole harmo-
> nious body, being no greater in all than in each, since He is
> neither expanded nor divided . . . to Him we offer on the altar of
> our heart the sacrifice of humility and praise, kindled by the fire
> of burning love.[5]

Sacrifice is a religious duty that honors God through praise and worship, and honors the presence of God in God's people by caring for
them. In this "harmonious body," care for the self does not compete
with the interests of the other. Augustine also mentions the care due
to oneself as to another, anticipating a contentious aspect of sacrifice
encountered in today's literature. Augustine's quest for God, which
is made concrete through the language of sacrifice, is cast as the philosopher's search for happiness. It is thus natural that the intellectual
soul will seek the highest good, and love it with all its heart.

> For, that man might be intelligent in his self-love, there was ap-
> pointed for him an end to which he might refer all his actions,
> that he might be blessed. For he who loves himself wishes noth-
> ing else than this. And the end set before him is "to draw near
> to God."

Self-love need not be an aggressive and perverse act of pride, but
expresses the wisdom of seeking the soul's only true fulfillment. The
Christian who follows the great commandment to love the neighbor
as oneself expresses this love not by denying the true desires of his
heart, but by leading the neighbor also to the love of God, to this
holy and uniting sacrifice. "And so, when one who has this intelligent
self-love is commanded to love his neighbor as himself, what else is
enjoined than that he shall do all in his power to commend to him
the love of God?" Despite the complex, occasionally severely negative
and often contradictory way Augustine refers to self-love, Augustine

is able to find in the contemplative inner awareness of self-love and self-awareness the very image of God.[6]

Augustine's reflection on self-love offers a historical perspective that shows the long association of sacrifice with love of God, love of neighbor, and love of self. Despite Augustine's pious and eudaemonistic identification of one's own good with the love of God and with sacrifice, sacrifice implies cost or difficulty. Sacrifice implies accepting a loss of one's own goals, time, or values, and so conveys a nuance of difficulty not conveyed in self-gift. Because Christian love is classically described as the imitation of Christ, whose death is venerated and interpreted traditionally as a sacrifice, reflection upon self-offering is not addressed satisfactorily as a separate, "ethical" idea of self-gift apart from the rich language of sacrifice that permeates Christian tradition.

## The Risks of Sacrifice

Criticism of the dangers of "sacrifice" has led some contemporary theologians to assert that we must seriously question, if not eliminate, the idea of "sacrifice" as a valued part of Christian life and identity. They charge that the risks of self-giving include a destructive loss of self, misuse of Christian imagery, and uncritical acceptance of an ideology of self-abnegation. Early feminists like Elizabeth Cady Stanton expressed suspicion of male praise for female self-sacrifice as the ideal virtue. Later thinkers such as Mary Daly called attention to a one-sided emphasis on self-abnegation and sacrifice in theory, and an imbalanced designation of women to accept the task of self-abnegation in practice. Feminists who analyze female psychosocial development make a strong case for women's predisposition to self-denial. Still, the power problem is not played out exclusively along gender lines. The son who is controlled by his mother into adulthood, or the elder sister whose habit of authority outlives childhood, demonstrate that power imbalances exist between men and may favor women.

Such criticism discerns acceptable from unwanted sacrifice, not assuming that all sacrifice is meaningful or pleasing to God. The criticisms of sacrifice in response to its exaggerated forms are central to the present argument. This critique provides a hermeneutic of suspicion that questions self-sacrifice and investigates its proper boundaries. Still, the critique risks distortion itself if it exaggerates an ideal of narcissistic self-fulfillment, portrays mutuality without conflict, or abandons the classic Christian language of sacrifice. To remove "sacrifice" from the Christian lexicon of life eviscerates the radical gospel message, and obscures a profound Christian insight that self-realization is often discovered in service and dedication to the other. Critics rightly reject the negative forms of sacrifice, but risk losing sight of the valuable contribution of sacrifice to self-realization.

## Preserving the Insight of Sacrifice

Both the idealization and the rejection of sacrifice frame self-sacrifice and self-realization as incompatible opposites, separating what is mysteriously united in the ideal paradox. A critical retrieval restores both self-sacrifice and self-realization in a balance of self-regard and other-regard. Commitment to the other should not destroy, but realizes one's own Christian identity. The value of sacrifice resonates in the relational contexts of religious life, friendship, marriage, experience of parenthood, citizenship, and membership in the earth community. Separating what is destructive from what is difficult may help to renew sacrifice as an important symbol of Christian life, and criteria for distinguishing "destructive" and "difficult" need to be developed. Initially, it can be said that these criteria should protect the fulfillment of one's vocation and values — but perhaps not always one's life. Christian witness does recognize the call for the ultimate sacrifice.

Revisionist theologies appropriately reinterpret the meaning of sacrifice to avoid oppressive usage and assure its relevance in the contemporary situation, but the idea of sacrifice should not be eliminated. The positive heritage of this tradition expresses an ideal of love which transforms the individual and the community into the Body of Christ. That language deserves to be preserved and renewed so that its depth is not discarded along with the problematic elements of sacrifice. Like any human act, an offering of self inspired by theological reflection on sacrifice is guided by interpretation, and so is also subject to confusion and distortion. The purification of sacrifice as a religious act circumscribing the identity of the believer is never totally complete. The liberating sacrifice of Jesus needs to be engaged and rearticulated for each generation.

The twentieth century has seen striking models of sacrifice. Dietrich Bonhoeffer, Mother Teresa, Gandhi, and Martin Luther King Jr. are among the most vivid faces of this century. Each is known for a sacrificial life that led some of them to a violent death. New arenas for the struggle of sacrifice emerge in our times. Globalization, nationalism, ecological destruction, and the technological transformation of life call for a new understanding of the costs and challenges of coexistence. Sacrifice is also needed for the well-being of the planet. Any realistic assessment of our situation must address the ecological devastation of exploitative consumption and the need for globally shared sacrifice. This message has been expressed as a religious and a moral issue by the 1993 Parliament of World's Religions and many other religious coalitions and leaders, including Pope John Paul II and Benedict XVI.[7] New ecological problems raise the question of how to view the earth as integrally bound to human identity, and thus sharing in the economy of sacrifice by which persons care for their children and community. The themes of identity and sacrifice intertwine. Sacrifice shapes Christian identity, and that identity leads in various ways to sacrifice.

## Outline of Chapters

To pursue a reexamination of self-sacrifice, I will engage the work of scriptural exegetes, of selected feminist scholars, of the philosopher Paul Ricoeur, and of the Catholic theologian Edward Schillebeeckx, OP. These thinkers share a concern for human liberation. They are part of contemporary discourse that has sought new ways to envision the self-in-relation that are credible today. Each attends to the impact of religious language upon identity, the risk that

that language can be distorted, and the subsequent need for hermeneutical principles and approaches. Indeed, they draw on each other as resources and discourse partners.

I begin by exploring what it means to describe Jesus' life and Christian life as sacrificial. Scriptural studies of how the early Christian writers used familiar sacrificial terms and symbols show how traditional sacrificial images and themes are transformed by Christian reflection into a profoundly new way to see sacrifice as a powerful symbol of God's reconciling love.

Chapter 2 examines feminist and womanist readings of theologies of atonement, love, and sin, and how they shape the model of sacrificial discipleship. Their work provides new ways of recognizing excessive loss of self, envisioning sin, and defending self-regard. The risk of self-loss inherent in sacrifice has been particularly well articulated by feminist theologians. Joanne Carlson Brown and Rebecca Parker critique theologies of the cross in specific relationship to feminist concern about women's tendency to accept a destructive loss of self. They contend that a specifically Christian ideal of sacrifice is distorted by religious language that sanctions the passivity, suffering, and violence involved in Jesus' sacrifice. Barbara Hilkert Andolsen contends that there is an imbalance in views of Christian love, and hence of sacrifice as an expression of love, resulting from assumptions within an inadequate theological anthropology. Her exposition provides the foundation for my analysis of the effect of theologies of Christian love on the interrelationship of self-sacrifice and self-realization, and provides a second look at agape that includes self-love. The last major feminist figure, Marjorie Hewitt Suchocki, critically examines assumptions about sin in a way that can illuminate its positive and negative correlation with self-sacrifice. She contends that imbalanced views of sin derive from the assumption that pride is the dominant mode of sin and contributes a theory of sin that is capable of judging when self-limiting is sinful. Constructively, she demonstrates how forgiveness opens self and other into a more fully realized relation.

As these thinkers probe the impact of weak attention to self-realization, they forge a cumulatively powerful critique and an invitation to right the balance. Equivocal teaching about sacrifice affects all persons who take seriously the task of Christian disciple-ship. Feminist consciousness asserts that the problem is magnified for women in particular, on whom the model of submissive service is cast by sexist societal pressures. Thus the already problematic and ambiguous question about right sacrifice is further warped by patriar-chally ordered social situations. In such contexts the need for careful interpretation is greater.

The necessary critique of the risks of sacrifice clear the ground to ask, how then does losing one's life lead to saving it? For this, in the third chapter I engage relevant work by Paul Ricoeur, who situates the problem of sacrifice and the self as the challenge of interpreting one's religious and ethical identity within the context of the other. Rejecting the immediacy posited of the "modern" self, Ricoeur grounds the identity of the self over time in commitment to promises made to the other. Ricoeur treats selfhood as a hermeneutical topic because of his conviction that human existence is fundamentally intersubjective, and that self-understanding requires a reflective detour through in-terpretation. One's identity is not transparently self-evident, but is interpreted through the experience of living within multiple relation-ships. Responding to the other, in turn, realizes our capacity to act. Self-realization, in other words, is discovered in the paradoxical pro-cess of surrender and self-creation involved in hearing the summons of the other.

Furthermore, for Ricoeur, the relationship of self and other is an equal relationship. One's self is also worthy of respect and whole-ness — oneself, in this sense also, *is* an other. This framework points to the potentially constructive — or self-realizing — effects of sacri-fice. The central elements of a hermeneutics of sacrifice inspired by Ricoeur include the constituent role of the other in one's selfhood, the equality and primacy of the self and other, and the fact of being summoned by the other. These three elements will structure my dis-cussion of Ricoeur's hermeneutical phenomenology of selfhood as a resource for the interpretation of sacrifice.

I will then research the theological anthropology of Catholic scholar Edward Schillebeeckx for a theological vision that complements the relevant elements of Ricoeur's philosophic framework (without attempting to document Schillebeeckx's specific study and use of Ricoeur). Schillebeeckx's work will guide my rearticulation of self-sacrifice in the following ways. His description of salvation as human wholeness, both experienced in the present and hoped for in the future, will provide a positive criterion for judging the value of any act of self-sacrifice. More specifically, his use of "negative contrast experiences" will show how suffering, either imposed by forces outside the self or even accepted in self-sacrifice for the other, protests against injustice and also reveals humanity's hope for full flourishing. Convinced that God wills to be Creator *for us,* Schillebeeckx advocates a hopeful response to suffering and finitude in a spirit of creation faith, which acts to bring about the reign of God.

The final chapter explores the deeper ground of the self-giving life of Jesus in the self-giving love of God as Creator. Contemporary theological interpretations of divine creativity as kenotic enable a vision of Christian sacrificial giving that is both in the image of Jesus and a reflection of God's sacrificial creativity.

These sources contribute to a critically self-conscious view of sacrifice that links the self and other, in expression of Christian identity. Changing oppressive structures into egalitarian relationships does not by itself remove the need for healthy sacrifice. Interdependence in this world of limited resources, fragile ecosystems, and finite time and space still calls for sacrifice. The challenge of self-sacrifice and self-realization may be worsened by cultural expectation and social oppression, yet the paradox is internal to Christian identity. Therefore, articulating a coherent Christian identity requires a creative and healthy way to understand sacrifice, rather than rejecting sacrifice as inevitably limiting or victimizing. Vital symbols for sacrifice guided by the Christian vision of communal life that are adequate to contemporary consciousness are sorely needed. Sacrifice is a necessary part of Christian identity and may be creative if carefully chosen by the self to express its commitment to discipleship.

Chapter One

# THE SACRIFICIAL NATURE
# OF CHRISTIAN LIFE

*If I then, your Lord and Teacher, have washed your feet, you
also ought to wash one another's feet. For I have given you an
example, that you also should do as I have done to you.*
—John 13:14–15

Sacrifice is fundamental to Christian life. Scripture writers and early
church theologians — and Jesus himself — used the language of sacrifice to describe Jesus' death. The symbolism of sacrifice was also
used to describe the life of the Christian who seeks to follow Jesus.
The language of sacrifice has an ancient power, yet its symbolism
and meaning must be reinterpreted for every generation and for every
Christian. The application of sacrificial language to the work of Jesus,
and by extension to the believer, is itself an interpretation which identifies the dedication to God shown by Jesus and his followers as a
sacrifice. While sacrificial imagery has shaped theological language
throughout centuries of Christian tradition, a sacrificial interpretation of Jesus or of discipleship is not inevitable. There are many ways
to understand the life and death of Jesus, and to envision the pattern of Christian life. More importantly, the vocabulary of sacrifice
is dangerous: sacrificial language has a potentially negative effect on
the integrity of personal identity, in the name of love for the other.
Awareness of these risks enables a critical hermeneutics of the central Christian insight of sacrifice and calls for a deeper investigation
of how identity relates to sacrifice, and to the other for whom one

sacrifices. These themes are relevant to the power and fruitfulness of sacrificial language for Christian identity today.

I do not intend primarily to address the question of the meaning or mystery of Jesus' saving work as a sacrifice — what it means or what it accomplishes. To bracket the question of soteriology from the main focus of theological anthropology is not to deny that the Christian community shares in the very life and death of Jesus through baptism and Eucharist and receives its identity from this communion. My question is rather how the believer is called to imitate Jesus and appropriate the experience of sacrifice in his or her life. I focus on interpreting the meaning of sacrifice for Christian life today. However, the question about discipleship begins with consideration of how the language of sacrifice has framed an interpretation of Jesus' life. Without that consideration we cannot see how or why sacrifice should shape Christian discipleship.

I employ three working definitions of sacrifice in this chapter: general, Christian, and existential. My working definition of sacrifice in its most general theistic sense is that sacrifice is an action that seeks to establish or transform one's relationship with the divine, often with a material offering or visible ritual, whose goal is the transformation of one's own religious identity. Exceptions to this general statement include Buddhist views of bloodless sacrifice in the form of generosity that are not understood in relation to the divine. For example, the Kutadanta Sutta teaches that the most perfect sacrifice is to practice morality and attain insight, but does not refer to this sacrifice as creating a relationship with a divinity.[8] Within a Christian religious framework, sacrifice means an act that responds to the encounter of God's grace in Jesus, and expresses one's dedication to God by caring for the neighbor. From a contemporary ethical perspective, sacrifice is understood as an act that is costly or burdensome, but needed as a means to an important end, and undertaken out of love for the other. This is the common, colloquial sense of "sacrifice" spoken of in ordinary life, separated from religious rituals. It may or may not be oriented to God religiously. The willingness to bear a burden or undertake a difficult act can express dedication to a larger, meaningful whole, even if not interpreted in explicitly theistic terms. For example, dedication to one's family, commitment to a cause, or concern for the good of humanity may inspire sacrifice.

In this chapter I will sketch how the religious significance of Jesus and Christian discipleship is expressed in the New Testament through the vocabulary of sacrifice. Understanding how sacrificial language describes Jesus in the tradition is necessary to identify how this language shapes Christian identity. For Jesus and the Christian believer, there is a dynamic relationship between sacrifice and identity mediated by symbolic language. The sacrificial language that describes Jesus and comes to be applied to the disciple takes up even older sacrificial symbols from ancient traditions. To analyze this dynamic relationship between sacrifice and identity I will first briefly explore some characteristics of religious sacrifice as studied from a history-of-religions point of view. Second, I will examine how New Testament texts identify Jesus with sacrificial images. Third, I will trace the association of sacrificial images with the disciple, and conclude with some contemporary reflection on the sacrificial nature of Christian witness.

## I. Sacrifice and Religious Identity

Before analyzing what sacrificial language means in relation to Jesus, it is helpful to consider the wider context of how sacrifice functions in relation to religious identity in general, as well as its meaning for the Hebrew prophets. Though the central concern is to identify how the language of sacrifice will describe the Christian believer, it is necessary first to explore a connection between sacrifice and religious identity in general, and then account for the application of sacrificial language to Jesus himself. The point we are moving toward is how early Christianity came to recognize the believer's life as sacrificial, precisely because the early movement had come to identify Jesus as a sacrificial offering, within a tradition that gave sacrifice a special religious meaning. As Frances Young has shown, Christian claims developed in particular ways as the experience of salvation found expression in different cultures. In the ancient Mediterranean world, sacrifice provided the most important religious images. Indeed, sacrifice was so widespread that the practice became synonymous with worship itself.

> Christianity was born into an age and culture saturated with religion, and if it is true to say that there is hardly a religion of man which has not involved the practice of sacrifice, this general statement is even more applicable to the period and culture in which Christianity grew up.[9]

Sacrifice was an inescapable aspect of religious life in the ancient world and constituted its chief form of worship.

In this religious milieu, Christianity had to come to terms with its Jewish religious heritage, confront cultural attitudes about sacrifice in the Hellenized Roman Empire, and articulate its own distinctive understanding of sacrifice. Even though Christians did not offer animal sacrifices, Christianity adopted the vocabulary of sacrifice for its worship, while continuing to revise the meaning of this vocabulary. One approach to understanding this distinctive approach involves what Robert Daly calls the "incarnational spiritualization of sacrifice" as the chief defining mode of Christian life.[10] This idea will be a guiding lens for the Christian reframing of sacrifice as worship that is made incarnate through love of neighbor, discussed in the second part of this chapter.

The spiritualizing transformation of cultic sacrifice in Christian experience takes its starting point from the radical monotheism of the Hebrews. Its more ancient roots lie in the widespread practice of sacrifice across human history. These remarks will provide the barest of contexts and set forth the vocabulary of sacrifice that shapes identity. The most important elements of that vocabulary express the realities of relationship: the self and the other; dedication to the other; the cost and healing of renewal. In this broad sense, sacrifice may be described as a widespread human impulse that affirms one's relationship to the divine with a visible action or offering, and seeks a transformation of one's identity before the divinity.

## Ancient Cultic Patterns of Sacrifice

*Sacrifice as a Means for Relating to the Divine*

Vivid examples of sacrifice are familiar from popular culture and reading history, yet often fascination with such practices belies how strange, even irrational, they can appear to a modern Westerner. Sacrificial rituals range from harvest celebrations, to simple offerings of oranges and incense before a home altar, to appalling images of humans disemboweled on top of Mayan temples. Child sacrifice, that most haunting of practices, figures even in the remote memory of the Jewish faith, as prophetic denunciations hint at offerings once widespread and now forbidden. Gravestones in the diaspora of the Roman Empire suggest that child sacrifice among non-Jews persisted until the second century BCE, and possibly later.[11] Ritual sacrifice endures in some cultures. Practitioners of candomble, Santeria, and vodun or voodoo offer animal sacrifices. There are present-day Samaritans who slaughter lambs to observe Passover.[12] In more personal terms, many can recall examples of childlike instinctive barter with God to plead for some good fortune and offer a tangible trade-in: "God, let my mother/brother/spouse get better and I'll give away my baseball glove/dollhouse/smoking habit." Is sacrifice fundamentally akin to a bribe, an ethical commitment, or a gift of thanks? What is the link between these widely divergent practices? Is there a shared inner logic or common impulse that defines sacrifice? While the purpose and experience of sacrifice vary greatly across cultures, at a very basic level sacrifice can be defined as a cultural and religious practice that seeks to forge or deepen a relationship with the divine. Sacrificial acts visibly express that sacred relationship and mediate personal transformation in relation to the divinity. Sacrifice hints at a deep human need to connect with God and communicate one's hopes and needs in a tangible, visible way.

*Theories of Sacrifice*

Within this overarching impulse to connect with the divine, ancient processes of sacrifice held many specific functions in diverse cultures.

There are many theories about the functions and origins of sacrifice. The term itself is derived from the Latin *sacrificium,* meaning "the action of making sacred (*sacer*)." As Victor Turner indicates, possible etymological origins include the Indo-European *sak-,* which means "to sanctify, make a compact." Related derivations include the Old Norse *sattr,* meaning "reconciled," and the Hittite *saklis,* a term for law or ritual. These may be cognates of *sacer.*[13] Theories of sacrifice include the evolutionist, diffusionist, functionalist, and structuralist schools. Each school focuses on a certain aspect of a complex total process, including "gift exchange, tribute, propitiation, penitence, atonement, submission, purification, communion, symbolic parricide or filiocide, impetration, etc."[14] Anthropologists and cultural scholars such as Henri Hubert, Marcel Mauss, Victor Turner, and René Girard identify several categories of sacrificial function: communion, thanksgiving, expiation of sins, and prophylactic sacrifice for social stability.[15] Each of these functions acknowledges the power of the divine over different aspects of life. Through different mechanisms, those who sacrifice seek to be in harmony with that power.

Sacrifices often intend to change the moral state of the sacrificer by means of the victim. Sacrifice may involve individuals or groups. It may involve offering a gift or immolating a victim. The aspects of sacrifice cannot be clearly separated and distinguished. In Turner's view, it is futile to attempt a chronology or phylogeny of sacrificial forms.[16] Daly concludes that the complexity of the ancient experience of sacrifice yields five ideas: gift, homage, expiation, communion, life released and transferred.[17] For Joseph Henninger, the term expresses the connotation of "the religious act in the highest or fullest sense," or the act of "sanctifying or consecrating an object."[18] While some scholars view blood sacrifice as the purest form of sacrifice — René Girard, for example, established his theories of religion and culture on blood sacrifice — there are numerous other forms of sacrifice, including firstfruits offerings of grains, fruits, milk, and alcohol. It is important to acknowledge the diverse forms of sacrifice, especially as sacrificial terms come to be applied to ethical actions without a tangible offering. Nonetheless, blood is a powerful element in the symbolism of sacrifice and a key to interpreting the logic of sacrifice.

Because religious persons recognize the power of the divinity over life, life itself — identified with blood — appears logically to be the most fitting offering. Blood gives life and flows at birth as well as death. Leviticus 17:10–12 declares:

> Any Israelite or any alien living among them who eats any blood — I will set my face against that person who eats blood and will cut him off from his people. For the life of a creature is in the blood, and I have given it to you to make atonement for yourselves on the altar; it is the blood that makes atonement for one's life. Therefore I say to the Israelites, "None of you may eat blood, nor may an alien living among you eat blood."

Leviticus 17:11 contains the most complete statement of the connection between blood and atonement: God has given the Israelites the blood of the offered creature to make atonement.[19] Blood was identified with life because it was believed to contain the living breath. Blood is sacred to God; it is the gift of life God has already given. To the ancient world, the blood of sacrifice was an appropriate part of a joyful event that served the deity with thanksgiving. Daly stresses that the actual death of the slaughtered victim means nothing, and effects nothing. It is the giving that matters, for which the death is needed primarily in an incidental or preliminary sense. The symbolic logic of blood offerings does not depend on death or on a symbolic substitution of the victim for the offerer. The blood atones because it contains life — not because the victim's blood or life substitutes for the life of another.

Blood was shed not as a vicarious punishment, but as a symbolic dedication of the animal in place of the person. The life in the blood symbolically dedicates the life of the offerer to God, and unites him to God. "The 'life' of the animal was consecrated to Yahweh (Lev. 16:8–9); it was a symbolic dedication of the life of the person who sacrificed it to Yahweh; it cleansed him of his faults in Yahweh's sight and reconciled him once more."[20]

It is important to distinguish between atonement and propitiation. Propitiation is an offering that tries to placate the deity and avoid its anger. Atonement is the process whereby the Creator restores harmony to the creature-Creator relationship. In Hebraic culture after the Babylonian exile, atonement was associated with the sin offering and holocaust, and especially the blood rite. Sin offerings became more prominent in a nation greatly sensitized to their collective sin and judgment. The sin offerings were not meant as a propitiation, an attempt to change God and stave off God's righteous anger. The sin offerings were a means given by God to take away sin and restore the covenant relationship. God is the true subject who reconciles the people to God; the means of doing so is the blood of the sacrifice offering. To the ancients, it was widely accepted that blood brings about atonement, but how it did so was never exactly explained. Frances Young hypothesizes that confusion between atonement and propitiation developed as Christians moved apart from their Jewish roots and were increasingly influenced by pagan ideas. As a result, the mechanism of expiation became overlaid with the somewhat more primitive ideas of propitiation and aversion, by which humans seek to change God.[21]

The bloody nature of ancient sacrifice that has always fascinated humanity still echoes in the term. However, even in ancient times a spiritual or existential meaning lay beneath the ritualistic details of sacrificial activity. It is this meaning of sacrifice as expression of dedication that is both preserved and changed in today's understanding of that term.

As an expression of commitment to the deity, sacrifice indicates a desire to share somehow in the divine life, however that is understood within the religious worldview. This may involve purification, forgiveness, or a desire for acceptance and signs of favor. As such, a key effect of sacrifice is to transform the individual's religious status before God. Sacrifice also transforms one's relationship to the community through incorporation or reconciliation.[22]

The classic work of Henri Hubert and Marcel Mauss, *Sacrifice: Its Nature and Function* defines the purpose of sacrifice as "to affect the religious state of the sacrifier or the object of sacrifice."[23] "Sacrifier" is a term that Hubert and Mauss devise to denote the one concerned with the purpose and effect of the sacrifice, as distinct from the priest, denoted as "sacrificer," who may offer a victim on behalf of the sacrifier. Diverse forms and purposes of sacrifice have a common procedure — "establishing a means of communication between the sacred and the profane worlds through the mediation of a victim."[24] The victim concentrates religious feeling, "expresses and incarnates" its dangerous energy, allowing it to be directed, absorbed, or expelled. The mediation of the victim is needed because the life forces are by definition awesome and powerful. The victim absorbs the peril, thus protecting the sacrifier.[25]

Sacrifices that remove sin or impurity transform the individual through the ritual and mediation of the victim. The victim allows the sacrifier to draw close to the god without actually yielding his own blood. The sacrifier abnegates and submits, through the offering of the sacrifice, in order to receive favor from the gods. Such sacrifices, though contractual and perhaps temporary, affect the agent's religious state, and express his or her religious identity and desire to attain a certain new form of religious identity.

Hubert and Mauss's reductive interpretation of sacrifice makes sacrifice the mainstay of a religious-force barter system. This system centers on the sacrifier and his or her needs.[26] It is a closed cycle about the sacrifier. The character and identity of the divine is dimly specified. The holy exists as the larger numinous background toward which the sacrifier directs his sacrificial transactions, of which he is the prime beneficiary. Frances Young notes the transactional quality of such sacrifices. She describes such votive offerings, extremely common in the ancient and pagan world, as bribes that obligate the gods to grant the petitioner their request.[27] This contrasts sharply with a focus on the transforming effect of sacrifice upon religious identity.

## Transformation of Identity through Sacrifice

Sacrifice is a social institution as well as a dynamic that shapes individual identity. Sacrificial practices function as a social institution that organizes customs, values, concepts, social forms, and public religious practice. Yet Victor Turner believes that the ambiguity of sacrifice is not adequately explained by reducing it to the mechanisms of society, or to human manipulation of the deity.[28] Sacrifices do not create a sacred state in the subject out of nothing, through contact with the victim; they heighten a sacred character that is already present.[29] Working with an anthropological methodology, Turner primarily approaches sacrifice as a social practice and interprets sacrifice as effecting a mutual transformation among the community.[30] Still, he acknowledges that one form of sacrifice is internal sacrifice, "the inward offering of oneself or something one deeply cherishes to God, the God, or other transcendental beings or powers."[31] Here again, the idea of dedication appears.

Turner divides the many forms of sacrifice into roughly two types. One model, the "sacrifice of prophylactics," is a mechanism of self-interest. This model applies to the cultic process described by Hubert and Mauss, in which a victim or offering mediates the agents' petitions to the gods in what appears to be a barter system of offerings and favors. The second model, or sacrifice that resolves conflict and restores community harmony, is the "sacrifice of abandonment." The sacrifice of abandonment dissolves hierarchical structures, abandoning mundane power in order to access the flow of divine power that resolves community conflicts.[32] This model of sacrifice includes the process of sin, redemption, and atonement, which fundamentally expresses divine action, not human petition.

Interestingly, Turner chooses to use suggestively Christian language to label the two models of sacrifice. He attributes the motivations of sacrifice to membership in either an "earthly city," or a "heavenly city." The assignation of citizenship depends on whether disinterested or manipulative motives are applied to the sacrificer. "One destructures, the other restructures, soul and city. Both renew, both respond to the human condition, oscillant and liminal between the Visible and the Invisible, the Many and the One."[33] The abandonment model probes a dynamic of self and other mediated by sacrifice, similar to

the self-renunciation of later Christian ideas of sacrifice. "Renunciatory sacrifices stress the interiority of the act; prophylactic sacrifices,
the performative, institutionalized details."[34] The sacrifice of abandonment allows divine power to flow, transforming the identity of
individuals, joining them to their God, and healing communities.
The mysterious dynamic of unity and transformation between individual and larger societies or powers is a recurring characteristic of
sacrifice.

The poles of abandonment and prophylactics mark the range
of sacrificial experiences. "At one pole, self is immolated for the
other; at the opposite pole, the other is immolated for self." Turner's
dichotomy of the sacrifice of prophylaxis and the sacrifice of abandonment offers a framework for identifying models of sacrifice that
center upon communal and individual transformation. The model
is somewhat fluid and simplified. As I shall show, the Hebrew model
of sacrifice combines performance and interiority, without necessarily
viewing the performance of a cultic sacrifice as manipulative or as de-
void of renunciatory character. Still, as a schema of sacrifice, Turner's
perception bridges a reductionist view of sacrifice and a theological
vision oriented to God. In addition to terms of petition and barter, the
vocabulary of sacrifice thus speaks of the individual, the community,
transformation, and new identity.

Sacrifice thus contributes in an important way to religious identity.
This is true not simply as a habitual practice or a characteristic cus-
tom of one's culture. As an expression of commitment to the deity,
sacrifice indicates a desire to share in divine life, however that is
understood within the religious worldview. When viewed existen-
tially beyond a sociological perspective, sacrifice has meaning not
only as a public action, but as a reality that shapes the life and
role of the initiate. The connection of religious identity and sacrifice shows that a fundamental impulse of sacrifice is to affirm one's
relationship with the divine and to accept a transformation of one's
religious identity as the consequence of that relationship. Sacrifice
is a means of effecting and expressing that sacred relationship and
personal transformation.

## Hebrew Renewal of Sacrifice

The origin of Christian understandings of sacrifice lies within the Hebrew religion and prophetic tradition. Israel's religious identity was
marked by enduring sacrificial practices, and also by changing interpretations of sacrifice. The prophetic critique of sacrifice in Hebrew
monotheism flowed from their reverence of God's justice, identified
obedience as the essential element of sacrifice, and was reinforced by
a philosophical critique. In the Hebrew religious worldview, religious
identity is formed by faith in one transcendent God who liberates his
chosen people, makes a covenant with this people, establishes the law
and the cult, and enjoins them to justice. Israel's sacrifice meant to
honor the transcendent God who cannot be bribed by material offerings. The prophets rejected a manipulative, self-directed mode of
sacrifice as idolatry. In time, material offerings are displaced from the
center of the sacrificial act. Jesus' own concern for justice and for the
inbreaking reign of God consciously reflects the prophets' thirst for
justice.

That the language of sacrifice evolves over time testifies to the importance of ongoing religious reflection on the meaning of sacrifice
in new contexts. The spiritualization of sacrificial language is an important reinterpretation of sacrifice and religious life that begins in
the Hebrew prophetic tradition. The formal, external activity of sacrifice is not the focus of reinterpretation. Rather, reformers attacked
treating sacrifice as *only* a formal, exterior act that excuses ethical
failure. The Hebrew prophets called for a more faithful observance
of the same sacrificial rituals to emphasize that these rituals were the
vehicle of religious veneration and righteousness, which could not be
omitted.

### Justice

Abraham Heschel reflects upon the interrelationship of justice and
sacrifice as part of the transforming relationship Israel experienced
with God, and thus underscores the characterization of sacrifice in
the previous section as establishing a relationship and transforming

one's identity. "The person was transformed, a communion vital to man and precious to God was established. In the sacrifice of homage, God was a participant; in the sacrifice of expiation, God was a recipient. The sacrificial act was a form of personal association with God, a way of entering into communion with Him."[35] God's righteousness is not a quality separable from God, or a moral code apart from piety, but "inherent in His essence and identified with His ways."[36] As the personal way of being of God, justice is not an abstract or immutable law, but a relatedness and concern for God's people that overflows with mercy. "Pathos, concern for the world, is the very ethos of God.... indeed, *righteousness wrapped in mystery, togetherness in holy otherness.*"[37] God's personal nature demands of the human partner in this relationship a true heart that is centered on the Lord and takes seriously God's concerns for the poor. Justice as the mode of a relationship with God transcends the individual's relationship with God. Justice is an interpersonal, community concern, and so sacrifice must foster right relations in the community.[38]

Revering God's justice, the prophets intuited that acceptance of sacrifice is not automatic. God may or may not accept an offering, depending on one's inner attitude.[39] This awareness formed the basis of a theology of the acceptance of sacrifice.[40] Jeremiah warns: "Do not trust in these deceptive words: 'This is the temple of the LORD, the temple of the LORD, the temple of the LORD'" (Jer. 7:4). The act of sacrifice is not effective of itself; the sanctuary does not issue automatic blessings. When God is understood as the champion and liberator of the poor, right worship requires living justly. True sacrifice comes to be seen as an act of obedience and of justice.

> What to me is the multitude of your sacrifices? says the LORD; I have had enough of burnt offerings of rams and the fat of well-fed beasts; I do not delight in the blood of bulls, or of lambs, or of goats.... Cease to do evil, learn to do good; seek justice, correct oppression; bring justice to the fatherless, plead the widow's cause. (Isa. 1:11, 17)

The prophets denounce empty and corrupt sacrifices and call for compassion. Hosea cries, "For I desire steadfast love and not sacrifice, the knowledge of God rather than burnt offerings" (Hos. 6:6). Amos's God overturns the sacrificial economy that manipulates the deity while scorning the poor:

> I hate, I despise your feasts, and I take no delight in your solemn assemblies. Even though you offer me your burnt offerings and grain offerings, I will not accept them; and the peace offerings of your fattened animals, I will not look upon them. Take away from me the noise of your songs; to the melody of your harps I will not listen. But let justice roll down like waters, and righteousness like an ever-flowing stream. (Amos 5:21–24)

## The Inner Sacrifice

The Israelites' developing awareness of God's transcendent justice was a key factor transforming Hebrew ideas about sacrifice.[41] The prophetic insight about the centrality of justice led to a turn to the interior of the religious subject, that is, to a focus on right sacrifice as the offering of the sincere intention of worship in one's heart. Awareness of God's transcendence prohibited attempts to manipulate God by human acts of sacrifice assumed to have unfailing efficacy. This theological insight is the basis for the Hebrew internalization of sacrifice.

The Hebrew critique of sacrifice insists that justice accompany sacrifice. "Love the Lord your God with all your heart and with all your soul and with all your strength and with all your mind" (Deut. 6:5); and, "Love your neighbor as yourself" (Lev. 19:18). These commandments charge the individual to realize his or her religious faith in action, among the whole community. As a consequence, the locus of true sacrifice shifts from the external act of the ritual to the internal spirit of the actor *and* his or her consequent sacrificial action. Terms and practices from cultic sacrifice's acts of violent slaughter and fiery immolation begin to refer also to inner, spiritual actions. The technical vocabulary of sacrifice took on a metaphorical meaning in addition to the literal referents, for sacrificial practices continued during the Second Temple period until the destruction of the Temple (70 CE).[42] For example, the phrase "sweet savour," used to express God's pleasure in an offering, increasingly alluded not so much to the holocaust smoke rising as to the sincerity of the worshippers' devotion. These shifts in meaning signal the reinterpretation of sacrifice.

Sacrifice was not rejected outright, but its practice is counterbalanced by a call for justice. The sacrificial system was never officially rejected in theory by unambiguous prophetic negation or rabbinic teaching. The prophets confirmed that God required service in the form of worship but refused to allow the sacrificer to neglect the care of the poor. However, the practice of Israelite sacrifice was abruptly terminated when the Temple was destroyed and never rebuilt. The contemporary Jewish theologian Jon Levenson also acknowledges that there is no religious reason why sacrifice should not be a part of Jewish life today, never having been repudiated — except that there is no Temple.[43] Diaspora Jews without access to the Temple had already shifted their attention to inner repentance. Repentance was the essential act for atonement, and where sacrifices were not possible, they were not essential.[44] Both Jews and Christians built upon the prophetic moralizing tradition, Jews because they no longer had (or have) the Temple, or lived in the diaspora, and Christians to support their spiritualizing movement.

The insight that true sacrifice is the contrite heart grounded the Hebrew internalization of sacrifice. This orientation toward obedience and sincere devotion became a foundation for both ancient and modern interpretations that interiorize sacrifice. This spiritualized orientation toward obedience and devotion later "established a theological principle by which Christians could look upon various activities of Christian living, and the Christian life itself, as sacrificial."[45]

## The Philosophical Critique

The spiritualization of sacrifice was driven not only by the Hebraic sense of social justice, but also by a philosophical critique. Pagan philosophers found overly literal language about God savoring animal flesh unworthy. The Platonic emphasis on the pure spirituality of the divine, understanding the holy as the unchangeable One, or Stoic dedication to an impersonal Providence, reinforced the interpretation of sacrifice as a spiritual action.[46] Jews, Christians, and Greeks influenced by these philosophers experienced a cross-fertilizing of these ideas in various ways. (Indeed, many Jews and Christians were Greek themselves.) At times practice lagged behind theory, as each group made compromises with the social and political customs that sanctioned sacrifices. These ancient wisdoms came to conclude, at least in their highest forms, that God did not need material offerings. The preference for good interior dispositions is reinforced by similar sentiments in Hellenistic culture, Jewish or pagan. Louis-Marie Chauvet cites Philo and Seneca as examples.[47]

One way both Christians and Jews sought to offer sacrifice that was pleasing to God, other than through acts of charity, was by fasting. In fasting they experienced a self-denial that offered up their abstinence without placing meals inappropriately before the transcendent God. Diaspora Jews encouraged the interpretation of sacrifice as an ethical stance, which they could justify using the prophetic language that at times suggested that God did reject sacrifice.[48] Christians would also cite parts of the psalms that appeared to denounce sacrifice: e.g., verse 17 of Psalm 51 — "The sacrifices of God are a broken spirit; a broken and contrite heart, O God, you will not despise" — while neglecting the following affirmation of sacrifice in verses 18 and 19: "Do good to Zion in your good pleasure; build up the walls of Jerusalem; then will you delight in right sacrifices, in burnt offerings and whole burnt offerings; then bulls will be offered on your altar."[49]

By the time of Jesus, the spiritualization of sacrifice in Judaism is evident in the *todah*. This term for a "sacrifice of praise" was also translated in the second century as a sacrifice of thanksgiving or Eucharist (*tes eucharistias thusia*). Thus, in Chauvet's words, " *'to make eucharist' is in the first place to confess God as savior; and this confession of thanksgiving has an immediately sacrificial connotation"* (emphasis in original).[50] In this liturgy, the emphasis shifts from the victim to prayer. Some groups, such as the followers of John the Baptist, dispensed with animal victims entirely.

The existence of the prophetic and philosophical critiques of sacrifice demonstrates how the meaning of sacrifice changed over time, even before the Christian era. Atoning sacrifice comes to mean inner piety as much as, if not more than, the material offering or action. To sacrifice rightly is to respond to the holiness of God with personal holiness, expressed by caring for the widow and the stranger. Sacrifice refers not just to the ritual act but also to the repentant motivation or purpose that is spiritual and internal, centering on sincere dedication to God and ethical actions toward others. The prophetic critique of sacrifice in Hebrew monotheism identifies obedience as the essential element of sacrifice, thus "spiritualizing" sacrifice without abandoning the material practice — until forced by circumstance.

## Transitional Crosscurrents

### Classic Symbols in Christian Settings

Early followers of Jesus lived in the crosscurrents of Jewish belief and new Christian convictions. To the ancient Hebrews, sacrifice belonged to a way of living that expressed their identity as the people of the law. This traditional understanding of sacrifice shaped the interpretation of Jesus as a sacrifice, and ultimately, the vocation of the Christian, in complex ways. In the early Christian period, the classic sacrificial symbols existed in a shifting matrix of development, appropriation, and criticism by Christian-Jewish, mainstream-Jewish, and separatist-Jewish sects. This mobile symbolic material is taken up by Christian evangelists and preachers in a unique way to form their interpretations of Jesus' life and death, guided by their new creed. These symbols include the binding of Isaac, or the *Aqedah*, the Passover lamb, the suffering servant songs of Isaiah, and the Maccabean martyrs. Another important development of Jewish views of sacrifice that I will address is Jesus' own view of the cult and Last Supper.

Former ideas of sacrifice exert influence in at least two ways. Traditional material can be determinative; that is, it provides details and shapes the emerging story positively. The influence can also be affirmative, as when a detail about Jesus calls to mind a pattern already known elsewhere in the tradition, which then reinforces the Jesus material. New experiences also revise the current assessment of one's inheritance from the past. Therefore it is not enough to ask how existing views of sacrifice and other non-cultic symbols of dedication and death (like the suffering servant and the Maccabean martyrs) shaped the interpretation of Jesus. For the early Christians, the life and death of Jesus impelled a change in their religious views of sacrifice. How did their experience of Jesus as a life-giving healer make it necessary to revise the meaning and interpretation of sacrifice? On the one hand, they viewed Jesus as a sacrifice in terms inherited from Jewish life. Sacrificial images play into the interpretive and reflective process by which the disciples respond to Jesus. On the other hand, their experiences will emerge in a new tradition that reflects on the meaning of sacrifice itself, as a religious activity. I will return to this question at the conclusion of this chapter.

The Binding of Isaac is a tradition which became known as the *Aqedah*. This Jewish symbol deserves special attention because it inspired new interpretations of the Passover lamb's expiatory significance and promoted the spiritualization of sacrifice: both key precedents in understanding Jesus as a sacrifice. A full *Aqedah* theology includes Isaac's willingness to suffer and God's acceptance of his trial as an expiation for future generations. Consequently, central to the theology of the *Aqedah* is the good will and full consent of a righteous victim. It is implied that the *Aqedah* is linked to historical deliverance, and its Haggadah is liturgically set in the Passover feast. The *Aqedah* teaches that Isaac's death expiates sin, although the Passover lamb is not technically a sin offering.[51] But after the exile, Israel had a renewed concern with expiation and added expiatory significance to other types of sacrifices. Bruce H. Grigsby affirms that by New Testament times, the paschal lamb was widely considered expiatory, and rabbinic thought encouraged extending expiatory significance to all sacrifices.[52]

The extent of the influence of rabbinic development of the *Aqedah* on New Testament sacrificial soteriology is disputed. Some scholars, including Robert Daly, believe that the tradition of Isaac's expiatory death directly influenced the gospel writers. Some feel the Isaac tradition developed too late to have a clear impact.[53] Others suggest that the expiatory significance of the *Aqedah* developed to fill the void left by the destruction of the Temple, which extinguished the sacrificial cult. Philip R. Davies and Bruce D. Chilton propose that the *Aqedah* was a post-Temple theological invention developed by the Tannaic rabbis as a replacement for the vicarious atonement formerly provided by the daily offerings.[54]

To some extent questions about dating and precedence become moot in the crosscurrents of mutual influence. Jon Levenson takes an interesting approach to the parallels between Jesus and Isaac. He sees a supersessionist typology behind Paul's substitution of Jesus for Isaac, the sacrifice on which is contingent the blessings to all nations, as was the sacrifice of Isaac for the blessings given through Abraham. In both cases the beloved son brings hope and forgiveness of sins.[55] The influence may go both ways, as Davies and Chilton believe. Then the *Aqedah* tradition would represent a mutual flow of influences, as Christian teaching shapes the model of Isaac as expiating servant.[56] If so, in a chiastic reversal and reflection of the Christian praise given to God *by casting God in the image of Abraham* (Rom. 8:32), this Jewish *Aqedah* tradition appeals not to Abraham's faith, but *honors the obedience of Isaac in the image of Jesus,* whom Christians claimed as God's son.

Christianity was perhaps one influential factor enhancing the meaning of the Isaac story; the loss of the Temple was another. The destruction of the Temple led to a crisis for many forms of Judaism, including early Christianity (again, however, not for Paul, who died before the Temple's collapse). Justification by Isaac, if Davies and Chilton's theory of the Aqedah is correct, offered a Jewish version of justification by faith. New ways to express the security of forgiveness of sins apart from the Temple — or new applications for sacrificial images — were needed by the different currents of Abraham's descendents.

Other Jewish images used by the evangelists are not specifically cultic. For example, allusions to Isaiah express the theme of being handed over, of suffering and dying, which are not properly cultic models.[57] The lives of the Maccabean martyrs provided another noncultic way to reinterpret sacrifice. The belief that a martyr's death could expiate sin was widely held and was probably used to interpret the death of Christ very early. The righteous king praised in Psalms 50–51 also shapes these ideas.[58] The evolution of the tradition of the expiatory martyr (that a person can be a sacrifice) connected with the specification of Isaiah 53 about what type of person offers his life (a suffering servant). The evolution and coincidence of these ideas shows how the shameful death of Jesus, a suffering servant, expiates sin as did the sacrifice of the martyrs.

The classic Hebrew images of sacrifice are reoriented in the new Christian constellation, distinguished not so much by their "spiritual" nature, but by their arrangement into the Christian symbolic system. The necessity of reinterpreting these images in a non-sacrificial way was also inescapably affected by the destruction of the Temple, and the ushering in of the post-sacrificial era for Christians and Jews. It is hard to say how the development might have unfolded had the Temple remained standing. This backward review of theological developments necessarily takes the perspective of the currents that survived. Fredriksen astutely perceives the importance of moving behind our awareness of what has actually transpired in history to attempt to recapture the events as they were understood before their consequent influences and interpretations came to full fruit. This approach attempts to reconstruct a historical snapshot, before incipient implications develop into themes and other historical options come to an end. In attempting to confront the standpoint of past actors, it is also necessary to allow the past to truly be other. "It is not our world at all, but a place where leprosy and death defile, where ashes and water make clean, where one approaches the altar of God with purifications, blood offerings, and awe."[59]

The ethical development, or "spiritualization," of sacrifice need not imply a supersessionist trajectory from Hebrew faith into Christian belief. Each tradition experiences both formalization and renewal. Formalization may mean retrenched or corrupt cultic practice such as the Pharisaic practices that Luke portrays Jesus as criticizing. Louis-Marie Chauvet suggests that Christian formalization includes the risk of "sacerdotalizing" the Christian Eucharistic sacrifice, focusing on the minister and the institution at the expense of the participating community. Both traditions have a heritage of prophetic renewal that calls the people to the faith that sacrifice embodies, which becomes recognized as the true act of sacrifice.[60] Worship in Spirit and truth is not a Hellenizing philosophical development or a Christian innovation, but an authentically Judaic focus on proper ethical and religious attitudes.[61]

## Jesus' View of the Cult

Similarly, Jesus' own view of the cult emerges from a Jewish tradition of critiquing the cult. According to Chauvet, Jesus' critiques of the Temple are not original but echo the prophets' message.[62] In texts such as Mark 7:6–7, Matthew 15:8–9, Matthew 9:13, 12:7, and Mark 12:28–34 Jesus cites the prophets. For example, he alludes to Isaiah 29:13 ("this people draw near with their mouth and honor me with their lips, while their hearts are far from me"), using the technical sacrificial terminology "draw near." Jesus' attitude toward the cult is perhaps best recognized as a compromise. He was critical of formalism, abuse, and corruption; he associated with unclean persons and included women in his fellowship; yet he accommodated the lepers' offering and the expectation to pay tax.[63] Overall, the synoptic Gospels contain some favorable texts, but generally show Jesus criticizing the sacrificial system.[64] Similar criticism came from Philo and certain Jewish renewal groups, such as the Qumran community, which had lost control of the priestly Temple succession for political reasons. They were critical of the current leadership, but unlike Jesus, in fact wished to intensify the purity codes.[65]

Scholars are divided on the extent of Jesus' criticism of the cult: did he wish to provoke renewal, but not reject the system entirely? Or did he intend to foster a new spiritual program?[66] Unlike Daly, Fredriksen downplays the extent to which Jesus rejected the Temple cult and purity system. She does not identify this system with the reification of hierarchical exclusion, which Jesus attacked by healing on the Sabbath or touching women. As she sees it, these actions are unconventional and incur impurity, but because impurity can be cleansed, Jesus has not necessarily rejected the system.[67] In other words, Jesus rejected exclusivity, but not the cult. In my view, she is underestimating the socially subversive and compassionate inclusivity that Jesus demonstrated specifically by a willingness to flaunt the cultic codes as less important than the dignity of those he affirmed, whether or not he was ultimately concerned with overturning the system of washing and defilement. Chauvet recommends that scholars attempt to judge what is unique by Ernst Käsemann's criteria of difference (that which is not derived from Jewish or Christian groups) and coherence (that which fits with the overall message), without the illusion of portraying the historical Jesus apart from the church or his Jewish world.[68] This recommendation places Jesus alongside other Jewish critics of the cult: different from some, like-minded to others.

## Jesus' View of His Death in Relation to the Cult

Scholars also offer a range of opinions about Jesus' view of his own death as a sacrifice. Jonathan Klawans proposes that the purpose of "metaphorical" action such as Jesus employed at the Last Supper is to signal "this too is divine service." Jesus most likely did not act deliberately to attempt to launch a new sacrificial program. However, Klawans's assertion that *all* Jesus intended with his symbolic action at the Last Supper was that *this too is divine service* is too subtle. The Last Supper was a symbolic confrontation with his fate, haunted by the context of the Passover slaughter. Jesus' words likely reflected his awareness of his crisis more than a desire for cultic reform. Yet in the moment of crisis, did Jesus explicitly expect that his death would be an expiatory sacrifice? With some differences, Paul Fiddes, Edward Schillebeeckx, and Paula Fredriksen agree that "Jesus' whole life is the hermeneusis of his death."[69]

Paul Fiddes believes that, according to Jesus, salvation requires repentance but not sacrifice. In his way of interacting and ministering, Jesus freely adapts the requirements of the law. Yet at his last supper, he finds meaning in sacrificial symbolism. Fiddes argues that Jesus' message during his active ministry is continuous with the meaning of his death, providing a heuristic clue into the meaning of the atonement. Forgiveness and acceptance were the overriding themes in Jesus' message as a teacher and healer, and also provide the meaning of atonement.[70] Schillebeeckx notes that no "certain logion" in which Jesus anticipates his death contains "any allusion to the death as salvation or propitiation."[71] Instead, the shared cup is a final extension of fellowship, an integration of his death into his entire ministry, all of which has been "for you." Fredriksen takes a stronger view of the earliest words of commission in 1 Corinthians 11:23–26 and Mark 14:22–25 as presupposing Jesus' anticipation of his death as an expiatory sacrifice. She agrees that the commemoration of this meal is linked to the future kingdom of God, the subject of his preaching throughout his life.[72] In the final analysis, Jesus' own feelings about his death are inaccessible to history. Any assessment is a revisable interpretation.

A metaphorical or "spiritual" reading of sacrifice is a legitimate strand within the core symbolic tradition, already reframed on inner-Jewish grounds by prophetic critique, exile, diaspora, philosophizing (Philo), radical spiritualizing (Qumran), and finally crushed by the physical destruction of the Temple. The shifting status of sacrifice is further qualified for Christians by Jesus' own ethical critique, then marginalized somewhat by the influx of Gentiles into the church. Yet in important ways, Christian interpretations will apply the ancient sacrificial language to Jesus Christ. By extension to themselves, Christians will also ask what the sacrificial identity of Jesus means for the disciple. The tide of an evolving understanding moves forward and backward. Former ideas of sacrifice shape new experience; at the same time, new experiences impel changes in the understanding of the original form that framed the reception of these new experiences.

## II. First Christian Interpretation: Jesus Christ

### Early New Testament Traditions

A brief excursus into New Testament exegesis is risky for the non-specialist, but necessary. The purpose of the review of scriptural scholarship in this section is to show that sacrifice is a deliberate interpretation of Jesus and of discipleship that emerges in different forms in various strands of the early church tradition, but generally serves to express Jesus' dedication. New Testament authors speak differently about how Jesus is a sacrifice. For example, the synoptic Gospels at times allude to the suffering servant theme of Isaiah or to Passover motifs. John employs the symbolism of blood and water and Passover details. Paul develops a theology of Christ as the paschal lamb and Christians as the new Temple. Hebrews in particular creates an original interpretation of Jesus using Temple and cult terminology, which is also found in 1 Peter. Thus, early interpretations of Jesus take different approaches. There is, in fact, an embarrassment of riches available in the multiple scriptural interpretations of Jesus as a sacrifice.

One way to consider multiple interpretive options is as root metaphors that express a religion's central truths. Such metaphors are the heart of each religious classic. As such, they express the excess of meaning contained in a classic. The challenge for the reader is to pinpoint the central metaphor, while also accepting the possibility of plural modes of Christian being.[73] One proceeds through this multiplicity of meaning by correlating one's current questions with the text, allowing hermeneutic criteria of appropriateness to the situation and adequate meaning to guide conflicts of interpretation, and assess claims to truth.[74] Later chapters will begin to seek these criteria of appropriateness for Christian sacrifice today. Here, I identify the metaphors or canons of texts that comprise the plurality of scriptural descriptions of sacrifice. Within this plurality, there is a common core meaning. At the end of this chapter I will consider the core meaning of sacrifice in relationship to Jesus and conclude that the core meaning of sacrificial metaphors is "dedication."

Different early Christian communities framed their understanding of Jesus according to the religious and cultural values that carried their sense of ultimate meaning. Each way of understanding Jesus entailed characteristic hopes, diverse titles, and varied eschatological scenarios. For example, Schillebeeckx identified several distinctive horizons of early Christian communities which developed particular christologies. These included *maranatha,* miracle-worker, Wisdom, and Easter christologies. Each understood salvation in different terms, had particular characterizations for the expected messiah, etc. Despite this variety, Jesus represented definitive salvation for each group.[75] Each group knew him to be the fulfillment of the hopes their various religious and cultural backgrounds had led them to expect, but also experience Jesus as the overturning of long-held ideas that framed their hope.

This process of recognition was not without challenges. A crucified Messiah was not expected. The shock of Jesus' death was a blow to the disciples and their messianic expectations.[76] Their hopes, however framed, were still not annihilated by the death of Jesus. In life and death, Jesus transcended and transformed their expectations. The Easter experience confirmed that the salvation known in Jesus during his life was a continuous living reality. Despite his death — and now, in some ways, because of it — Jesus could still be recognized and experienced as the Christ.

The many details within the traditional sacrificial metaphors are exchanged, highlighted, or recontextualized by the evangelists. Jesus' followers perceived a meaning in his life, which led them to retrieve symbols from their Scriptures. They sought deeper interpretations from their traditional wisdom to understand these central features of Jesus' life. The texts and symbols they retrieved are a clue to which aspect of Jesus struck the writers as most important. The changes each made show what details are relatively inconsequential. What is central for one evangelist is absent in another. The relative fluidity of sacrificial details makes it hard to sift out a definitive element in the concrete sacrificial details. The underlying structure seems to be that sacrifice is a gift given by God for reconciliation, salvation, and communion, which is now recognized in Jesus.

I will review how Jesus' death was interpreted in the New Testament in both sacrificial and non-sacrificial ways. There is a distinct place for sacrificial language about Jesus. Nevertheless, a sacrificial interpretation of his death does not provide the exclusive foundation for Christian discipleship. The scholarly literature on sacrifice in the New Testament authors is enormously vast. I will focus my remarks on each author by considering what sacrificial images are highlighted, how the function of sacrifice is described, and what tone is taken toward sacrifice.

## Pre-Gospel Traditions

As they sought to explain how Jesus was savior in spite of, or because of, his violent death, the evangelists drew upon traditions that included sacrificial and non-sacrificial views of the death of Jesus. Among New Testament sources, Edward Schillebeeckx identifies three early frameworks for interpreting the death of Jesus. These frameworks contain distinctive strands of material, or textual canons that constitute different approaches to the meaning of Jesus' death. These texts are very old and difficult to prioritize chronologically.[77] Only the third strand definitely interprets his death as a sacrifice.

According to the first strand, the "prophet-martyr contrast scheme," Jesus is a prophet in the Deuteronomic pattern. He confronts the people with their disobedience, calls them to conversion, but is then condemned as a pseudo-prophet. The prophet-martyr contrast scheme is so called because the prophet's ignominious death contrasts with the favor he receives from God. In this view, his death is not salvific. The prophet-martyr canon is found mostly in Luke and Acts, though pre-Lucan units are present elsewhere independently.[78] Luke does not emphasize the sacrificial and atoning nature of Jesus' death, though he uses the servant theme.[79]

The second framework, found in the earliest layer of the passion narrative, reveals a divine plan of salvation. Here Jesus teaches his disciples that he "must suffer" to "enter into glory." There is no soteriological explanation for his death, which functions only as a call to decision (to faith) and discipleship. His death is not absurd, it must occur; yet it does not have a saving function. Suffering confronts the disciples with the decision to recognize God's actions and follow. The passages in the "salvation history canon" cite the psalms of the suffering righteous one only (Ps. 22:2, 8, 9, 19; Ps. 41, Ps. 42, Ps. 69), not the Isaiah 53 tradition.[80]

For many disciples, the death of Jesus was a shattering challenge. But the third strand no longer judges the death to be an obstacle to affirming Jesus as savior, but in fact states that his death is the reason to affirm him as savior. The third framework is the atoning death–soteriological scheme. Here Jesus' death is salvific and redemptive in itself. The third atoning death model is more likely to use sacrificial symbolism. Reflection upon Jesus' death and his identity as savior finds a positive and causal relationship between the two. It is an "atoning death for human beings, as a vicarious propitiatory sacrifice whereby human beings are redeemed." The decisive term is "for" (the *hyper* formula): Jesus dies "for" sinners. While the evidence for this strand is sparse, it is very old and very influential.[81] Its attestation in early layers of the gospel traditions is slight but it becomes a governing factor for the theme of redemption in a later stage.

The texts of the "atoning death canon" include Mark 14:24, Mark 10:45, 1 Corinthians 15:3b–5, Romans 4:25, 5:8, 8:32, Galatians 1:4, Ephesians 5:2, 1 Peter 2:21–24, Mark 14:61, Matthew 8:17, Acts 8:32–33, and Hebrews. These earliest pre-synoptic and pre-Pauline soteriological formulae later shaped soteriological interpretations in Paul, Hebrews, the Deutero-Pauline texts, the Apocalypse and John's Gospel. Why this third strand interprets Jesus' death as meaningful is an important question. A natural response is to look for influences and sources among the symbols of the Hebrew tradition and perhaps especially to the suffering servant figures, yet allusions to the suffering servant are inconsistent.[82] Paul is a major shaper of the "atoning death" tradition. Yet Paul does not use the Isaiah tradition in reference to Jesus' death.

Scholars dispute the extent to which this "atoning death" interpretation depends upon Isaiah 53 or a vicarious martyr tradition. Raymund Schwager agrees that the atoning death tradition, which he calls the Palestinian tradition, did not rely heavily upon the Isaiah tradition or Hellenistic Jewish ideas of atonement. He argues for the origins of the atoning-death interpretation with Jesus.[83] Schwager does not see a conflict between Jesus' message of salvation in the kingdom of God and his death because of the necessary continuity between Jesus' life and death. Jesus' existence for sinners is the most emphasized point of his preaching, and he always spoke of being sent. Therefore, if the message is the messenger, Jesus' fate continues to affect his significance. Similarly, Schillebeeckx believes the soteriological formulae are a self-contained tradition — perhaps ultimately based in a saying of Jesus. This possibility turns the reader away from searches through the overlapping layers of tradition back to the historical Jesus.[84] John Galvin takes a slightly different view, commenting that Jesus at least anticipated his own vindication (Matt. 14:25), but did not definitively interpret his death as salvific.[85]

## Editorial Emphases in Gospel Views of Jesus' Death

A comparison of Mark and Luke's portrayal of Jesus' death cry and the rending of the veil of the Temple illustrates the meaning added by editorial selection. Each evangelist crafts a passion narrative that draws on pre-gospel traditions and material from the Hebrew Scriptures to express his theological understanding of the death of Jesus. Their selective use of the Hebrew Scriptures reveals what is most significant in their experience of Jesus. The cry shows how diverse theological approaches to the meaning of Jesus' death employ different scriptural allusions. Allusions to Psalm 22, Zechariah, Jeremiah, Psalm 31, and other Psalms shape or reinforce the structure of the passion narrative. The rending of the veil shows more specifically how the evangelists treat the sacrificial cult in relationship to Jesus.[86]

For Mark, the passion is an experience of human failure. God's power is demonstrated only after Jesus' death.[87] The Marcan narrative is structured to show the fulfillment of the Hebrew Scriptures in Jesus' claims.[88] Mark's Jesus utters a cry with the words of Psalm 22, which begins with lamentation. After deliverance comes, the Psalmist gives praise in the second half. The message of the psalmist is that God vindicates the just in the end, even if he is not spared from suffering.

Psalm 22 has long been known in the tradition as the "passion psalm." Raymond Brown believes that the actual location of citations merits instead the label the "crucifixion psalm." Brown takes a conservative approach to assessing influence, crediting as parallels only those Hebrew Scripture passages whose vocabulary is precisely echoed in the New Testament passion narrative. The correlation of Psalm 22 and the passion narratives centers on the setting of the crucifixion, the mockery, and appeals to God. The literary similarities suggest that appeals to the Psalms caused certain details of the memory of the passion to be highlighted. Brown observes that some scholars believe the second half of Psalm 22 refers to the *todah*, thus calling the hearer to complete Jesus' cry of abandonment with the liturgy of praise.[89] However, Brown accepts the literal meaning of Jesus' cry of abandonment and does not invoke the full context of Psalm 22 with its final rejoicing except insofar as that greater context makes the cry appropriate to Jesus. That is, the citation confirms Jesus as one who ultimately has hope and who has been faithful to God all his life. The association would represent an appeal to see God's plan in the events of crucifixion. But the cry of alienation is real. It is not even addressed to Abba any longer, and is not a cipher for confident victory.[90] In Mark and Matthew, Jesus does not appear to invoke the victory and thanksgiving of the second part of the psalm. If the allusions were stronger, the case could be made that the *todah* is a model for resurrection narratives and the Eucharist.[91] But most of the gospel references allude to the first part of the psalm. The references to Psalm 22 in the resurrection part of the passion narrative are dubious. While Brown's conservative estimation of direct reference to Psalm

22 in the resurrection narrative is wise, it does not seem that the vindication half of the psalm needs to be quoted explicitly to invoke the
theme of victory that follows lament. The anticipated glory may still
reasonably echo in the reader familiar with the psalm's ending and
form part of the reader's expectation.

In Brown's view, Luke reworks the Marcan structure to emphasize
forgiveness, peace with God, and the sympathetic crowds. This is evident most of all in his prayer for forgiveness of enemies (23:34).[92] In
Luke's Gospel, God's love and healing are manifest in the events of
the crucifixion. Many people see and are drawn into Jesus' story as
followers (for example, Simon as disciple, one thief, the centurion,
the crowds, and the women).[93] The Lucan theology of salvation and
the authoritative gracious offer of forgiveness are shown even as Jesus
speaks to a penitent wrongdoer — a final saving offer is made even
before the moment of his death.[94] In Luke's passion narrative, the veil
is rent before Jesus' death and expresses judgment on the mockers.
The tearing of the veil does not desacralize the Temple, in accord with
Luke's positive view of the Temple, but nevertheless shows that the
sanctuary is no longer to be preserved.[95] By contrast, Mark's treatment of the rent veil expresses an anti-sacrificial tone, indicating that
the sanctuary is no longer a holy place. The sign confirms Jesus' pre-
dictions of destroying the sanctuary. The last words in Luke's Gospel
also contrast to Mark's: Jesus utters words of trust from Psalm 31,
not Psalm 22. In the end, Jesus falls into the hands of his Father, not
the priests or sinners. His spirit so commended completes the mission
of the Spirit in Jesus' life, beginning with his birth and baptism.

Another interesting example of editorial shaping is the contrast of
victim and priestly images in John's use of sacrificial symbols. For
John, the cross is a victory, a place to rule and gather the believing
community, in a deliverance ritual marked by Passover symbolism.[96]
Jesus' church is gathered at the cross and his work surveyed and
finished. The climax of the theology of John's Gospel is the revelation of Jesus' unity with the Father, not a vicarious and expiatory
sacrifice. Death is a return to the Father (13:1, 17:4–5).[97] Grigsby
agrees that the Incarnation is the primary saving fact. "The exact

relationship between Christ's death and the elimination of sin is not explicit." Nevertheless John employs "hints" of an "expiatory rationale."[98] Among these hints are many sacrificial details. John specifies hyssop to allude to the paschal lamb's blood sprinkled on lintels at first Passover. (Hebrews also recapitulates the image of hyssop.) John also includes Passover details like the noon hour as the time of judgment — which was also the time of the Temple slaughter.[99] Other details are that his bones are left unbroken (Exod. 12:10); he accepts the vinegar, drinks the cup, and completes his role as the paschal lamb, taking away sin (although the paschal lamb is not originally a sin offering but a ransom for redemption). Grigsby sees a possible influence of the Aqedah behind the expiatory effect connected to the title "Lamb of God" and in the famous passage John 3:16. John 19:34 contains the innovation of depicting a flow of blood and water from Christ's side. This image combines the blood of Jesus' saving death and the living water he promised to the Samaritan woman, and perhaps the water that washed the disciples' feet.[100] In these ways John combines the images of sublime priest with paschal victim to portray Jesus.

According to Raymond Brown, the "community of the Beloved Disciple," originally Jewish Christian followers of Jesus and John the Baptist, were soon joined by a newer group. This group had Samaritan connections and a uniquely high christology. Their christology acclaimed the savior of the world who is not a Davidic messiah but a figure like Moses, reflecting Samaritan theology.[101] Because Samaritans did not share the Jerusalem view of the significance of the Temple, the new association with them caused the Johannine community to become increasingly identified as anti-Temple by other Jewish communities. The community became defensive and their theology developed a way to replace the Temple with Jesus: God is tabernacled among us in Jesus (John 1:14).[102]

In some sections of the Johannine community, reverence for the revelation of the Word in Jesus meant that Jesus' humanity and ministry are reduced — especially in certain extreme positions represented by the opponents of the author of 1 John. Their anti-Jewish polemics

spurred a new, non-cultic view of Jesus as the supreme religious sacrifice. First John attempted to rein in such factions by reemphasizing
the life and death of the historical Jesus.[103] The first epistle stresses the
saving earthly career and ministry of Jesus, emphasizing the meaning
of his death with its sacrificial imagery to preserve the importance
of Jesus' particular human life. The revelation of the Word is the key
meaning of his death, yet the historic details of his life as portrayed in
the gospel show the salvific import of his concrete death. The symbol
of the lamb shows that this death is redemptive, yet highly deliberate.[104] "Much more clearly, then, than in the Gospel, the Jesus of
1 John is a redeemer, even if as a true Johannine the author never
forgets the role of Jesus as a revealer: 'Christ revealed himself to take
away sins' (3:5)"[105] The author of 1 John highlights Jesus' humanity
and the significance of his saving death as a victim by emphasizing
elements that are indeed present in the Gospel of John, which symbolically portrays Jesus as victim, using the sacrificial details of blood,
hour of death, hyssop, etc. In both Johannine texts, if to different
degrees, the representation of Jesus as victim is transformed by the
revelation of the priestly purpose he evidences throughout the events
of the Passion.

## Paul

The Pauline material comes from an early stage of written Christian
reflection — significantly, Paul is the only Christian author whose
writing is completed before the destruction of the Temple. Paul uses
sacrificial images to refer to Jesus' death. A chief source of his imagery is the Passover Lamb. Christians very early connected Passover
symbols and the death of Jesus, and Paul expresses this directly in
1 Corinthians 5:7: "Christ, our Passover, is sacrificed." This is the
only time the verb for "sacrifice" (*thyo*) is applied to Jesus in connection with his death in Paul's writing.[106] However, as he ponders the
mystery of salvation in Jesus, Paul presents legal, rather than cultic,
explanations, and he celebrates the mystery in terms of victory. His
attitude toward sacrifice, as toward the law, can be described as loyal
ambivalence.

Robert Daly observes a strong sacrificial vocabulary in Paul's treatment of the cross. The death of Jesus is "for" us: it is a sin offering. The Pauline theology of sacrifice has three themes. First, the sacrifice of Christ as Passover lamb and sin offering, which stresses forgiveness and redemption.[107] Second, Christians are viewed as the new Temple. Third, as such, the lives of Christians and the demonstration of Christian love constitute the new sacrifice of the church. Young agrees that Paul uses sacrificial language for worship and also to explain Christ's death. She points out that Paul himself fulfilled Temple practices (Acts 21:23–26).[108]

On the contrary, Bradley H. McLean denies that Paul's soteriology represents "a sacrificially based interpretation of Christ's atoning death."[109] By this he means that Paul does not correlate Christ's death specifically with the *hatta't,* the sin offering or reparation offering. McLean makes a complex, if not watertight, case against a sacrificial interpretation of Christ's death in Paul. Reviewing his argument is useful to show how a tangle of sacrificial allusions enables a variety of legitimately different interpretations of sacrificial references. McLean writes: "the solitary reference in 1 Cor. 5:7 to Christ being sacrificed cannot be interpreted as an *expiatory* sacrifice. Paul is alluding to the freedom purchased for Christians by the slaughter of Christ, God's Passover lamb."[110] Ephesians 5:2 ("as a fragrant offering and sacrifice") is the only place in the Pauline corpus the noun *thusia* ("sacrifice") applies to Christ, and the text does not refer to expiation.[111] In the Eucharistic passage of 1 Corinthians 11:24–25, Christ's sacrificial death is expressed as a *covenant* sacrifice.

McLean's claim that "Paul's interpretation of the suffering and death of Christ is incompatible with sacrificial theology" rests upon the assumption that the Levitical sacrifices do not atone for personal sin. McLean further argues that only the scapegoat ritual atones for personal sins — and this ritual is not a sacrifice. In particular the *hatta't* is misunderstood as an offering for personal sin, since it is an offering that purifies the Temple sanctuary.[112] He disputes the interpretation by other scholars that the *hatta't* does effect personal atonement, claiming these interpretations illegitimately use the scapegoat ritual as the interpretive paradigm.[113]

Other scholars disagree, arguing that the sin offerings do effect personal forgiveness. Though McLean cites Roland de Vaux to show that the laying on of one hand (as opposed to the two hands used in the scapegoat rite) does not make the victim a *substitute* for the individual, even de Vaux indicates that the sacrifice is "offered in his name [that is, in the name of the individual presenting the animal to the high priest for sacrifice], and that the fruits of the sacrifice shall be his."[114] Likewise, Richard D. Nelson argues that even for the author of Hebrews, for whom the heavenly sanctuary and the action of Jesus provide a much superior form of atonement, the Levitical sin offerings were nevertheless understood to benefit the sinners themselves, in a moral as well as ritual or cultic sense (e.g., Lev. 4:20b: "and the priest shall make atonement for them, and they shall be forgiven").[115]

McLean also overlooks the increasing attention given to sin in post-exilic Judaism, with the concomitant tendency to ascribe expiatory significance to all sacrifices.[116] Furthermore, Christ's self-proclaimed identity as "being sent to sinners" continues to relate the purpose of his actions to the forgiveness of sins, regardless of the ancient purpose of specific cultic sacrifices. These points cannot be settled here, although it does appear that the least contentious sacrificial source for Paul is the paschal lamb. To a certain extent McLean appears to be splitting hairs. He acknowledges as much by stating that

> While it is undeniable that a number of NT books such as Hebrews and the Johannine epistles (e.g., 1 John 1:7) portray Christ's expiatory death as a sacrifice, this fact is only evidence for the adaptation and transformation of Levitical theology.[117]

Clearly, such adaptation is exactly what New Testament theology represents. McLean correctly states that the Christian transformation cannot and should not be used to reconstruct Levitical theology. Such transformation is, however, a defining feature of the emerging, novel synthesis of new beliefs and appropriation of old symbols that is early Christianity. Furthermore, a combination of allusions and references can tend to cohere in a powerful, if not historically accurate, impression of sacrificial symbolism in the mind of the Christian reader of the scriptures in any era. The reader's imagination naturally synthesizes powerful and overlapping sacrificial imagery to create impressions less precise than the exact Levitical definitions. It is less likely that Paul, the brilliantly trained Pharisee, would confuse the purpose of various sacrifices, if indeed McLean's thesis is correct and the sin offering fails to explain Paul's language. The lack of congruence would then explain why Paul appears to choose legal, not cultic, explanations for the meaning of Jesus' death.

Perhaps it is best to say that while the fact of Christ's saving death is central to the gospel, "the mystery of atonement Paul does not attempt to solve."[118] Multiple metaphors are at work in Paul's way of thinking. Fitzmyer in fact offers four ways of representing the effect of the death of Jesus in Paul's understanding. By speaking of the effects of sacrifice, Fitzmyer signifies that sacrifice has to be explained in other terms: that is, Paul uses other models to explain the sacrificial model. Sacrifice thus works by reconciling, expiating, liberating, and justifying.[119] In Fitzmyer's view, the theme of justification is not as central to Paul as it was to the debates of the Reformation. For Paul, this aspect of salvation was provoked by Judaizing opponents. It is another metaphor that suffers if its judicial aspects are overstressed.

X. Léon-Dufour proposes that sacrifice was not the earliest interpretation of the death of Jesus, even in Paul. He identifies three symbolic patterns that interpret the cross, asserting that none is based on sacrifice or cult. These are (1) a covenant-judicial model, under which humanity is condemned, but justified by the mediation of Christ, the new Adam; (2) a political framework, in which humanity is dominated by sin under the law, but ransomed by Jesus to become free heirs; and (3) an interpersonal model, in which alienated humanity is reconciled by Jesus from enmity with God to peace.[120] Léon-Dufour has accounted for three of Fitzmyer's models above. The covenant-judicial model relates to what Fitzmyer calls justification,

the political framework seems to be Fitzmyer's redemptive liberation, and the interpersonal model speaks of reconciliation. However,
he overlooks the sacrificial elements in them. The covenant is ratified
by sacrifice; the ransom of the Israelites by the Passover lamb is a sacrificial image applied to Jesus (although he correctly notes that the
ransom motif attached to the kinsman-redeemer, or *go-el,* is not sacrificial); and atoning sacrifices effect reconciliation. Dufour also leaves
out the expiation model when describing a judicial model of justification, but these sacrificial metaphors of covenant and expiation
cannot be overlooked.

John A. T. Robinson makes the case that Paul generally uses the
language of the legal courts. Obedience is the chief virtue of Christ's
death, which simply absorbs or defeats evil. The use of the idea of
expiation is one of the "rare uses of sacrificial categories."[121] Robinson believes that a major way Paul (and Jesus himself) viewed Jesus'
death is as a baptism (Mark 10:38, Luke 12:50). The baptism of the
believer then shares in this death.[122] In Romans 8:3, a text which
identifies Jesus as a sacrifice for sin, Robinson points out that its
meaning is again explained with a law metaphor:

> Yet the sacrificial imagery if present is not explicit. Paul draws
> out the meaning rather in his preferred categories of the law-
> courts: "He condemned sin in the flesh." It is the same juridical
> metaphor that he used in 6:7: "The dead man has his quittance
> from anything that sin can bring against him." Sin is regarded
> as the prosecution, man as the defendant, in God's court.[123]

When explaining how Christ's death saves, Paul resorts to a legal explanation of the process and expresses the effect in terms of battle
victory. Cleansing and purification are not vital themes in Paul's
thought. Even baptism is likened to burial rather than washing.[124]

Fitzmyer observes that Paul's central theological position is the
divine plan of salvation in the passion, death, and resurrection of
Christ. While Christocentric, Paul's is a functional Christology, recognizing Jesus as the power of God. The work of Christ always points
back to the Father.[125] Christ suffers and dies for humanity. This is at

times described as a form of sacrifice that expresses Christ's love. The disciple experiences that death and glorification through baptism. The life of Jesus receives less attention from Paul: it is not that the believer is tempted or baptized with Christ, but that he is crucified and raised with Christ.[126] Fitzmyer believes that what is most characteristically Pauline is his celebration of the saving event of Jesus' death and resurrection.[127] Chauvet also concludes that "the interpretation of Jesus' death as a sacrifice is not, in the New Testament, either the earliest (which does not mean it has less theological relevance than others) nor EVEN the most important."

In conclusion, Paul uses sacrificial images, but his thinking about how Christ saves lacks a detailed, procedural, ritual explanation of the process of sacrifice. Sacrificial language is present and well attested, but clearly exists within the plurality of images in Paul. In summary, Paul uses sacrificial images — indeed a bounty of sacrificial images — but he explains them legally and celebrates the meaning of Christ's death in terms of victory.

The cognitive dissonance Paul experienced through his associations with different social and religious groups may shed some insight into his complex view of the history of Jews and Gentiles. In his dual identity as observant Pharisee and Apostle to the Gentiles, Paul alternates between theologies of history. As seen in Romans, he considers three arguments, never perfectly reconciled: the remnant theme, the supersession of the law, and the final validity of the Abrahamic covenant in which the temporary dispossession of Israel ends and the Gentiles find salvation.[128] Tormented by the legitimacy and dispensability of the law, Paul resorts not to supersession but digs to more ancient foundations: the justification of Abraham by faith before the law.

For Paul, while the law is somewhat ambiguous, it is still good. Hebrews will more confidently dismiss the old covenant, indifferent to its central liberating symbol, the Passover Lamb. Perhaps despairing of symbols connected to Israel in the wilderness, its author chooses to center its spiritualizing upon the Day of Atonement rite. When Hebrews retrieves a more ancient tradition, prior to the law, it turns to the Melchizedek tradition.

## Later Developments of Sacrificial Imagery

*The Letter to the Hebrews*

In contrast to Paul, the chief symbol of sacrifice in the Letter to the Hebrews is the Day of Atonement, and also unlike Paul, the author of Hebrews works out his argument by a detailed sacrificial mechanism. The Letter to the Hebrews makes the new claim that all of the sacrificial rituals of the Hebrew Scriptures have been fulfilled (Heb. 7:26–8, 8:6–7, 10:1–10). Hebrews portrays the death of Jesus as the new covenant sacrifice and the perfection of the cult of the Day of Atonement. The message of Hebrews is the real efficacy of the new sacrifice of Christ the eternal high priest. The Letter to the Hebrews makes a radical break with the sacrificial cult on the principle that Jesus has fulfilled the cult. Here is the first radically "spiritualizing" theology of sacrifice. The sacrificial practices that Jewish Christians may have continued to observe, though not obligatory for Gentile Christians, are now declared by its author to be abolished, once for all.[129] In Daly's words, "Jesus redeemed us by offering himself to God as a sin offering in the full, realistic, Old Testament sense of the word."[130] However, the details of that sacrifice and views on why it saves are disputed.

Ambivalence regarding sacrifice pervades the Letter to the Hebrews: the author's metaphorical strategy engages sacrifice while at the same time criticizing it. The letter was most probably intended for a community in Rome, with a nonconformist Jewish background (in contrast to what later became mainstream Judaism).[131] The extent of a Platonic influence in Hebrews, which would downplay Jesus' historical experience, has been debated. According to Richard D. Nelson,

> Hebrews deprecates sacrifice from the perspective of a spatial, temporal, and evaluative dualism that opposes transitory earthly phenomena over against eternal heavenly realities. This reflects the apocalyptic worldview of early Christianity and echoes platonic idealism.[132]

In contrast, Schillebeeckx argues that the writer accepts that a historical event — the death of Jesus — has unusual influence to change eternal reality, indeed to inaugurate the new ages.[133] At the same time his death is treated in an ahistorical fashion. Frederick Fyvie Bruce points out that Christ's burial is not mentioned, and his resurrection is not directly stated.[134] Nelson agrees that there is an ahistorical synthesizing of the resurrection and the exaltation.[135]

The sacrificial imagery in the Letter to the Hebrews represents an original development beyond the sacrificial imagery of the synoptic Gospels which associated Jesus with the slain lamb, the victim. Like John, Hebrews also identifies Jesus Christ as the priest. In this way, Hebrews simultaneously promotes a "Christology from above," in terms of the exalted and heavenly high priest, and a "Christology from below," portraying one who willingly and obediently suffered in flesh and body under circumstances of the deepest shame.[136] The innovation of the author of Hebrews is to connect the Davidic prophecy in Psalm 110:1 to the promise that the Davidic king serves in the line of Melchizedek (110:4). What were seen as two distinct roles are combined in Jesus, as Royal Messiah and Priestly Messiah.[137] The priesthood of Jesus inaugurates the new order, the blessings of the new covenant that Jeremiah prophesied, in which God no longer remembers the sins of his people. For the author of Hebrews, this new covenant "presents a contrast to the Levitical ritual which involved a recurrent and never-ending remembrance of sins."[138] The author of Hebrews is critical of the covenant given to the people in the wilderness (Heb. 10:4) and the cultic practices that must be constantly repeated. He views the Passover liberation as imperfect and transient, both in the eyes of Jeremiah and in the new Christian community. This may be the reason he bypasses the Passover image that Paul employs (1 Cor. 5:7), concentrating his transforming and superseding interpretation on a separate symbol of the "old" covenant, the Day of Atonement ritual noted in Leviticus 16 — without the scapegoat rite — and the covenant sacrifice described in Exodus 24:3–8.

The complex features of this model require an elaborate midrash of the Melchizedek tradition to provide a priestly genealogy which circumvents the Levitical priesthood (to which Jesus does not belong). For the most part, Hebrews builds upon formal models and types, not actual events from the life of Jesus. The resurrection is not a central part of this message. Hebrews concentrates its christology into Christ's death and appearance before God in the heavenly sanctuary.[139] As with Pauline material, minute examinations of how the sacrifice functions in Hebrews result in varied explanations. Is the moment of death the decisive act? Other views minimize the importance of death, arguing that it is Jesus' entrance into heaven that saves.[140] Whether in one decisive offering on Calvary or in a three-stage ritual drama culminating with presentation of his blood in the heavenly Temple, the author of Hebrews declares that Christ's sacrifice is unique because it is spiritual offering of obedience, the dedication of Christ to the will of God: "the sacrifice of himself" (Heb. 9:26). Bruce insists the blood is not significant itself as an offering to God, not even metaphorically. By contrast to the Levitical priest who enters the holy place with the blood of goats, Christ enters through his own blood — that is, because of his self-sacrifice, not in order to offer his blood, whether figuratively or not. Bruce acknowledges that the author of Hebrews does not directly explain "how the self-sacrifice of Jesus removes the pollution of sin from the conscience of those who place their trust in him."[141] The mechanics of sacrifice remain obscure, in the spiritual as well as the original cultic form. This obscurity coheres with remarks cited above by Daly, Levenson, Robinson, Grigsby, and McLean that blood atones for sins without clearly explaining why or how. Accepting this model was part of an ancient worldview. Within that model, if an animal's sacrificial death had no meaning, as argued before, then Christ's can have no meaning. This is precisely why an existential understanding is necessary. Hebrews provides this with attention to obedience and solidarity.[142]

Interpretations of Hebrews that highlight Jesus' solidarity with those who suffer surmount the lack of a precisely defined sacrificial mechanism by emphasizing Jesus' care for God's people. Jesus' heavenly ministry is possible "only because he is the same Jesus now as he was then."[143] Jesus became

> . . . like his brothers and sisters in every respect, so that he might be a merciful and faithful high priest in the service of God, to make a sacrifice of atonement for sins of the people. Because he himself was tested by what he suffered, he is able to help those who are being tested. (Heb. 2:17–18)

The sacrificial act takes its meaning from the circumstances of Jesus' death, the suffering and supplication of one who lived in the flesh (Heb. 2:14), knew the miseries of his brothers and sisters (Heb. 2:10–11), and cried out to God (Heb. 5:7).[144] The priestly interpretation does not absorb Jesus Christ into a sacral model, minutely replicating cultic activity. Schillebeeckx reads Hebrews as in fact "demythologizing" sacrifice. To be priest means to relate to both God and humanity as intercessor. Jesus as priest is the image of God and the brother of humanity.

> These two characteristics — that Jesus takes up God's cause and at the same time shows solidarity with mankind and defends their cause — makes the author of Hebrews realize that what apostolic Christian experience calls salvation from God in Jesus can equally well be expressed in *priestly* terms. Evidently he does not mean to say anything new.[145]

Hebrews articulates the basic Christian affirmation of salvation in Jesus in priestly terms. His priesthood expresses a "philanthropic Christology." This view, which "seems to us to be a sacral reinterpretation of the *layman* Jesus in terms of Jewish priesthood is a demythologization of the Jewish image of priesthood."[146]

The letter stresses Jesus' participation in the suffering condition of humanity ("We have a high priest who can sympathize with our weaknesses" [4:15]). This participation gives the historical event of his death an eternal validity, a striking, determinatively Christian note against the "two-worlds" framework of the letter, which otherwise sees the future world as the real and enduring one. Suffering also provides the mode of salvation. Because suffering appears to be an inevitable aspect of human existence, it is fitting and compassionate that suffering mark the life of the savior of humanity. So according to Schillebeeckx, Hebrews is at once the most cultic and most radically non-cultic interpretation of Jesus and his saving death.

## The Complexity of Sacrificial Symbolism in the New Testament Writers

Comparing New Testament writers on sacrifice shows the complex development of sacrificial symbolism in the New Testament, a development that is both radically new and yet for a time still Jewish, at once strongly shaped by and painfully different from its traditional sources. This newness, which can be symbolized by the metaphor of tearing fabric, thus has different senses. Chauvet finds eschatological significance in the metaphor of the heavens torn apart at Jesus' baptism (Mark 1:10), in the metaphor of the torn garment or wineskin (Mark 2:21), and in the tearing of the Temple veil (Mark 15:38, Matt. 27:51, and Luke 23:45).[147] The experience of "tearing" could be the painful loss of the Temple as a judgment on the Jews (perhaps in bitter reaction to controversy and rejection by Temple and synagogues), or a genuine newness of spiritual practice. Matthew and Mark express the finality of the end of the sacrificial system via the torn veil. Paul, John, and Hebrews, however, maintain sacrificial symbolism in their own ways to refer to Jesus' death and to describe the sacrifice of discipleship.

New Testament references to Jesus as a sacrifice, priest, or victim indicate ways early Christians began to re-vision the presence of God in comparison with the Temple as the traditional place for God's presence. Brown points to the intriguing possibility of an early tradition affirming God's presence with the community. This independent tradition saw in Jesus the presence of God among God's people, as in the Holy of Holies.[148] Mark and the author of Hebrews reacted differently to this tradition, as symbolized in their treatment of the veil covering the Holy of Holies. In Mark, the rejection and failure of the crucifixion causes the veil to rend, destroying the Temple as the dwelling of God. In Hebrews, the Temple's function is preserved and transformed by Jesus as high priest, its old significance transformed by a new christological meaning. Hebrews depicts Jesus as the high priest of Yom Kippur going behind the veil to the Holy of Holies to sprinkle the ark with blood (Lev. 16:11–19), as the spiritualized heavenly sacrifice.[149] For Paul, the Temple presence of God is now identified with the community. For John, the presence of God is now found in the risen Lord.

The painful apprehension of Jesus' death as a historical failure in Mark and Matthew accompanies their use of sacrificial imagery, which casts Jesus as the victim. By contrast, John and Hebrews focus less directly on Jesus' historical life. John's Christ is a deliberate, victorious Lamb who sees his work completed from the cross. In Hebrews, Christ's saving work is accomplished as priest in the heavenly Temple. It seems that as the interpretation becomes more triumphant and heavenly, as in the case of Hebrews, it also envisions Jesus' sacrificial role as that of the priest (using formal models and types such as Melchizedek instead of gospel details of Jesus' life). Once again, it seems that those who, like Paul and John, emphasize sacrificial imagery, seem also to deemphasize the events of Jesus' life. Or, in the case of John, portray a deliberate and calm victim who is as much agent as patient. Paul also focuses directly upon Jesus' death and resurrection and does not highlight Jesus' ministry.

Something about Jesus' life summoned sacrificial images to describe his death. In the experience of his Jewish disciples, those images belong to a cult of sacrifice that is a gift of God's covenant for reconciliation. The symbol of the gift of sacrifice is brought forth by the evangelists, applied directly to his death, or interpreted in a new, post-cultic way. However interpreted, sacrifice remains a means of reconciliation, graciously given by God, and marked with blood. The grace and loss together create the ambiguity of the sacrificial symbol. Outside of a worldview accustomed to the logic of sacrifice, to require blood in ways that arguably are arbitrary (i.e., not shown to have medicinal value) is no longer accepted without question. To anticipate the challenge of the next chapter, many would abandon the symbolism as fatally incongruent in an era largely unfamiliar with blood sacrifice. Yet the reality of the cost of change, restitution, and new life keeps the symbol alive. Even if the blood or suffering is not inflicted by God — a view rightly rejected — suffering is often still somehow unavoidable in life. The chronicles of martyrdom are but one witness to this painful reality. There is often a cost to discipleship. Dietrich Bonhoeffer taught that suffering and rejection are essential to Christian life, since Christian life is committed to sharing the cross and suffering of Christ. "When Christ calls a man, he bids him come and die."[150] Dedication has its price. The use of sacrificial imagery for this aspect of discipleship remains meaningful not because blood is sought by God, but because suffering is inevitable.

### Interpreting Jesus' Death Together with His Life

The affirmation of the event of Jesus Christ, his death and resurrection as the final meaning for his life, and his life as the reason to take note of his death, took many forms. Sacrifice is not the earliest, nor the only, interpretation for the death of Jesus. Non-sacrificial interpretations include (1) the theme that one must "lose one's life to save it," an existential willingness to humble oneself also invoked by Hebrews and Philippians; (2) the three contexts suggested by Dufour (covenant, ransom, and reconciliation — even if these seem to employ motifs of sacrifice); (3) the servant theme; and (4) the prophet-martyr scheme and salvation history plan as seen by Schillebeeckx.[151]

That there are multiple ways to express the significance of Jesus' death indicates that this single point cannot be the source of all the meaning of his life. Jesus' death alone does not establish the meaning of his ministry. In ages less marked by historic consciousness, this was not necessarily the case. The meaning of the incarnation and passion as the pure fact of God's taking on human existence, aside from the details of Jesus' historical life, had great salvific importance. But for a modern, historically conscious generation, the interpretation of Jesus' death as a sacrifice makes sense only in the context of his life.[152] Jesus must have first lived and offered people hope in the reign of God to make his death meaningful. Otherwise his life is an ahistorical blank that simply precedes his death. Jesus himself may have understood his death as the final service of a lifelong offer of salvation.

The interpretations of Jesus in the diverse early Christian writings are answers to his own question: who do you say that I am? It is when contemplating discipleship that one needs to ask who Jesus is, what sacrifice means, and how one is to live that paradox in one's own life. The symbol of sacrifice belongs to the hermeneutical circle of understanding discipleship. Each early Christian community had a characteristic answer; each new age will also have an answer. Each believer also interprets sacrifice within the terms of his or her own life story, guided by the Christian narrative.

The review of scriptural scholarship in this section showed that sacrifice is a deliberate interpretation of Jesus by some strands of the early church tradition, utilizing the symbolic heritage of Scripture in varied ways. In the final New Testament canon, sacrifice does become a governing interpretation of Jesus, and one that is also appropriated in a significant way to talk about the life of the disciple. How does sacrifice apply to the disciple's own narrative?

## III. Second Christian Interpretation: Application to the Disciple

### New Testament Representations: Sacrifice as a Liturgy of Life

Sacrificial imagery plays a role in key texts of the New Testament that describe the life of the Christian, though compared to the sacrificial imagery applied to Christ, sacrificial references for the disciple are sparse.[153] For Paul, Christians are the new Temple, individually and as a community, because of the indwelling of the Holy Spirit. Paul's theology of Christians as "the new Temple" recapitulates the language of sacrifice for the life of the community.

Paul uses the metaphor of "becoming" the Temple to describe the continuous process of becoming holy. The sacrifice of Christians occurs in apostolic service, and in the disciple's life and death. Both are offerings of service described in the technical sacrificial language as "fragrant" and "acceptable" (Phil. 4:18).[154] The text of Romans 15 shows that sacrifice includes the apostolic service of preaching, which is, in Daly's words, "the obedience of faith in giving oneself to God for the sake of one's neighbor."[155]

> But on some points I have written to you very boldly by way of reminder, because of the grace given me by God to be a minister of Christ Jesus to the Gentiles in the priestly service of the gospel of God, so that the offering of the Gentiles may be acceptable, sanctified by the Holy Spirit. (Rom. 15:15–16)

Paul's interpretation of the life of the disciple has three core elements: (1) its foundation in the sacrifice of Jesus as Passover lamb and sin offering, stressing forgiveness and redemption, (2) Christians as the new Temple, individually and as a community, because of the indwelling Spirit, and (3) the sacrifice of Christians that occurs in a disciple's life and death.[156] Romans 12 describes Christian life as cultic service, applying to Christ and to each Christian.

> appeal to you therefore, brothers, by the mercies of God, to present your bodies as a living sacrifice, holy and acceptable to God, which is your spiritual worship. Do not be conformed to this world, but be transformed by the renewal of your mind, that by testing you may discern what is the will of God, what is good and acceptable and perfect. (Rom. 12:1–3)

Paul's use of the phrase "spiritual worship" (*logiken latreian*) echoes a term from Hellenistic religious philosophy, *logike thusia,* or "spiritual/reasonable sacrifice." On the other hand, the Greek term *soma* emphasizes the bodily, concrete form of the offering, and may carry for Jewish-speaking hearers the Semitic connotations of an offering of one's total bodily self. This term affirms the centrality of creation and incarnation in Christian faith.

> Paul thus combines the irreconcilable in order to bring out the true nature of Christian sacrifice. He combines the most elevated ethical and spiritual ideas of the Greeks with the Semitic ideas of his Jewish experience and Christian existence. This enables him to reject the Hellenistic mistrust of matter and emphasize

two cardinal points of Christian faith: creation and incarnation. The rest of this passage thus falls harmoniously into place as describing Christian life in terms of cultic service — terms which, significantly, are as applicable to Christ as to the individual Christian.[157]

Sacrifice is thus not primarily about the destruction of life, but its sanctification and dedication for others. Paul's claiming of sacrificial language for discipleship is perhaps more striking since in his time the Temple still existed, and his audience was largely Gentile non-participants in Temple sacrifice (although they may well have been familiar with "pagan" cults outside Judaism).

Another important source for the description of Christian discipleship is 1 Peter; 1 Peter 2:4–10 has been called the "richest single source for a New Testament theology of sacrifice":[158]

[4]As you come to him, a living stone rejected by men but in the sight of God chosen and precious, [5]you yourselves like living stones are being built up as a spiritual house, to be a holy priesthood, to offer spiritual sacrifices acceptable to God through Jesus Christ. [6]For it stands in Scripture: "Behold, I am laying in Zion a stone, a cornerstone chosen and precious, and whoever believes in him will not be put to shame." [7]So the honor is for you who believe, but for those who do not believe, "The stone that the builders rejected has become the cornerstone," [8]and "A stone of stumbling, and a rock of offense." They stumble because they disobey the word, as they were destined to do. [9]But you are a chosen race, a royal priesthood, a holy nation, a people for his own possession, that you may proclaim the excellencies of him who called you out of darkness into his marvelous light. [10]Once you were not a people, but now you are God's people; once you had not received mercy, but now you have received mercy. (1 Pet. 2:4–10)

This passage echoes with technical phrases. The epistle summons the disciple to "come to him," that is, believe in Christ, with the verb used for priests approaching the altar of sacrifice. Belief is likened to a sacrificial attitude, realized by offering spiritual sacrifice. Christian sacrifice is a gift of the whole self, which becomes a living stone in the Temple of the community. Verse 5b teaches that sacrifice is spiritual, accepted by God, mediated by Christ. Verse 9 calls Christians to be a universal priesthood, whose cultic offerings are spiritual sacrifice and proclaiming the good news of God's salvation.[159]

The author of 1 Peter uses a great many scriptural quotations; in number proportionate to length only Revelation exceeds it.[160] The purpose of this passage with its scriptural echoes is to illustrate the continuity of the new people of God with Israel. Best demonstrates that the author draws on material common to the primitive tradition. References to Jesus and believers as stones or buildings are common. Another source for this author may be the Qumran tradition, which also associates a new Temple with spiritual sacrifice and symbolizes its members as its stones. Interestingly, 1 Peter alludes to a non-Levitical text — Exodus 19:6 — in expressing his idea of Christians as a royal priesthood ("and you shall be to me a kingdom of priests and a holy nation"). This allusion may also derive from the Qumran community, known to read the Book of Jubilees, which also quotes the Exodus text.[161] The Exodus verse applies to all Israel, unlike the restricted Levitical priesthood.[162] Hebrews overcame this restriction by appeal to the priesthood of Melchizedek and by the general spiritualizing of Christian worship. While still interested in "spiritual sacrifice," 1 Peter appeals to an already universalized, non-Levitical scriptural vision of priesthood as the background for the holy service of Christian life.

First Peter teaches that salvation is gained not only through the proclamation of the death and resurrection of Jesus, but also through living Christian life. The difficult nature of Christian discipleship reflects the life of Jesus: the Christian will suffer and will serve the world through suffering in a Christ-like, priestly fashion. The community serves the world in a priestly fashion by suffering for others, as the suffering of the innocent may lead others to conversion. In this way the community imitates Jesus' patient suffering, and this action is an acceptable sacrifice to God. The sacrifices of Christians are described in general terms. Unlike the Qumran belief, nowhere are these sacrifices of Christians held to atone for sins.[163] New life in Christ transforms one's entire identity. It is patterned on the event of Jesus: his once-for-all sacrifice marks the newly baptized whose break with sin is irreversible.[164]

The Gospel and First Letter of John also develop a theology of the Christian community as the new Temple. Worship in Spirit and in truth is a spiritualization in specifically christological terms. The theme of sacrificial self-giving occurs in many Johannine texts. Sacrificial self-giving describes the activity of Jesus and Christians who also should serve and lay down their lives for the community. Sacrificial self-giving is voluntary and shows obedience to God.[165] Faith is expressed via a distinctively Johannine image of the blood and water flowing from Jesus' side, which evokes the wine and water that poured over the stone of foundation beneath the altar. By drinking (by having faith) we may share the living water it offers and embody the Temple of God.

Obedience, the crux of the earlier prophetic renewal of sacrifice, links the sacrifice of Jesus and the disciple in the Letter to the Hebrews. Frances Young writes that for the early church, "there was an intimate relationship between the sacrifice of Christ and the sacrificial worship and service of the church; there was an indissoluble bond linking Christ's sacrifice of obedience to the spiritual sacrifices of the saint and the martyr. For the sacrifice of Christ was itself more than an atoning sacrifice; it was a sacrifice of worship and obedience."[166] The Letter to the Hebrews depicts the Christian who participates in Jesus' sacrifice as "drawing near," using the technical term for approaching the altar. The sacrifice here is the spiritual offering of Christian life — love, good works, encouraging and being in communion:[167]

> Let us draw near with a true heart in full assurance of faith, with our hearts sprinkled clean from an evil conscience and our bodies washed with pure water. Let us hold fast the confession of our hope without wavering, for he who promised is faithful.

> And let us consider how to stir up one another to love and good
> works, not neglecting to meet together, as is the habit of some,
> but encouraging one another, and all the more as you see the
> Day drawing near. (Heb. 10:22–25)

This is a sacrifice of praise: "Through him then let us continually
offer up a sacrifice of praise to God, that is, the fruit of lips that
acknowledge his name. Do not neglect to do good and to share what
you have, for such sacrifices are pleasing to God" (Heb. 13:15–16).

There may be a parallel between the Pauline theology of Christians as the new Temple and the heavenly sanctuary in Hebrews.
The sanctuary in Hebrews where Christians draw near to God and
where Jesus is exalted at God's right hand is akin to the fellowship
of saints, or Paul's description of the disciples as the Temple.[168] Both
symbols suggest the eternal and present fellowship of Christians in
communion with God in Jesus. The spiritual Temple/sanctuary symbol emphasizes God's closeness to human conscience. Conscience
is thus purified by sacrifice and cleansed by sprinkling blood. A
similar idea occurs in 1 Peter 2:5: so cleansed, the disciple may
offer "spiritual sacrifices."[169] With the sacrifice of praise, Hebrews
also alludes to the communal worship of the Day of Atonement,
the covenant sacrifice, the Sabbath, and the eschatological gather-
ing at Mount Zion.[170] At these gatherings, all share the banquet, not
priests alone consuming the sacrifice. This is the blessing of Christian
community.

Hebrews made a shift from sacrifice as cultic practice to sacrifice as
spiritual obedience. The letter insisted also, equally significantly, on
the single sufficient sacrifice of Christ. The first development prepared
the way to view spiritual acts of worship and charity, not cultic offerings, as sacrifice. The second prevents viewing sacrifice as an imitation
or repetition of Christ's ultimate sacrifice in death. The theological
move in Hebrews ends the Jewish cult system of the Aaronic priesthood and replaces it with the incommensurate priesthood of Christ.
This difference is not moral, as if Jewish sacrifice was irredeemably
legalistic or a form of cultic sin barter. The theological difference is

that "Christians' thanksgiving is Christ himself."[171] Christian justification is Christ and his gift of the Spirit. The new mode of justification is in the Spirit dwelling in us through faith in Christ.

Daly concludes that "the sacrifices which Christians offer have primarily an ethical rather than ritual or liturgical meaning;... sacrifice is understood as the practical living of the life of Christian virtue and Christian mission."[172] The offering of self is the supreme sacrifice, which could mean Christian virtue, monasticism, or martyrdom. Spiritual worship, praise, and charity constitute the new language of sacrificial discipleship. Its message is "to do good and to share what you have, for such sacrifices are pleasing to God" (Heb. 15:16). The new law and new cult ordain the Christian, in imitation of Jesus, to be a holy sacrifice and a holy priesthood. As such, sacrifice is a metaphorical vehicle for the role and drama of Christian identity. In this rich imagery, the multivalent nature of sacrificial symbolism again appears. Drawing on the active and passive roles within a sacrificial model enables *self*-offering. Within a sacrificial metaphor, the one who gives offers a priestly service and is himself the offering. The advantage of symbolically combining victim and priest, or offering and subject, or gift and giver, is to eliminate violence, scapegoating, exploitation, and oppression. This dual meaning reflects into the sacrificial symbolism of both Christ and the disciple, as the choice and the subjectivity of the one making the sacrifice is clear. This theme can be expressed without cultic resonances when the victim and priest are described as the gift and the giver. Love understood as the incarnational spiritualization of sacrifice unites the actions of Jesus and the believer. Both offer obedience and love (right dispositions) *to* God, and offer self-sacrificing love and service *for* others. Through sacrifice, one expresses one's dedication to God.

## Defining the Core Meaning of the Metaphor of Sacrifice

How does the event of Jesus Christ change the meaning of sacrifice for the communities that followed him? It can be argued that Jesus' own death — whether or not understood as a sacrifice in the cultic sense and whether he intended all the changes that unfolded in history, beyond his Jewish world — radically changes the possibility and function of sacrifice in the life of the Christian church. There are several elements to this change. First, *salvation is offered in the person of Jesus Christ.* Second, it is offered definitively and finally. Third, salvation is offered continuously in the church. Finally, all the baptized belong to the holy priesthood.

Nonetheless, the interpretation of Jesus' death as a sacrifice does not alone establish the meaning of his ministry. In fact, it is his life that provides a reason to seek meaning in his death. Paul's theology of the Christian as a "living sacrifice" shows that dying does not exhaust the options for following Jesus. The theology of sacrifice for the disciple will also flow from an imitation of Jesus' life. The paradox of finding one's self by losing it becomes a pointed question for the disciple at this point. Jesus' words about suffering were not the whole of his message. Jesus summoned the people to accept that their lives were meaningful and treasured by God, and his healing acts confirmed his consoling words. He continually called his followers to the fullness of life, to the joy of friends in the presence of the bridegroom, trusting in God's constant love. The texts that show Jesus healing, teaching love of self and neighbor, and calling the disciples to live with king-dom fruitfulness constitute a "canon of self-realization." There are many stories of healing: Mark 1:25, 1:31, 1:34, 1:41, 2:11, 3:5, 3:10, 5:13, 5:21, 6:5, 7:29, 7:34, 9:25, 9:43, 10:52, and parallels. The great command to love the neighbor *as oneself* recurs in Mat-thew 22:34, Mark 12:28, and Luke 10:25. The great quality of the coming kingdom is its fruitfulness, as exemplified in many parables (the Sower parable: Matt. 13:1–9, Mark 4:1–9, Luke 8:4–8; and the seed parables: Mark 4:26–32, Luke 13:18, Matt. 13:24–34).

The image of a healing savior is retrieved by an important reference to Isaiah 53, a text usually employed to give meaning to Jesus' death. One of the few direct citations of Isaiah's suffering servant poems is found not in the passion narratives, but in the story of healing Peter's mother-in-law. Matthew 8:17 describes Jesus as the fulfill-ment of the prophet's words: "This was to fulfil what was spoken by the prophet Isaiah, 'He took our infirmities and bore our diseases.' "

John McKenzie shows that Matthew quotes Isaiah 53:4 and alters the meaning by a wordplay: "Matthew interprets the words 'take' and 'carry' as take away, which Jesus does by healing."[173] Matthew does not apply this text for an explanation of Jesus' death, but shows what manner of servant Jesus is: one who heals. Geza Vermes argues that Jesus' strongest sense of his own identity was as a healer in the context of first-century charismatic Judaism.[174] The evangelist recognizes him as the savior because of his marvelous healing. Similarly, when John's disciples asked if he is the expected one, Jesus offers the proof of the blind, lame, and deaf who are healed (Matt. 11:2–6). Luke's Jesus proclaims the initiation of his ministry by claiming the prophet's description of one who brings good news and heals the blind (Luke 4:18).

Each of the gospel writers' congregations remembered and celebrated a particular aspect of Jesus' historical life and death. Each focused on a particular, historical aspect of his ministry and sought ways to continue that ministry in their own lives. Continuing to live by this memory is what Schillebeeckx called the continuance principle. Based on the principle of continuance, Christians do not imitate his saving death only, but continue the practices of his healing ministry, transforming the religious intent of sacrifice as an offering for atonement into an offering for love of neighbor. Implications for an ongoing discipleship of sacrifice can then be drawn from Jesus' historical ministry, and should seek to imitate his work of healing, inclusion, and offering fulfillment.

Is it necessary to interpret the life of discipleship as a sacrifice? The plurality of New Testament expressions of Christian life, as briefly reviewed here, indicates that while significant and even dominant, sacrifice is not an essential or unavoidable characterization of discipleship. But there are extensive grounds for retrieving the symbolic description of Christian witness with the imagery of sacrifice. In the brief examples given, New Testament language expresses sacrifice as a sign of love, of inner dedication, as an act that transforms the believer. The believer's identity is united to Christ's and confirmed through love of neighbor. Furthermore, because the need to sacrifice and to dedicate one's self to another recurs frequently in human experience, a model of sacrificial Christian life can draw richly from the New Testament message of Jesus' life and death for understanding its own identity. The themes of transformation and connection to others through sacrifice form a continuous thread.

The relative fluidity of sacrificial details makes it hard to sift out a definitive element in the concrete sacrificial details. Common to most expressions of sacrifice is that sacrifice is a gift given by God for reconciliation, salvation, and communion, which is now recognized in Jesus. I propose that the core meaning of the sacrificial symbol that unites the canon of metaphors is neither blood nor death, but dedication. The basic meaning of Jesus' life is dedicated self-gift, whether expressed in sacrificial symbols or not. This theme of dedication continues to be a central message and essential mode of discipleship. The expression of dedication may or may not always use the term "sacrifice." Use of the term "sacrifice" today is usually interpreted in an ethical sense without any cultic reference. Christian communities applied the sacrificial language of "offering" to actions that, if described without metaphors, would be spoken of as "giving and serving."

Through baptism, initiated into Jesus Christ's life and death, the disciple now shares in the reconciliation offered to all. The death of Jesus — interpreted as a sacrifice, or not — frees the Christian to live by the Spirit of Jesus Christ and by grace share in the economy of divine love. This gracious invitation into the life of the Trinity means that sacrifice reflects not only the historical life of Jesus Christ, much less only his death, but is a mirror of the outpouring love of God the Father, Son, and Holy Spirit. That is the ground for a theological anthropology of sacrifice that is not only christological, but also Trinitarian. The sacramental cycle and all the circles of life participate in accepting and giving back what God has first given.

R. Kevin Seasoltz interprets this gift as God's self-sacrificing love.

As Irenaeus said so powerfully, "The glory of God is the human person fully alive" — alive with God's own gift of life. As a result *we are empowered to act in relation to others as God relates to us — with self-sacrificing love. It is only in that sense that we can speak of praising God* [emphasis added].[175]

Love and thanksgiving, receptivity and dependence, giftedness and grace, self-giving and self-sacrifice form a unity in the Christian experience.

## Sacrifice as Existential Response and Dedication

At the outset of this chapter I suggested three working definitions of sacrifice outlined at the beginning of this chapter: general, Christian, and existential. My working definition of sacrifice in its most general theistic sense was that sacrifice is an action that seeks to establish or transform one's relationship with the divine, which may result in the transformation of one's own religious identity. Within a Christian religious framework, sacrifice means an act that responds to the encounter of God's grace in Jesus Christ and expresses one's dedication to God through worship and by caring for the neighbor. In a modern, existential worldview, sacrifice is understood as an act that is costly or burdensome but undertaken out of love for the other. This is the common, colloquial sense of "sacrifice" spoken of in ordinary life, separated from religious rituals. The next section explores a Christian view of sacrifice in existential terms, as a way to bridge the discussion of Christian discipleship in Palestinian and Graeco-Roman antiquity to modern times.

Otto Semmelroth defines Christian sacrifice as that which enables humans to experience and express their relationship to God. He describes human participation in God's self-giving in existential and transcendental terms. The capacity to sacrifice demonstrates "esteem ...as a sort of readiness for self-dedication — a token of one's belonging to another." Sacrifice represents an attitude that expresses love, in the way a gift to another person shows affection.[176] More precisely, it is an expression or designation of humanity's dedication to God. Sacrifice thus makes the human relationship to God visible.

Consistent with a transcendental approach, Semmelroth offers a formal view of Christian sacrifice, rather than identifying a material act. Semmelroth criticizes an exaggerated interest in the modes of symbolic sacrificial gift. This misplaced concern categorizes objects rather than recognizing the relational encounter. It is the formal view that structures the "core metaphor." In this light, sacrifice reveals the personal encounter that has taken place, resulting in confession of faith and offering of gifts to be dedicated to God. Sacrifice from this formal light *is* the interpersonal relationship. Sacrifice acknowledges humanity's encounter with God and, without manipulation, responds to the initiative of grace. Sacrifice presupposes being gifted by God, not only by an awareness of grace, but by the very gift of creation itself. The truth of being created and loved impels a response — yet faith humbly acknowledges that even the response is given by God.

> Hence there are only two ways in the NT order of salvation in which man can respond to his being enriched by God. There is the sacrifice which Christ offered once and for all as head of the human race, inviting men to share in it. And there is love of the neighbour, in which the love of God is passed on.[177]

Christian sacrifice is the response to an encounter with God that is expressed outwardly by loving the neighbor. Sacrifice is an interpretation of our relationship with God; it is a loving acknowledgment of the transcendent God as creator and holy power. The dedication of humanity to God is a decision that informs all aspects of life. The inner decision is expressed outwardly by its embodiment in action. Sacrifice is not a gift that substitutes for giving of oneself; it is this very self-giving and dedication.

> But sacrifice is this act of dedication, which is also a programme of life, in its most forcible expression. It is this character of programme or design for living which makes it appropriate that sacrifice should be used to represent the wholeness of man's self-dedication, by bringing in visibly the plurality of the dimensions of man's existence — in the body, in society and in the world.[178]

Sacrifice is the gift of the whole self; it includes and integrates all dimensions of life. Its core is the decision to love God, but the decision is embodied by visible sacrifice. The commitment to dedicate oneself to God radiates through all of life and shows the wholeness of self-dedication. That sacrifice unites religious devotion throughout all dimensions of life makes an important statement about Christian identity and spirituality.[179] Sacrifice ultimately remains a mystery of love. It is a mystery that cannot be satisfactorily sustained by secularization. There are many possible ways to secularize the dynamics of sacrifice, in psychological theories of scapegoating, art, and literary criticism.[180] Yet Christian theology may prophetically refuse to secularize sacrifice. Sacrifice for the church remains an intimate connection between God who shares life with the people who depend upon God, and because of God's giving are able to respond to each other with love.

This brief existential reflection on the sacrificial nature of Christian life suggests how the multiple meanings of sacrifice proposed by New Testament authors can be translated into a contemporary mode. The complexity of New Testament descriptions of Jesus as a sacrifice and the consequent application of sacrificial language to Christian identity provide a foundation for viewing religious identity through the lens of sacrifice. Sacrificial images of discipleship derive from legitimate, ancient, and contemporary descriptions of Christian life. Semmelroth's transcendental definition strongly connects sacrifice to Christian identity, echoing Augustine's focus on the uniting power of sacrifice.

As significant as it is, the sacrificial description of Christian life is only one aspect of discipleship. The call to sacrifice accompanies the promise of the fullness of life. Indeed, Jesus teaches that one's realization is achieved *through* sacrifice. I will explore how sacrifice supports the realization of Christian identity in chapter 3. A more complete and careful examination of the implications of sacrifice for the realization of the self is needed first. Because of the unity of love of God and neighbor, dedication to God expressed by sacrifice involves care for the other. The possibility that care for the other may threaten one's own integrity requires further interpretation of the problematic of Christian sacrifice. This interpretation addresses the lived experience of sacrifice as a mode of relationship between self and neighbor. The conflicts and struggles within this relationship bring the paradox of self-sacrifice and self-realization to the fore. The real challenge of a contemporary retrieval of sacrifice is now to examine some of the legitimate critiques and objections to the rhetoric and practice of sacrifice. This brings us, first of all, to the feminist critique of a distorted ideal of sacrifice.

# Chapter Two

# THE FEMINIST CRITIQUE OF A DISTORTED IDEAL OF SACRIFICE

*Are not two sparrows sold for a penny? And not one of them falls to the ground without your Father's will.... You are of more value than many sparrows.* — Matthew 10:29–31

Among his reflections on sacrifice cited in the previous chapter, Dietrich Bonhoeffer issued a severe warning to anyone posing the very kind of question I am about to raise. In *The Cost of Discipleship* he writes that the word calls for work and obedience, not puzzling and pondering. Disobedience makes union with Christ impossible. "If we start asking questions, posing problems, and offering interpretations, we are not doing his word."[181] Bonhoeffer emphasizes that the word does not call for discernment, but for faith. At the risk of ignoring Bonhoeffer's caution and falling into the trap of the lawyer who delayed doing good to ask Jesus to define the neighbor (Luke 10:29), it must be acknowledged that authentic sacrifice does call for discernment. A realistic effort to be obedient should be aware that false interpretations of Jesus' message are possible. Every action is based on some interpretation of the word and of the situation. The need for discernment is the justification for this chapter. The Syro-Phoenician woman risked an interpretation of whom Jesus identified as his people, hoping his concern extended to herself (Mark 7:24–30; Matt. 15:21–28). She dared to ask Jesus if he would care for her, and for her daughter. She chose to define herself as the neighbor, and her interpretation was praised by Jesus. The woman with an

71

issue of blood also dared to ask for her own healing (Mark 6:25–43). Both women are recalled by the Gospels as models of faith, and their example inspires the present discussion of self-love.[182]

The ideal of self-sacrifice expresses one side of the summons to discipleship. Jesus' invitation to his followers is also a call to healing and the fullness of life. Together self-sacrifice and self-realization describe a paradox within Christian life. In Jesus' paradoxical teaching, self-sacrifice is a means of self-realization. "For whoever would save his life will lose it; and whoever loses his life for my sake and the gospel's will save it" (Mark 8:35). This insight represents a tension that is not meant to be resolved by eliminating one pole or the other. If the message of sacrifice contained within Jesus' words and actions is complex and subject to grave misinterpretation, the message of fulfillment and healing in the other pole of the paradox, the pole of self-realization, also requires interpretation.

How do specific aspects of Christian theology present an ambiguous context for the interpretation and lived experience of sacrifice, so that sacrifice may either build or erode identity? In what ways might theological use of sacrificial symbolism obstruct or overwhelm the gospel promise of having "life to the fullest"? Feminist scholars in particular contend that the tension between self-sacrifice and self-realization that is the paradox of Christian wisdom has imploded; too often, the effort to live sacrificially instead destroys the realization of the richness of life. Sacrifice attains a problematic weight for people when their choices are weighed with an intolerably high acceptance of suffering and loss of well-being. Sacrifice then fails to be a means of self-realization but instead thwarts the fulfillment of the gospel paradox.

Theological ideas integral to guiding Christian sacrifice can fail to construct a sufficient support for self-realization. The frequency of theological attention to sacrifice makes sacrifice appear to be a very important and valuable thing by virtue of sheer ubiquity. The greater weight of theological attention given to sacrifice overpowers the potential for a fruitful tension between self-sacrifice and self-realization in the life of discipleship. The problem of sacrifice is not that the ideal is hollow, or false, or that its practice in all cases must be malicious or naive. However, theological reflection on the cross, Christian love, and sin — central topics that establish the model for and implications of sacrifice — often views suffering as salutary and corrective. Traditional theological reflection on the cross, love, and sin that assumes suffering is redemptive in itself may overlook the negative impact of suffering upon self-realization. When Christian language sanctions the passivity, suffering, and violence involved in Jesus' death, the Christian ideal of sacrifice can encourage the loss of self and erosion of identity. As a direct consequence of these views of the Passion, ideas about love and sin as models for the believer incorporate the same tolerance of suffering.

Influenced by a theological tolerance of suffering, persons may undertake sacrifices that are not primarily chosen to express dedication to God and neighbor. Swayed by the idealization of sacrifice, they may accept the cost or suffering in their acts as meaningful. Such sacrifices result in meaningless suffering, undermine the individual's purpose and agency, and confound the development of identity. Religious language that approves of passivity and suffering per se distorts the Christian ideal of sacrifice as dedicated giving that expresses one's love of God, and thus confirms and strengthens one's identity. By insisting upon a careful assessment of suffering in the discernment of sacrifice, I do not mean to delegitimize any sacrifice that has the potential for suffering. In some cases suffering may be redemptive. Part of my interest in retrieving the symbolism of sacrifice stems from recognizing that difficult and painful sacrifices are often important and necessary. Furthermore, although martyrdom is a special topic not treated here, it remains the fate of Christians even today.

Aware that sacrifice takes place in a historical and social context, two analyses precede an exposition of the theological traditions that contextualize sacrifice. First, appropriate historical theory will enable a hermeneutic approach to the changes in the meaning of sacrifice over time. Next, the claims of feminist thinkers about the particular social situation of women illuminate distortions in the

experience of sacrifice. These two preliminary sections on historical and social context enable a more nuanced investigation of how
theologies of atonement, Christian love, and sin have served as the
sometimes unsteady framework in which the balance of sacrifice and
self-realization is at stake.

Important critiques of atonement theologies emerge from feminist concern about women's tendency to accept a destructive loss
of self. Theologies of Christian love and of sin also impact the
interrelationship of self-sacrifice and self-realization. Outdated or inadequate views of the human person result in imbalanced ideas about
Christian love and of sacrifice as an expression of love.

## I. A Hermeneutic Approach to Freeing
## the Symbol of Sacrifice

### Historical Developments in Sacrificial Language

A theory of historical change and continuity can help explain the enduring power of sacrificial language — and its capacity to be often
misunderstood. The meaning of a religious practice or symbol may
evolve over time until it eventually takes on a substantively new
meaning. Or it may be reformed within the accepted meaning of
a given time through critique. Both types of historical change can
be accommodated by a view of history which accounts for the divisions and connections between social eras. Looking at history as a
continuity punctuated by fractures explains why meanings and practices change over time, yet retain forms and emphases from the past.
Such a theoretical model of history also identifies the point of contact
where feminist critique strikes the problem of sacrifice.

Tradition is a living reality. But because tradition spans from one
historical age to another, the theologian must ask how traditional
statements can bear meaning today.[183] The philosophy of historical
continuity and change formulated by Fernand Braudel and the *Annales* school establishes several key points. First, change is rarely so
total so as to bar comprehension. Old things may be strange, but
often they are still intelligible. Communication of a sort thus exists

between eras. Second, change is nonsynchronous. The complex factors that make up a society — political, economic, cultural, moral, artistic, linguistic — do not change all together, all at once. Things change, and they stay the same — only not always all the same things, at the same times.

This theory of historical continuity and discontinuity proposes three levels of historical change. These levels may be envisioned as periods of time which last either for a millennium, occupy hundreds of years, or pass daily. Similarly, they can be viewed as rates of change that are either glacially slow, revolve with the centuries, or spin at the speed of daily events. Braudel refers to these as the structural, conjunctural, and ephemeral levels of history. Structural history persists for centuries. It is in motion, but these changes are almost imperceptible. These fundamental structures provide the deep continuity underlying successive conjunctures. Conjunctural history includes the more comprehensive patterns of interpenetrating layers that form a coherent society.

> "Social movement" can be taken to refer to all the movements at work in a given society, the combination of movements which forms the *conjuncture* or rather the *conjunctures*. For there may be different conjunctural rhythms affecting the economy, political life, demography and indeed collective attitudes, preoccupations, crime, the different schools of art or literature, even fashion.[184]

Lastly, ephemeral history includes the day-to-day events and facts that are replaced quickly by new ones.

The multiple elements of society do not all change together, or at the same pace. For example, political structures may be very long-lasting, while social customs shift more quickly, or vice versa. This nonsynchronous change creates different connections or breaks between the whole fabric of culture and the past from which it is evolving. Some structures hold, and some things break as the syncopated beats of historical change prolong inheritances from the past and incorporate new influences. The hermeneutical circle in which the individual encounters tradition is borne by this complex movement of history. The believer makes sense of the tradition's interpretive models within his or her conjunctural level.

At the structural level, sacrifice has evolved from a primarily cultic meaning to a primarily ethical sense over the course of centuries. Of course, important cultic patterns still persist and develop in ways that need not be considered primitive. This theory of history nevertheless explains how certain aspects of a religious tradition can be both intelligible and strange, as in the tension and interplay between views of sacrifice as cultic and as ethical dedication. At the conjunctural level, shifts within a fairly constant paradigm appear. Thus the prophets maintained a legitimate view of sacrifice as a material offering according to the law. Yet, without challenging that basic view, they perceived corruption in practices that called for renewal. The New Testament texts take up themes about sacrifice and reshaped them according to the context and concerns of the community, as well as to reflect new philosophical or cultural attitudes. For example, each evangelical community viewed Jesus and his actions in relationship to their particular views of sacrifice and their messianic expectations. These are interpretations that operate at the conjunctural level.

A religious theme is also appropriated within the hermeneutical circle of an individual life, becoming a new work. Meaning is colored by context and takes form in the individual's understanding, where it is conditioned by that individual's experience. Even then meaning is not closed or final, since ongoing experiences may revise one's understanding, if one is open to new outlooks. Again, like all interpretive experience, this phenomenon is also communal. The individual understands as a member of a community. She both receives and shapes the group's views. Every individual shares the effect of a moment that ripples through his or her historical situation and may pass into the conjunctural changes affecting society.[185]

One source of false interpretations is the loss of sacrifice's original vibrant cultural context as societies evolved and languages changed. The New Testament saw Christ as the model of self-giving and expressed this belief with sacrificial imagery drawing on Jewish patterns. Their larger society was alive with the sacrificial cults of other rites and traditions also. However, the cultic scenes which are the original context of the term "sacrifice" have virtually vanished from sight in modern Western society. Traces of the term's original bloody connotation remain, however, and give rise to the anachronistic difficulties I will address later in the chapter. This contributes to the sense of inadequacy that calls for critique.

The shift in context requires that ideas be not simply translated, but re-instanciated. To interpret sacrifice is not to match terms across centuries. Doctrines and ideas cannot be simply lifted into the language of a new time, but must be "re-enacted." As Schillebeeckx observes, capturing the authentic meaning of a message requires determining its relationship with its culture at any given time. Therefore, the interpretive challenge is to understand what sacrifice meant to Jesus and to his hearers, in proportion to sacrifice's impact or implications upon existing mores. A distinct, but parallel, effect of sacrifice upon the believers and societies of today can then be imagined. In this practical and reflective process, critical responses to negative contrast experiences can clarify our understanding.[186]

Human ways of knowing overlap with the theory of historical change in a very complex way. Human knowledge, which includes the encounter with religious traditions, is borne by the multiple tempos of these paces of historical change. Persons know what they know in changing historical periods. By viewing religious models against their historical and epistemological contexts, both the continuity and change of such language across epochs becomes more intelligible. It also becomes possible to explain the dynamic of interpretation and critique within a single epoch. The call for reform within a tradition may thus represent an upheaval caused by the breaks between more enduring structural patterns, a critical impulse within a conjunctural period, or a combination of both.

When the ongoing tradition of the church regarding sacrifice is carried into new cultures, time periods, or generations in an encounter that requires a translation, interpretation occurs. Changes occur within the same culture as patterns of thought emerge from catalysts like the civil rights movement or women's movement. Such changes affect individuals through social and religious institutions and mores. My focus on sacrifice in relationship to suffering and passivity centers on the individual experience of sacrifice. Different individuals may interpret, appropriate, and experience religious teaching as destructive or salutary. At this level, what harms one person may benefit another. This conflict of horizons explains the difficulty for some to credit the criticisms of others.

The feminist critique of sacrifice as a damaging ideology demonstrates that the message of Jesus about sacrifice can lose its proper relationship to our society when self-realization is overlooked. This argument claims that the memory of Jesus' ministry invites both the joyful discovery of new life and the costly commitments of discipleship. To neglect either memory when bringing this message to the culture of today weakens the gospel's power to engage our times. Second, the feminist critique shows that sexism intensifies an imbalanced understanding of sacrifice. Both of these are calls for reform within the given understanding of sacrifice as an ethical action in contemporary society.

## Interpreting Social Factors That Intensify a Distorted View of Sacrifice

Social contexts significantly affect sacrificial behavior. While the interpretation of the paradox is a challenge for men and women across the centuries of Christian experience, feminist thought discerns a gendered history in which women's experience of sacrifice is marked by sexism. Social patterns in a sexist society exacerbate the imbalanced effect of some exhortations to sacrifice. Using a hermeneutic of suspicion, feminist theology discerns the fingerprints of power upon the traditions that are effectively handed down. The term "hermeneutic of suspicion" derives from Paul Ricoeur, whose work has investigated the sources and interpretation of meaning in many fields, and whose philosophical reflection on self-giving will be examined in the next chapter. Influenced by Marx, Nietzsche, and Freud, Ricoeur realized that "sources of signification may exist that are removed from the immediate grasp of consciousness" and that must be critically examined to fully understand them.[187] Feminist analyses of society probe for such subconscious meanings, or ideological presuppositions, that obscure an authentic representation of the gospel message. The turbulent effects of the tension between self-sacrifice and self-realization, caught between conflicting ideologies of self-worth, emerge as distortions in different theological themes. Many feminist activists and scholars judge that sacrifice is a tool of social inequality and sexist discrimination that does oppose women's flourishing.

Socially, suffragettes and social critics have long been concerned that even valuable forms of self-sacrifice have been unequally urged upon women. In 1895, Elizabeth Cady Stanton, one of the central leaders of early feminism, expressed suspicion of male praise for female self-sacrifice as the ideal virtue. She wrote, "Men think that self-sacrifice is the most charming of all the Cardinal virtues for women...and in order to keep it in healthy working order they make opportunities for its illustration as often as possible."[188] She suggested that male recommendation of self-sacrifice failed to appreciate women's distinctive patterns of psychological development. More cynically, she suspected that promoting this ideal for women was expedient for men, who were able to exploit often pathologically low female self-regard.

Mary Grey has noted even more pernicious strands of sexism intertwined with theological justification that found women responsible for evil and suffering because of their descent from Eve. Therefore, women are thought to be justly punished by self-sacrifice because of their original sin and deserve to take up their crosses. Grey cites 1 Timothy 3:11–15, which assigns to all women blame for Eve's transgression, and offers women salvation through childbearing and submissive acceptance of subordination in the patriarchal household.[189]

For Adam was formed first, then Eve: and Adam was not deceived, but the woman was deceived and became a transgressor.

Yet woman will be saved through bearing children, if she continues in faith and love and holiness, with modesty. (1 Tim.
3:11–15)

Grey also shows how Martin Luther likewise identifies all women
with Eve, confers Eve's guilt upon all women, and finds fitting punishment in women's confinement to the home. "The wife should stay at
home . . . as one who has been deprived of the ability of administering
those affairs that are outside. . . . In this way is Eve punished."[190]

The groundbreaking feminist writer Mary Daly illustrates both the
theoretical imbalance and the social distortion of self-sacrifice. She
declared,

> there has been a *theoretical* one-sided emphasis upon charity,
> meekness, obedience, humility, self-abnegation, sacrifice, ser-
> vice. Part of the problem with this moral ideology is that it
> became accepted not by men, but by women, who hardly have
> been helped by an ethic which reinforces the abject female
> situation.[191]

A theoretical one-sidedness exists when self-regard is delegitimated,
by emphasizing sacrifice to the expense of realization. Socially, Daly
detects a further imbalance as gender discrimination and sexism pressure women in particular to accept this distorted emphasis upon
self-sacrifice. Women are more likely than men to be pushed into
self-sacrificing positions by the structures and mores of society. Betty
Friedan famously depicted this crisis of wasted female energy in the
trapped American housewife in *The Feminine Mystique*.[192] Women
entering the workforce half a generation later encountered a new
inequity that invited their sacrifices. This new, unequal distribution
of self-sacrifice has been documented in the concrete social patterns
of the "second shift."[193] This phrase refers to the unequal burden
of domestic labor, traditionally considered to be "women's work,"
added to the schedule of women who also work outside the home.
Working women who return home to complete the vast majority of
domestic chores in effect face a "second shift." Other effects could

be examined which I will not explore explicitly; for example, the impact of oppressive forms of sacrifice on women's physical well-being, economic independence, political leadership, or artistic expression.

While the pioneering figures of feminist thought point to the intensification of this imbalance in women's social experience, the profound disequilibrium of the paradox may unsettle all Christian believers, men and women. When the paradox of self-sacrifice and self-realization loses its necessary tension, then sacrifice is no longer a pruning hook that stimulates new life, but a spear that drains away one's lifeblood. The balance between self-sacrifice and self-realization collapses when suffering and passivity are viewed as redemptive, and when the importance of well-being is overlooked. This imbalance draws upon deep sources in Christian theological reflection on atonement, love, and sin. These themes intertwined with sacrifice form the subject of the next three sections.

## II. Critique of Atonement Theories as a Theological Justification of Victimization

### Critiques of Atonement Theologies That Promote Self-Sacrifice

Because sacrificial images of Jesus shape the sacrificial model for Christian life, the feminist charge that sacralized self-destruction is rooted in the cross is critically relevant. Feminist thinkers question whether atonement models are necessarily violent or arbitrary, or if it is simply sacrificial images for the atonement that are inappropriate. Joanne Carlson Brown and Rebecca Parker, among many others, have criticized theologies of the cross that reinforce women's tendency to accept a destructive loss of self.[194] They contend that a specifically Christian ideal of sacrifice encourages the loss of self and erosion of identity when religious language sanctions the passivity, suffering, and violence involved in Jesus' sacrifice. They criticize an assumption that Jesus' experience of suffering and violence is in itself salvific. Brown and Parker argue that this assumption is flawed because it associates divinity with violence and minimizes the value of self-realization. They argue that traditional teaching about self-sacrifice based on this assumption creates a history of damaging effects and demand a revision of this teaching and a new interpretation of self-sacrifice. In effect, their critical reading of atonement theologies that glorify passive suffering revisits the ideal expression of sacrificial Christian identity traced in chapter 1, but exposes the potential of that same ideal for harm.

Brown and Parker charge that Christianity has acculturated women to accept abuse by framing the acceptance of abuse as virtuous self-sacrifice, and then teaches women to believe that their suffering is divinely justified.

> The central image of Christ on the cross as the savior of the world communicates the message that suffering is redemptive. ...Any sense that we have a right to care for our needs is in conflict with being a faithful follower of Jesus....Those whose lives have been deeply shaped by the Christian tradition feel that self-sacrifice and obedience are not only virtues but the definition of a faithful identity.[195]

This ideology has victimized many, especially women, by thwarting their full personhood and the right freely to seek self-determination and wholeness. "The promise of resurrection persuades us to endure pain, humiliation, and violation of our sacred rights to self-determination, wholeness, and freedom."[196] They assert that according to this ideology, self-sacrifice, simply stated, without context or qualification, is the defining virtue of "faithful identity."

Brown and Parker locate the root of this destructive theology in a view of the cross that asserts that Jesus' suffering and death are fundamental to our salvation. They analyze how three major versions of atonement theory describe suffering and its role in the life of the believer. The first of these three strands is the *Christus Victor* tradition found in patristic teaching, in which the greater power of God triumphs over death and the devil in Jesus. Brown and Parker argue that the *Christus Victor* tradition encourages the believer to look for new life coming through the endurance of pain. If Jesus' suffering brought about the resurrection, then the believer may try to earn new life not only through, but because of, pain. Second, there is the satisfaction theory, in which Jesus dies to pay the price for our sins and satisfy the demands of justice. They cite Anselm as the formulator of this theory, and question whether it hinges upon payment by the "human" side of Christ to restore God's honor. The satisfaction theory shows that by one's suffering, another may be freed from pain. This view is linked with biblical images of sacrifice and the power of blood. Finally, the third theory is that the moral persuasion effected by the demonstration of God's mercy on the cross moves the beholder to faith and trust in God. Abelard exemplifies this model.[197] Adherents of this view believe the victimization of the innocent may motivate an oppressor to convert. In fact, Brown and Parker counter, the innocent themselves are denied relief from their own suffering, finding their victimization justified and their concerns silenced.[198] Feminism is rightly hard put to find redemption in this cross. In this light, traditional doctrines of atonement appear uncongenial at best and deliberately repressive and punitive at worst.[199]

Brown and Parker approve of developments in twentieth-century theology that reconsider divine impassibility. However, according to their review, these developments may not relieve the believer who is still shown that suffering leads to greater life. "Suffering God" theologies may valorize suffering even further because if even God suffers, suffering must be good.[200] Liberation theology places suffering within a larger view of historical change. In other words, for the struggles to occur that challenge injustice and increase political options for the disenfranchised, the poor and the powerless must first suffer of necessity. Brown and Parker are concerned that some liberation theologians have taken up a new version of a moral influence theory. In this contemporary form, suffering is instrumental to awaken change in history, and the victims become "the servants of the evildoers' salvation."[201] However, in Brown and Parker's view, suffering may be inevitable but it cannot be instrumental to salvation. The cross is a sign of tragedy. The true resurrection is the deathless commitment to life that Jesus made in the garden of Gethsemane — the "resurrected one was crucified."[202]

In summary, Brown and Parker criticize atonement theologies that make the cross something violent God does to Jesus, wherein Jesus is not the subject but truly the passive victim of the crucifixion — the victim not only of Pilate, but of God. Each model treats suffering as a cipher for another good: for obedience, for accepting a punishment that liberates, or for influence upon souls. Because obedience, liberation, and influence are positive goods, suffering is validated along with them.

Brown and Parker have important concerns about the dangers such ideology poses for many people. Parker's personal story provides a harrowing example of how Jesus' example of bearing suffering can be twisted into an internalized system of torture.

> The gesture of sacrifice was familiar. I knew the rubrics of the ritual by heart: you cut away some part of yourself, then peace and security are restored, relationship is preserved, and shame is avoided. I could have drawn you a picture of the steps. First I bow my head. I cast my eyes down to indicate my subservience to the other whose will or needs I am obeying. I close my mouth. I do not speak. Then I kneel. I offer my head, my hands, or expose my breast or thighs to the executioner's blade, holding still. He swings, cuts. Then I rise, silently wrap the wound, and withdraw. Clearly this ritual is a horror. Where did the executioner come from who appeared so readily in my imagination? . . . I recognize that Christianity had taught me that sacrifice is the way of life. I forgot the neighbor who raped me, but I could see that when theology presents Jesus as God's sacrifice of his beloved child for the sake of the world, it teaches that the highest love is sacrifice. To make sacrifice or to be sacrificed is virtuous and redemptive. But what if this is not true? What if nothing, or very little, is saved? What if the consequence of sacrifice is simply pain, the diminishment of life, fragmentation of the soul, abasement, shame? What if the severing of life is merely destructive of

life and is not the path of love, courage, trust, and faith? What if the performance of sacrifice is a ritual in which some human beings bear loss and others are protected from accountability or moral expectations?[203]

Brown and Parker protest that the symbol of the cross encourages victimization and negatively affects an interpretation of the paradox of self-sacrifice and self-realization.

Brown and Parker conclude that Christianity must eliminate the idea of the atonement in order to liberate the present. Maintaining this ancient symbol seems to exalt submission to violence. This kind of soteriology turns the loving God whom Jesus preached into a legalistic tyrant. To "argue that salvation can only come through the cross is to make God a divine sadist and a divine child abuser."[204] To see the violence of the cross as salvific subsequently colors the imitation of Christ by the disciple and glorifies accepting violence inflicted by self or other. Conscious of this idealized view of self-sacrifice, Christians lose the capacity to judge painful experience critically. The ideal permits them to justify violence and consider their own well-being expendable.

## Assessing Feminist Critiques of Atonement

### Anachronisms Affecting Interpretation

Certain anachronisms complicate the assessment of sacrificial theological language. Atonement is not interchangeable with sacrifice. A loose handling of this anachronism pervades and weakens Brown and Parker's argument. Atonement means "at-one-ment," the reconciliation and restoration of the Creator-creature relationship. Some process must explain how that relationship is restored. Sacrifice is one particular mechanism, established in the ancient context of the early church, that explains how the relationship is changed. Paul Fiddes emphasizes the creative and redemptive purpose of atonement. While the idea of a sin offering is strange to us today, to the early church, sin offerings and spiritual offerings were readily understood. This is a historical fact even if the early church's acceptance of the power of sacrifice does not easily translate into a contemporary worldview.[205] Ancient logic accepted that sacrifice removed sin, covered it over, and washed it away by blood. The spirituality and iconography of the Middle Ages found the blood and pain of Christ supremely moving, and not at all distasteful, as testified by the contorted statues with realistic tears and streaming blood in countless European and colonial churches. Perceiving such imagery negatively is in part a modern phenomenon. Brown and Parker's concern for the danger of the symbol of sacrifice, when taken apart from its detailed historical background, is legitimate. Unfortunately, they do not acknowledge the nuance within ancient sacrificial theory that suffering is never a meaningful or purposeful part of the sacrificial process.[206]

It is understandable that Brown and Parker might consider the distinction between the underlying gracious initiative of atonement and its ambiguous sacrificial symbolism to be excessively fine. Throwing out the baby with the bath water, they reject the idea of atonement together with its jarring sacrificial imagery. But to reject the imagery also discards potentially fruitful reflection on sacrifice as a symbol of discipleship in a non-cultic sense as self-giving and dedication. Brown and Parker's rejection of cultic imagery also negates the prominent role of the cultic representation of self-giving in Christian liturgy.

When the original cultic practices no longer provide the chief context for theological symbolism, the terminology will fall into disuse or radically change by taking on a new meaning. That is, when bloody cultic sacrifices fade from the practice of the early Jewish-Christians, the terminology and practice of sacrifice remains, available to be applied to new forms. Furthermore, by ultimately expressing Jesus as the final and consummate sacrifice (as in the Letter to the Hebrews), the cultic practices of the Jewish and early Jewish Christian sacrificial system themselves are undermined. Sacrifice may be best used to express our subjective response to God, as a gift offering, and a means of communion.[207] Brown and Parker are right that the anachronistic connotations of sacrifice as cultic offering seem difficult or even offensive to the modern ear, but such connotations do not exempt us from the task of searching for the value of self-sacrifice. This is why theology must recover a core metaphor below the imagery to preserve the meaning of sacrifice.

## Alternate Assessments of Passivity and Suffering in Atonement Theory

Aside from their aversion to sacrificial language, Brown and Parker critique the focus on Jesus as victim. The victim role justifies sacrifice as an experience of passivity, punishment, or suffering, upheld in turn by different forms of atonement theories. There are, however, important alternate readings of these atonement theologies more responsive to their specific concerns.

Gustav Aulén, a Swedish Lutheran theologian, has also reviewed these same three types of atonement theology. His 1932 book is named *Christus Victor* after the first of the three atonement models.[208] His goal is to explain their characteristic forms, not to defend atonement theologies from feminist critique. Most likely he did not anticipate the criticisms Brown and Parker have raised. He emphasizes the active participation of Christ in the drama of atonement as neither a passive victim, nor the object of the wrath of the Father. Aulén rejects any notion of the passivity of Jesus. Jesus and God the Father act together in the Passion and Resurrection. The subject of atonement is "God in Jesus." His orienting text is Colossians: "God was in Christ reconciling all things to himself." Aulén's description of God's "double-sided" action, offering and accepting reconciliation, mitigates the sense that sacrifice is something God "did to Jesus." Fiddes also believes that as difficult as the logic of sacrifice is to grasp today, the point is that God is the subject who offers sacrifice, and is offered, in Jesus. The message is that doing away with sin is costly to God. This model, counter to Brown and Parker's interpretation, is not inescapably dependent on Jesus' passivity.

Modern ideas of justice and penalty have negatively altered the legal metaphor of debt payment, resulting in the punitive theories that Brown and Parker abhor. Other scholars share this distaste. Fitzmyer concurred that to combine debt images with justice metaphors creates an excessively legalistic interpretation of Paul.[209] Chauvet also criticizes the "treacherous" vocabulary of sacrifice, which perverts the giving of Christ into the punishment of the angry Father.[210] Chauvet rejects this notion as having a "frankly unacceptable character in authentically Christian theology." He cites Maurice Bellet's strong criticism of a punitive soteriology: "The 'Strike, Lord, strike!' addressed to God hurling his rage on his Son in order to save us, in the sermons of Bourdaloue and Bossuet, must be called by its name, a perversion of God."[211]

In Anselm's defense, Fiddes demonstrates that Anselm teaches not that Jesus was necessarily punished vicariously, but that he offered his life, a gift of honor "releasing us from punishment through satisfaction."[212] A law of penalties does not bind God to a necessary action — the penalty is removed when rebellion ends and the repentant sinner seeks to return to God.[213] Even so, Fiddes favors an Abelardian interpretation, the one type Brown does not thoroughly denounce. According to this model, by means of the atonement, God experiences the judgment against sin and precisely in this way can identify totally with humanity and share its desolation. God enters into the depths of human existence. This is the objective event. Christ is judged, not to take the penalty, but to create our penitence. As Paul Tillich stated: "Not substitution but free participation is the character of the divine suffering."[214] Suffering is not a necessary part of love or atonement. Simply because Jesus suffered, we should not accept suffering, societal evil, and disease. But because of sin, God willingly entered humanity's situation and in Jesus participated in the human experience of evil.[215]

Hans Urs von Balthasar reads Anselm's teaching as an aesthetic statement of harmony between God's justice and mercy. God the Father does not compel the sacrifice of his son but allows his obedience. The Son's sacrifice is divine, hence spontaneous — an essential quality of divinity that Anselm celebrates, quite opposed to any notion of necessity circumscribing God — and costly enough so as to outweigh all the world's sin. The point of the Son acting as a human has to do with the gracious gift of granting humanity salvation with dignity. Transferred merit would not erase the stain of sin, and the still-debting sinner comes to heaven as a beggar. The only just payment is that made by the guilty man paying for himself. God does not want to be paid, but seeks to renew humanity's love. God did not need his Son's abasement, but man needed Christ to meet and redeem him from the abyss of judgment, sin, and perdition.[216] Again, the passivity and punishment Brown and Parker reject are not essential to these readings of atonement. This is not to trivialize their criticisms. These theologies are open to ambiguous and distorted interpretations. In fact, such dangerous interpretations are arguably common and influential — a situation which Brown and Parker rightly protest.

Brown and Parker claim that theopaschite theologies in fact encourage passivity. If God suffers, then the disciple should suffer. Suffering need not be a passive experience, however. This is especially true in the case of the person who chooses sacrifice, and for theologies of the active compassion of God. When sacrifice is an active decision, the suffering that results is not so much chosen as accepted. Suffering thus results indirectly from an active commitment to sacrifice. Likewise, God's compassion does not recommend but rejects suffering. Their critiques of suffering God theologies are not entirely fair. Clear models of the active compassion of the suffering God exist, and certain existential philosophers teach that suffering may be transformed by choosing how to give painful experiences meaning for oneself. Elizabeth A. Johnson describes the compassion of God with the analogy of active suffering.[217] Victor Frankl locates the ultimate act of meaning in accepting suffering and transforming its significance for the sufferer.[218] The paradox of accepting the suffering that one passively receives finds ultimate form in Jesus' agony in the garden. He willed both to see the cup pass from him and also to do the will of his father. Faithfulness, not death, is shown to be Jesus' will by the evangelists.

Brown and Parker's concerns suggest an interesting schema of different types of passivity. There is the experience of violence and

suffering; also, there is the passivity of inaction and evasion of purpose. They suggest people should reject the passivity of violence,
endure or resist the passivity of suffering, and overcome the passivity
of subdued agency. These last examples of true passivity are forced
upon the individual. Passivity can also take the form of an evasion
of responsibility that is more appropriately viewed as the individual's
choice; this aspect will be analyzed in more detail in the final section
of this chapter as a form of sin. Yet another dimension of passivity is
the very coming into existence among others. This unchosen context
of one's life is the background for all relationships, actions, and sacrifices, and the context for sacrificial choices that shape one's identity.
(Chapter 3 examines this theme in greater depth.) The multiple dimensions of passivity contribute to the paradoxical and ambiguous
nature of sacrifice. Sacrifice is not necessarily the same thing as suffering. There is a difference between an act and its effect; an action
and its meaning to the agent and the observer. Sacrifice is an action,
an expression of dedication, an inner decision that must be voluntar-
ily chosen. Suffering may result from any willed sacrifice, unwilled
misfortune, or oppression. That women — and surely many men —
too easily accept suffering because of its religious validation is an
important concern. Veneration of the cross may encourage some to
choose a sacrifice partly because it entails suffering, suffering that is
considered holy. But when sacrifice is an active decision, the suffering that results might be considered chosen, but is really not so much
chosen as accepted. The glorification of suffering is not acceptable,
but neither should we overlook that mode of passivity or suffering
that results from fidelity.

Feminist scholars are correct to suspect that atonement theologies exalting the passive suffering of Jesus as the victim influence a
destructive theology of discipleship. Their past experience and observation confirm the prudence of rejecting such risky soteriologies.
Brown and Parker are right that many believe this is the message of
the Gospels. Further, while some are outraged and scandalized by
what strikes them as divine child abuse, others are deeply nourished

by Jesus dying *for me*. I agree with Brown and Parker that Christians are not called to imitate passive suffering and victimhood. But I disagree with them in that I do not believe that Jesus was a model of this victimhood, nor that atonement theology is necessarily arbitrary and violent. Jesus, in fact, was not entirely passive, though certainly a victim of historical and social forces and the enmity of specific individuals. The gospel scene in the garden of Gethsemane shows him to be conflicted, torn, and human, but committed to the Father's will. Through this unity and commitment Jesus was the subject of his own actions.

Atonement theology should intend to unite the action of God and Jesus, as they are united in spirit.[219] This approach ideally presents God as taking the initiative in both the incarnation and Jesus' victorious fidelity. Jesus is not simply a victim, but also the actor. Sacrifice rooted in imitation of Jesus is then risky but potentially meaningful. An imaginative presentation of redemption comes from Mary Grey's thoughtful feminist soteriology, which offers a reinterpretation of atonement. Her revisionist theology of redemption recasts the reality of conflict in life as the life-bringing pain of childbirth. Instead of using the cross against women non-redemptively, Grey lifts up the images of labor and birth to redeem atonement from destructive interpretations. Such images are an alternative to the death symbolism of the cross, and evoke the full meaning of atonement in relation to redemption and creation.[220] A birth image provides an alternate model of conflict, transformation, and victory without violence. The transformation of death is expressed differently in the conflict, separation, and still waiting of birth.[221] My intent here has not been to write a more adequate soteriology, but to assess sacrifice as an authentic mode of Christian discipleship, deeply affected by theological statements about the cross of Jesus Christ. Feminist writers have raised serious questions about the impact of certain theological formulations. Womanist theologians sharpen this critique from their particular perspective as voices of oppressed minority women.

## Womanist Critiques of the Cross as Surrogacy

Womanist theologians, or African American feminist theologians, have contributed in a significant way to critiques of the cross as a tool of sexist oppression. Womanist theology represents the distinctive voices gradually emerging from black male liberation theology, with significant differences from mainstream white feminist circles. Black male liberation theologians brought the Christian spirituality and resistance forged under slavery to critical consciousness and socio-political action. However, the dominant models were drawn from male experience, and black women's experiences of sexism were often overlooked. Feminist liberalism countering sexism often failed to account for racist oppression. Aware that black women labored under a double burden, black women theologians developed characteristic insights and methods of their own. JoAnne Marie Terrell expresses this distinction.

> While varieties of womanist theology are critical of black theologies of liberation, they do not oppose the project of black liberation; they place a more nuanced emphasis on the goals of *survival* and *quality of life* issues for African American people, male and female.[222]

The theme of survival became a lens for interpreting their own suffering and the story of Jesus. Delores Williams has restated the African American Christian sense of solidarity with Jesus as a shared experience of surrogacy. At the same time, she pointedly retrieves the *lack* of solidarity that persists in scriptural stories where the marginalized victims are not liberated. This painful contrast lies at the root of womanist ambivalence and struggle.

Williams rejects the claim of black liberation theology, as expressed by James Cone, that the Bible is an absolute witness to God's liberating activity on behalf of the poor. Instead, she argues, Scripture is an ambivalent witness to God's desire that all be free. "The Hagar-Sarah texts in Genesis and Galatians, however, demonstrate that the oppressed and abused do not always experience God's liberating power."²²³ The Bible contains a *non*-liberative strand, and therefore cannot function as a tool against oppression without careful questioning. It is not enough to correlate the liberating message of the Bible with the needs of society today (the method of liberation theology). Womanist exegetes and preachers must be conscious of the ambivalence in the sacred text and hence in the community's faith. Williams asks, "Does this kind of blindness with regard to non-Hebrew victims in the scripture also make it easy for black male theologians and biblical scholars to ignore the figures in the Bible whose experience is analogous to that of black women?"²²⁴ In other words, to overlook the victims in scripture may perpetuate turning a blind eye to women's oppression today.

Williams claims that mainline Protestantism often teaches that Jesus redeems by taking sin upon himself and dying in place of humans, thus becoming the ultimate surrogate. Accepting an idea of redemption as surrogacy brings with it the question of whether such an image reinforces black women's experience of surrogacy and compels a passive acceptance of its exploitation.²²⁵ Williams's critical approach to symbols of liberation enables her to bracket "ransom, satisfaction, substitution and moral theories of atonement [as...not] serviceable to African-American women's questions about redemption and surrogacy."²²⁶ Judged by the criterion of women's suffering, preaching the cross becomes a dangerous promotion of surrogacy. Instead of glorifying Jesus' death as the ultimate surrogate—and legitimating their own surrogacy—women must look for the salvific meaning of his life in his ministry, and in the "survival strategies" he offered on the conflicted path to gospel ethics and kingdom living. The resurrection vindicates Jesus, showing that God does not intend surrogacy for anyone: not Jesus, not the black woman. "Rather, with God's help, black women...will make a way out of no way."²²⁷

The charged symbol of surrogacy has drawn attention to fundamental problems in the doctrines of God, Christ, and the cross. As did the feminist thinkers already discussed, womanist theologians confront the troubling varieties of atonement theories—satisfaction,

substitution, or penal — with similar theological concerns. Their particular history of social and church-sanctioned oppression also calls
attention to the social, economic, and political contexts of oppression maintained by an appeal to legitimated suffering. The struggle
to emerge from state and socially sanctioned slavery often ends in
situations still marked by poverty and racism. The oppression is
ongoing.

> Thus, the church is historically guilty of inflicting and per-
> petuating abuse, allying with oppressors and imposing the
> hermeneutics of sacrifice on subjugated peoples in order to jus-
> tify the abusive polices of the state and of its own ministerium.[228]

JoAnne Marie Terrell shares my interest in sacrifice as a guiding
theme of Christian life, and one with ambiguous, even dangerous
implications. She has employed the same term — "hermeneutics of
sacrifice" — but uses it to refer only to what I am calling its negative pole. In her words, a womanist theological commitment engages
the "hermeneutics of sacrifice in the suffering that has pervaded my
experience as a poor African American woman who has also been
called into ministry."[229] The demonic power of false interpretations
marks Terrell's use of the term "hermeneutics of sacrifice." Sacrifice
should ideally be embodied in the praxis of nonviolence, but instead
is frequently applied to victims as a tool of oppression.[230]

Terrell defines womanist theology as not simply black feminist
thought, but as the commitment to exploring the contradictions of
life, as Williams has done with her study of scripture. Womanist
Christology begins with recognizing Jesus as the lowly born minister to the outcast, who suffered a *wrongful* death. For Jacquelyn
Grant, Jesus is the divine co-sufferer who died for women as well as
men. She identifies the image of the suffering Jesus with the suffering
of black Christians, and indeed goes beyond black liberation theologians to state that "Christ is a black woman."[231] Terrell argues that
Grant's assertions "have implications for understanding the Atonement as God's option for and empowerment of black women."[232]
Jesus' ministry and sacrificial death reveal God, in turn. In the words

of Kelly Brown Douglas: "God is as Christ does."[233] Like Grant, Douglas emphasizes that the sufferings of Jesus were easily affirmed by the slave communities as similar to their own suffering: Jesus is one like them. Terrell perceives that this sense of unity carried with it a one-sided moral obligation to be like Jesus: to adopt the "hermeneutics of sacrifice [which] proposed even higher standards for the slaves in relationship to the slaveholders."[234] She shows how a liberation perspective transforms this potentially repressive and quietist attitude by viewing holiness not as passive endurance, but as agency, the empowered spirit to endure, resist, and overcome suffering. The cross is a final sign of the lived solidarity of Jesus, God incarnate in the flesh and among victims.

The ambivalent edges in womanist thought pull back and forth like a cross-saw. Terrell questions if Williams's survival is too lowly a goal. Preaching survival may only maintain the status quo. Williams counters that preaching the cross as liberation can justify new life through pain. Williams is reluctant to distinguish the violent image of the cross from the empty cross signifying resurrection hope, lest Christians come to look for good from violence. The cross is a sign of struggle and realism, teaching us to look for survival. On the other hand, Terrell attempts a mediating perspective. As clergy, she acknowledges the challenges posed to revisionist preaching. New ideas can be resisted by both congregations' traditional beliefs and ecclesiastical censure. Therefore other scriptural images expressing Jesus' salvific ministry (such as the canon of realization noted in the previous chapter) can and should be brought to the fore. Other interpretations of why Jesus was sent — i.e., as the vineyard owner's son coming to care for the vineyard, not simply to die — should be recalled. Survivors still need to find meaning in their experiences — perhaps even in the suffering they have experienced, and in God's continued support. To that end Terrell holds up not the crucifix, nor the empty cross, but the ongoing intercession and solidarity of the Spirit of Christ as the sign of God's being at-one with us.[235] Furthermore, while the importance of Williams's critique of the violence affecting society sanctioned by traditional beliefs "cannot be overstated," Terrell contextualizes the crises of racism within global political and environmental threats.

Terrell describes her construction of a womanist sacrificial ethic as a "sacramental understanding." In this light, the command to love one's enemies should not diminish the one who has been victimized, but enables a creative response to the victimizers. She cites the testimony of Mamie Mobley, mother of the young Emmett Till, lynched in 1955. Mobley acknowledged that she did not love her son's murderers, but had no desire to hurt them. "If I had to, I could take their four little children... and I could raise those children as if they were my own."[236] Williams might see this as a startling new model of black maternal surrogacy. Terrell takes Mobley's statement as a courageous accompaniment to Mobley's ongoing work for justice. This "sacramental" witness is creative: "loving one's own, *not* loving others uncritically and, most important, *not* being defined by one's victimization but by one's commitments."[237] Marjorie Hewitt Suchocki also develops this idea of creative utilization of possibilities beyond the memories of victimization, as I will show below.

Like Terrell, Cheryl Townsend Gilkes agrees that one is not a womanist simply by being a black woman. The womanist ideal embodies a commitment to love of self and others despite the oppressions that work profoundly against such love. Alice Walker is credited with helping to shape the coalescing consciousness of womanist thought by coining the term "womanist." In reflecting upon the role of contradiction and ambivalence within this consciousness, Gilkes points out that Walker emphasized difference as a means to critical consciousness, and ambivalence that strives for heroism. As a result of racism and oppression, ambivalence reaches deep into the psyche and self-image.

> For African-American women, the pain of simply being embodied — coping with others' responses to our hair, skin, and size — can overshadow the strengths and options.... Walker makes the heroic and critical side of being black, female, poor, and oppressed most explicit in her definition of womanist. Where the

tension between the pathetic and the heroic fosters ambivalence, Walker pushes us toward clarity.[238]

It takes courage to struggle toward self-love, but this is the "first step toward our 'response-ability' to save our brothers and sisters."[239] Self-love grounds love of other. This womanist insight anticipates the work of Paul Ricoeur to be considered in the next chapter. For Gilkes, and Walker, self-love is the cornerstone of commitment to "survival and wholeness." These two terms together summarize the womanist contribution to a feminist analysis of the ambiguity of sacrifice. The goal of all Christian living, and sacrifice included, is wholeness, or salvation. The first step on that road is survival. Surviving with love of self intact seems contradictory to a program of sacrifice — at least, it raises questions about how sacrifice and self-love coexist. Barbara Hilkert Andolsen, suspicious of any ideal that rejects self-love, takes a second look at agape and sacrifice, and questions whether a sacrificial model of discipleship is still valid.

## III. Sources of Distortion in Sacrificial Discipleship

### Andolsen's Critique of Narrow Views of Agape

A sacrificial interpretation of Jesus Christ implies that the life of the disciple and the practice of Christian love be sacrificial. Theologies of Christian love directly affect the interpretation of how to balance self-sacrifice and self-realization. Feminists contend that an inadequate theological anthropology skews the understanding of Christian love, and hence of sacrifice as an expression of love. Specifically, the balance between self-sacrifice and self-realization collapses when suffering and passivity within the lived experience of Christian love are viewed as redemptive or virtuous. Influential theologians have rejected self-love as inappropriate to Christian discipleship. Barbara Hilkert Andolsen identifies contemporary Protestant theologians in whose writings about agape "emphasis on other regard has been accompanied by suspicion toward, or outright condemnation of self-love. . . . Agape as self-sacrifice has been rooted in a Christology which concentrates on Jesus' self-immolation upon the cross."[240]

Andolsen locates the modern-day connection between the idealization of agape as self-sacrifice and the de-legitimation of self-love in Anders Nygren's 1932 book, *Agape and Eros*. Nygren derives the virtue of sacrificial love from the revelation of divine sacrificial love manifested by Jesus on the cross. In other words, there is a direct link from the doctrine of the atonement to the teaching that exhorts the practice of sacrificial love.

> For Nygren, the sacrificial love for the neighbor displayed by Christians mirrors and is made possible by God's sacrificial love for human beings. . . . This divine love is made known on the cross. Hence Nygren rooted his ethical norm in the doctrine of the atonement.[241]

God pours out God's self, and so should the true Christian who seeks to follow the example of God's love in Jesus.

Nygren defines self-love as morally negative, and in fact unchristian. "Christianity does not recognize self-love as a legitimate form of love. Christian love moves in two directions, toward God and toward its neighbor; and in self-love it finds its chief adversary which must be fought and conquered."[242] According to Nygren, self-love expresses innate human selfishness and misdirects the will.

Nygren's idealization of self-sacrifice as the paradigm of Christian love is paralleled by the distrust of self-love in Reinhold Niebuhr's theology. Andolsen cites Niebuhr's statement that "man's self-love and self-centeredness is inevitable"; it is the source of human evil.[243] Humanity's competitive desire for survival and gain creates the natural self-centeredness at odds with the ideal harmony of Christian community. In the personal sphere, Christians may seek the religious ideal of agape's sacrificial love, which is love "poured out without seeking return."[244] Jesus' love is totally disinterested love. His cross "stands as a judgment against all egocentric self-assertion."[245] Self-sacrificing love perfects intimate relationships. In the public world, however, self-sacrificing love is not advisable. In the jungle of social and political strife, the best norm is justice based in equality and freedom. Thus, self-love is to be abandoned, as an offering in the private realm; it is to be feared and controlled in the public square.

The third critic of self-love whom Andolsen reviews is Gene Outka. In *Agape: An Ethical Analysis,* Outka dismisses self-love as a Christian duty, for "God will never think of blowing on this fire, which is bright enough already." Self-love is not necessarily the original sin, but it is a strong, innate tendency that can easily exceed appropriate limits. Love of neighbor is a command that corrects our natural self-assertion.[246] To Outka, agape means equal regard, a concern for others without consideration for their status, usefulness, or returned affection. Outka recognizes the need to balance the interests of persons and limits undue priority for the interests of the other, especially when their needs may be less pressing. But, as Andolsen points out, the norm that mediates these claims is justice — a public norm outside of specifically Christian values.

The idea of suffering is only implicit in Andolsen's discussion of these three authors. To the extent that any of the three acknowledge conflict and loss as part of the process of sacrificial giving, such conflict is expressed as a battle to conquer the adversary of self-love. It is as though a noble disdain of one's self makes light of loss in the desire to give oneself away to the other. The Christian is heedless of claims to self-interest, even to life itself.

## Retrieving Self-Love: Affirming Both Sides of the Paradox

Andolsen does highlight a fruitful theological discussion of the Trinitarian context for agape and sacrifice from Martin D'Arcy, who affirms the value of self-love.[247] For D'Arcy, self-love is part of an ideal balance between self-giving and self-respect. The balance is not easy to realize, but must depend upon personal dignity and one's own integrity. D'Arcy roots agape not in the atonement, but in the Trinity. Andolsen views D'Arcy's positive assessment of self-regard as a legitimate aspect of agape as a minority voice in the twentieth-century discourse on agape. He foreshadows later feminist thinkers,

who approach the theology of sacrifice with a critical eye, the resources of social science, the testimony of personal experience, and
often a rich reflection on Trinitarian theology.[248] This is a promising
avenue, which will be considered further in chapter 5.

Andolsen's useful analysis exposes the limitations of Nygren's and
Niebuhr's models as a guide for self-sacrifice. As Andolsen points
out, sacrifice is not always the appropriate response to every situation. Anna Howard Shaw, a Methodist suffragette writing during
the 1890s, approved of sacrifices for great moral causes. But she
insisted that women should have the freedom to determine when
to sacrifice their interests, for what causes, and in what manner.
The suffering that results from commitment should be endured for
the sake of the cause, not honored as an independent value. The
virtue of sacrifice is a *human* strength — certainly not only a female
virtue — together with "honesty, courage, and self-assertion." Shaw
thus points to the value of interpreting when sacrifice is important.[249]
Sacrifice is not always appropriate, just as self-love is not always
pernicious.

Andolsen's own constructive framework is compelling and offers
a template for many ethical situations. She concludes that sacrifices
must be mutual, and that mutuality can properly reorient self-
realization and self-sacrifice. "Neither self-sacrifice nor other-regard
captures the total meaning of agape. The full expression of the Christian ideal is mutuality."[250] She spells out some interesting concrete
implications of this principle. For example, mutuality should inform
public as well as private life. An economy which segregates women
into the home must be restructured. Parties in sustained relationships
should attempt to balance sacrifices. There should be a preferential
option for the privileged to undertake sacrifice. Basic human needs
should trump other concerns in the prioritization of sacrifices. Sys-
temic change should be sought to render sacrifice less frequently
necessary.

Andolsen also corrects a one-sided view of agape found in Nygren's
and Niebuhr's models by bringing female experience into focus.
Niebuhr's negative view of humanity as innately aggressive overlooks

models of human experience in which aggression is not a primary form of sin. Such generalized assumptions about the selfish nature of human personality tend to underplay self-realization in theological treatments of love. Andolsen appeals to Valerie Saiving's analysis of developmental patterns, which shows that in many cases self-love is a valuable corrective to passivity and irresolute personality, not a dangerous assertion of a self-centered will.

## Saiving's Critique of a One-Sided Anthropology That Exaggerates Sin as Pride

The watershed moment for an alternate articulation of love occurred in Valerie Saiving's 1960 article "Human Experience: A Feminine View," which rejected the delegitimation of self-regard as inadequate to women's experience. This breakthrough essay transformed the reading of theology by pointing to a different outlook that receives teachings in diverse ways: a "feminine view."[251] Feminists who analyze female psychosocial development make a powerful case for women's predisposition to self-denial. A number of writers have questioned whether women experience an inner tendency to identify with the concerns of the other, in addition to social pressure to conform to habits of self-denial and service.[252] Developmental tendencies are then exacerbated by one-sided theological presumptions that reject self-love in the name of Christian love. No matter how universally the message is preached — to men and women — women hear the message and internalize it more readily, according to the feminist argument.

Saiving shows that assessments of human personality and the human predicament embed particular conceptions of love and sin. Her essay also responds to Anders Nygren and Reinhold Niebuhr. If these theologians have not correctly described the human situation, then their interpretation of love and sin will also be inadequate. She challenges a definition of love that "according to these theologians, is completely self-giving, taking no thought for its own interests but seeking only the good of the other."[253]

Love and sin are the opposite potentials of the human condition. Yet because men and women experience the human condition in different ways, the potential for transcendence or vice takes different forms. The nature of love and sin may not be the same for men and women. Saiving asserts that

> contemporary theological doctrines of love have, I believe, been constructed primarily upon the basis of masculine experience and thus view the human condition from the male standpoint. Consequently, these doctrines do not provide an adequate interpretation of the situation of women — nor, for that matter, of men, especially in view of certain fundamental changes now taking place in our society.[254]

Saiving accepted Niebuhr's diagnosis of sin as an aggressive response to anxiety in men. However, her study of women's psychological development showed a different pattern of identity formation in women, which resulted in a different pattern of sin. Accordingly, as boys mature and separate from their mothers to become men, the "process of self-differentiation plays a stronger and more anxiety-provoking role" than it does for girls.[255] Girls more readily merge their interests and concerns with those of others. The risk for women, according to Saiving, is the failure to develop a distinctive personality, to lose themselves in concern for others, and to evade their own definition. Saiving thus proposes an alternate anthropology based in female experience, which supports assumptions about self-assertion contrary to those of Nygren. The ideal of self-giving love, framed in response to a purported male tendency to self-promotion, is not an appropriate virtue for women who tend to be selfless to a fault. For women, what appears to be giving is not always an active virtue, but the passive evasion of deliberately chosen action.

Women's natural strengths correlate with particular female weaknesses. The "passive" nature of female physical development is associated with a lack of creative drive; women's capacity to serve can founder in diffuseness of purpose; if women have a greater emotional receptivity, it may degenerate to dependence and intrusiveness; and a feminine capacity for forgiveness risks collapsing into an indiscriminating tolerance of mediocrity.[256]

> For the temptations of women as *women* are not the same as the temptations of man as *man,* and the specifically feminine forms of sin — "feminine" not because they are confined to women or because women are incapable of sinning in other ways but because they are outgrowths of the basic feminine character structure — the quality which can never be encompassed by such terms as "pride" and "will-to-power." They are better suggested by such terms as triviality, distractibility, and diffuseness; lack of an organizing center or focus; dependence on others for one's own self-definition; tolerance at the expense of standards of excellence; inability to respect boundaries of privacy; sentimentality, gossipy sensibility, and mistrust of reason — in short, underdevelopment or negation of the self.[257]

Gender does not determine human identity, nor dictate the experience of anxiety or passivity. But because women's experience has been overlooked, the tendency of male anxiety to define the self through assertion has provided the normative description of selfishness. The experience of modernity also highlights the individual's anxiety, heightened freedom, uncertainty, and need for achievement, and so reinforces the effectiveness of this normative description.[258] It is interesting that Saiving connects the greater freedom of the man, unburdened by constant physical nurture of children, to an anxiety about his freedom, which impels a drive for creativity.[259] Caregivers experience this creativity immediately and vitally — if indirectly — in the growth of children. On the other hand, women's self-sacrifice in the domestic realm prevents a more narrowly self-expressive creativity. The correlation between sacrifice and constricted freedom points directly to the need for criteria of healthy sacrifice that preserve freedom. Such freedom is precisely the ability to engage in sacrifices willingly and to view them as purposeful and creative.

## Assessing the Ambiguity of Psychological Evidence

Saiving's insights are valuable and inform my approach to passivity, self-giving, and identity. At the same time, generalizing about a "universal female nature" is risky. To assert a universal feminine norm of personality, sin, and virtue indeed challenges the hegemony of a male norm, but risks restricting women to a different norm in its stead.

Experience is a key source in feminist theology. Early modern liberal feminism focused on women's experience to counteract the presumed "neutral" character of human personality, suspecting that, in fact, such neutral norms often recapitulate male experience. Postmodern feminists, however, point out that to universalize "essential" female traits instead only reasserts the hegemony of a homogenized being. Such a model is especially limiting if it is grounded in biological phenomena. Furthermore, generalized norms obscure the flux of personality characteristics across both genders. Thus appears a chasm separating essentialist and postmodern views of "feminine nature."[260] Linell Elizabeth Cady observes a third, "historicist" approach that acknowledges the fragmented modern self as a stream of conflicting discourses but stresses the choices made as part of one's history.[261] This model views the cultural patterns and communities surrounding each person as concrete and particular social possibilities from which the subject draws. Her actions, however, confirm the chosen values that constitute her identity against her cultural background, though these may change in the flux of rejections and reinterpretations attending this life-long process. It is thus still possible to speak of a subject who is neither gender-determined nor culturally blank. As subject, she actively chooses to appropriate religious symbols and images to influence her spiritual identity. Cady's approach is a useful mediating stance.

Andolsen referred to Saiving's study because it depicted women's tendency to destructive self-abnegation. My intent is to show that feminist scholars have challenged a single assessment of human personality on a male model and have demonstrated the tendency of many persons — men and women alike — to retreat into passivity and self-sacrifice rather than aggression. Choices and failures need to be described more widely; so do sacrificial definitions of love.

## Enlarging the Scope of Agape

Andolsen showed that to cast agape exclusively as self-regard and then urge it upon women binds them with double fetters. Women's orientation to self-denial, whether psychological, socially conditioned, or both, is additionally chained by religious recommendations based on a narrow view of agape. Nygren states: "Christian love is essentially Agape" and rejects self-love as derived from Eros. Though the term "love" translates both *Agape* and *Eros,* these terms originally imply opposite impulses. While agape is ultimately equated with God, Eros is "the desire of the soul of man to attain salvation by detachment from earthly objects of desire and by seeking after heavenly things."[262] This desire is construed by Nygren to be self-seeking, self-benefiting, and self-originated. It follows that self-realization, even by seeking God, would be rejected by Nygren. This bizarrely self-defeating position clarifies, but does not justify, his extreme view of agape as self-negation.

I agree with Nygren's position that "the sacrificial love for the neighbor displayed by Christians mirrors and is made possible by God's sacrificial love for human beings.... This divine love is made known on the cross."[263] God's sacrificial love *is* the revelation and the condition of the possibility of human self-giving. Yet God's outpouring love, which is the model of Christian love, is larger than the doctrine of the atonement. The witness of Jesus' historical life is greater than the hours of his death. Important aspects of Jesus' teaching — especially words and deeds that call persons to the fullness of life — are lost if the atonement is the sole ground for Christian ethical norms.

A simplified, rigorist exaltation of other-regard alone is inadequate because it does not tolerate the tension set up in Jesus' call to love the self and other. Nygren's incomplete approach results from a selective use of scriptures, which overlooks the paradox of realization and sacrifice. For example, he cites Philippians 2:2 as evidence that self-interest is forbidden to Christians: "Agape pronounces judgment on all life that centers round the ego and its interest; hence Paul condemns those who seek their own things, not the things of Jesus Christ (Phil. 11:21)."[264] Philippians 2:21 reads: "They all look after their own interests, not those of Jesus Christ." But Nygren does not quote verse 4 of that same chapter, which states: "Let each of you look not only to his own interests, but also to the interests of others." The apostle censures caring *only* for one's own self-interest, not self-concern per se. The gravitational pull is not from self-regard to self-hatred, but from self-centeredness to other-regard. Furthermore, Nygren's argument appears illogical according to his own depiction of the mechanism of agape. If God's love embraces each person, and agape is God's love in us, it does not follow that the spirit of agape forbids love of oneself in particular, while commanding love of everyone else.

Andolsen appropriately criticizes Nygren's one-sided view of agape. By recovering the value and gospel call to self-realization, she helps prod a distorted view of Christian love away from unquestioned total self-denial and toward a centered position of mutuality. However, in the "hard cases" of sacrifice unable to meet the criteria of mutuality, other grounding values are needed. Persons today owe a legacy of a clean earth to future generations, but cannot receive repayment for the sacrifices that are required. Dependent disabled children and adults are unable to reciprocate the care and sacrifices they receive in kind. Regarding persons with special needs, Andolsen urges that those with greater needs have the first claim. She also hopes that such situations may be reduced by the transformation of society by human dedication so "that situations calling for sacrifice are reduced to a minimum."[265] While I share that hope, a great deal of discernment about present, pressing needs calling for sacrifice will be needed for a long time to come. Mutuality alone does not embody the paradox of Christian love. Furthermore, mutuality is not innocent of all ambiguity. There is the reality of mutual hate, of persons and groups locked together in mutual vengeance and resentment, and of nations committed to mutual conflict. These forms of mutual antipathy also bind and shape identities.

For Augustine, a love is determined not so much by its object simply as object, but in its orientation in relationship to God. It is not enough to love God, and to love one's neighbor. Love is not univocal. There are different loves whose quality is changed by context. "He who resolves to love God, and to love his neighbor as himself, not according to man but according to God, is on account of this love said to be of a good will."[266] Pride is an error in judgment that misdirects love, a craving that loses sight of God as a proper good.[267] Nygren and Niebuhr are right to condemn pride, but the solution is not to abolish self-love. Augustine recommends humility to the citizens of the city of God to correct that pride which exalts the self above God. Pride causes an erroneous evaluation of the centrality of the self. God is the center of the love of the self. To correct prideful self-centeredness, it is not necessary to end love of self, but to reorient love of self around God.

Augustine strongly distinguished the love of self and love of God, but also understands their complexity — this is the key to his eudaemonistic philosophy. "Accordingly, two cities have been formed by two loves: the earthly by the love of self, even to the contempt of God; the heavenly by the love of God, even to the contempt of self."[268] The opposition is not between love of self and neighbor, but between self and God. Still, self-love is appropriate in the proper place.

> For in its own kind and degree the flesh is good; but to desert the Creator good, and live according to the created good, is not good, whether a man choose to live according to the flesh, or according to the soul, or according to the whole human nature, which is composed of flesh and soul.[269]

Augustine's strong language of opposition should not, however, obscure his apposite evaluation of human life and creation in the proper relationship to God. By warning against self-absorption, he is trying to set the ones who seek happiness on the right path, toward the only true end of human happiness, which is God. Proportion and direction, rather than opposition and exclusion, are the more appropriate structures of Augustine's teaching on self-love. Love needs to be directed rightly, to God as the object of the love of one's heart and soul and mind, and to the neighbor as *oneself*.

Polarized models conceive of only two options: love of self, *or* love of neighbor; love of God, *or* love of self. Models such as this explain how Nygren can overlook the mutual regard Paul envisions, of caring for the interest of oneself and of others. The zero-sum approach sees in self-love only an exclusive self-interest. Such models overlook the potential of synergy, mutual benefit, and interdependence. This opposition ignores the parallel growth in human autonomy and nearness to God that Karl Rahner emphasizes.[270]

Reflection on agape expresses Christian values in positive form. Reflection on sin expresses the same values in negative form, which often reveals them more starkly. What are the sinful aspects of sacrificial other-regard and self-regard? To throw the details of that question into brighter view, we can examine the converse of the proposition that self-love is sinful: can it be said that a *lack* of self-love is sinful?

So far, we have considered whether sacrificial interpretations of the cross and of love oppose self-realization. The evident acceptance and even recommendation of passivity in some theological positions validates feminist and womanist concern that these interpretations validate suffering and surrogacy. According to some influential anthropologies, suffering is corrective, and passivity is salutary. Such views fail to support self-realization and contribute to the collapse of the paradox of self-love and self-giving in Christian sacrifice.

The balance of self-sacrifice and self-realization is unsteady at best. But some provisional answers seem appropriate. Is self-sacrifice an unqualified ideal deeply rooted in scripture, and an irretrievably violent vehicle of atonement theologies? (No.) Is it a blunt instrument in the hands of patriarchy and a tool that exploits empathetic and vulnerable personalities? (Sometimes.) Does it invalidate self-love? (Not according to at least possible readings of certain scriptural texts and sensitivity to multiple models of personality.) The relationship of sacrifice to atonement, to Christian love, and to Christian anthropology now leads to the examination of an interpretation of sin in relation to sacrifice. Sometimes, it appears, sacrifice may not be a heroic, virtuous gift of self or a transparent channeling of God's active agape, but the passive failure to express the values of the self.

## IV. A New Context for Sin and Transcendence

Marjorie Hewitt Suchocki critically examines assumptions about sin in a way that illuminates its positive and negative correlation with self-sacrifice. Suchocki contends that an imbalanced view of sin derives from the assumption that pride is the dominant mode of sin — an assumption similarly resulting from a one-sided anthropology. Such narrow views fail to account for other models of personality, inadequately grasp the horrific extent of violence, and overlook creation as the target of sin. Most relevantly, narrow views of sin overlook the potentially sinful practices of self-sacrifice.

In *The Fall to Violence: Original Sin in Relational Theology*, Suchocki develops the traditional categories of God, creation, sin, and redemption in light of humanity's interdependence, inspired by process thought.[271] Suchocki's holistic sense of a relational reality frames her approach to sin and redemption in light of life's rich possibilities and enriches a view of the creative act of sacrifice. Sin is considered as a shared bent toward violence. Forgiveness is its opposite, an expansive dynamic that opens the self and other into a more fully realized relation. Her study provides grounds for asserting that self-love is indeed a Christian virtue, on the one hand, and affirming that patterns of self-abnegation may in fact be sinful, on the other. The comprehensive model of sin she develops makes it possible to propose "negative criteria" for assessing acts of sacrifice, that is, indications that some sacrifices may be sinful rather than Christ-like.

### Rejecting Pride as Original Sin

Theories of original sin remain valuable for highlighting the social nature of behavior, which is the vehicle of humanity's complicity in sin before conscious consent. The organic relatedness of humanity and the social solidarity of sin are important aspects of a theory of original sin that effectively explain widespread human misery. However, the classic definition of original sin as pride, directed against God and rooted "solely in human freedom," is unconvincing to Suchocki.[272] She finds the Reformation version of original sin as unbelief to be no more credible. To posit a direct and clear-eyed rejection of God in each act of violence absurdly enlarges the meaning of unbelief.

Suchocki examines the formulation of sin expressed by Paul Tillich and Reinhold Niebuhr, engaging Niebuhr most directly. Niebuhr's worldview contains a classic distinction between nature and spirit, which grounds the individual's existential feeling of anxiety. Niebuhr posits that anxiety results from the nature/spirit duality — the instability of humankind being both finite and free. These two ways of being, as nature and spirit, limit each other. Spirit responds to anxiety through pride by attempting to secure the self and deify its freedom. Nature responds by ignoring the fear that freedom and awareness bring to a mortal creature, thus subsiding into sensuality or aggression. Both pride and sensuality are inevitable, but unnecessary. They are sins against God, in whom humanity should trust despite the creaturely condition of anxiety.

Suchocki rejects this view because it is inadequate to women's experience, it overlooks other sins, and it downplays violence. To define pride as the "normative" form of sin diminishes women's experience. Sin does not always thrust the soul into naked confrontation with God, but sometimes emerges through accommodation to social customs that constrict one's freedom and frown upon testing its limits. Sin may be the inertia that accepts the natural bent of violence, repeats the pain of the past, and passively settles for diminished agency and duller virtue. This is a major shift in the evaluation of boundaries from a feminist perspective. The limit that curtails the individual's growth is not God, but patriarchy. For women, the tempting sin is *not* to defy socially sanctioned limits. Thus, far from sin being the pride that launches humanity against God's limits, sin is instead the failure to transcend limits. For the oppressed, defining sin as religious rebellion against God has social implications. People who subscribe to authoritarian attitudes may identify any power with godliness, and condemn opposition against any form of political or individual power as against divine authority. Drawing all sin into rebellion against God also homogenizes the cruel diversity of sins ranging from genocide to child abuse. Finally, in a secular society where God is often "irrelevant to the consciousness or intentions of most perpetrators of evil," construing sin as rebellion against God suggests a "promethean defiance of deity which is probably remote from the experience of most people."[273]

Most significant from a feminist point of view, the personality defects observed by Saiving go unnoticed in this classic focus upon pride. As Saiving suggested, a more common model of sin for women is pride's opposite: an excessively humble evasion of responsibility.[274] If prideful assertion is the chief sin, then humility and its associated behaviors (like sacrifice) would logically appear to be the greatest virtue. Notably, humility is not generally the crowning Christian virtue, but rather what Paul calls love and Augustine, *caritas*.

One of Suchocki's goals is to account for the striking human capacity to harm. Violence is a surd she cannot adequately attribute to the anxious pride that rails against God's limits for humankind. According to Suchocki, anxiety should instead be attributed to the violence that constantly threatens life. This shift in focus effects Suchocki's first transposition of the classic view. She also redirects the target of sin, or the one sinned against, from God to creation. Under the classic model, the human victims of sin appear to be secondary targets, as it were, and God is the One most offended. Accordingly, those who suffer from sin recede from view and creation is devalued. "Naming sin as rebellion against God rather than creation implies that creation in and of itself is not significant enough that crimes directly intended against its well-being should merit the name of sin."[275] To her, the detour from pride to violence to God and then to creation appears unsatisfactory and incomplete. Acts of violence against creation are most directly acts of violence against creation.

## Thinking about Sin in Light of Natural Transcendence

Suchocki proposes a new model of transcendence and its failure. Humanity may rise above its violent instincts and passivity by using self-conscious gifts that open one to other modes of being. This openness she calls natural transcendence. If nature has a multiplicity of options represented by its many unique entities, to explore the options fully is to transcend one's given finite limits. Self-transcendence explores the infinite options within nature, and among the relationships in nature, imaged as a "horizontal" expansion of the self.[276] This model contrasts with Niebuhr's "vertical" understanding of self as spirit, with a consequent notion of sin as primarily directed against God.

Human activity engages its natural transcendence in terms of memory, empathy, and imagination. Empathy structures one's relationships with and perceptions of the other. When empathy is not properly developed, the self may absorb the other as an extension of itself — a "horizontal" error she calls pride. Alternately, there is the possibility of merging into the other, a failure to respect proper distance between self and other. She identifies this failing as the sin of hiding. This failure absolutizes the other, while at the same time overlooking that the other's inviolate mystery prohibits a totalizing merger. These are both failures of transcendence via empathy. Empathy should maintain and preserve one's own unique perspectives, while taking into account the perspectives of the other.

> A contrary mode of relating to the other that also fails to become empathic self-transcendence is not to make the self absolute, but to make the other absolute, or what the feminists point to as the sin of hiding. One can so identify with the other that one effectively loses — or never develops — a sense of self. To lose the self through absorbing the perspective of the other is doubly to lose, for on the one hand the aspect of infinity that pervades all finite selves means one can never completely identify with the other, since the fullness of the other is elusive. To pretend to do so is to absolutize an objectified other, which means one loses

sight of the real other. And on the other hand, one has also lost the rightful sense of self as the centered self who enters into relation. Whereas for Niebuhr the sin of sensuousness (or hiding) resulted from a refusal of one's freedom (and therefore a refusal of one's self-transcending possibilities), in this understanding the absolutization of the other is in fact the overreaching of self-transcendence to the point of losing the self.[277]

The multiple possibilities of human perspective are thus preserved, and the value of distinctive difference preserved. Memory, a second mode of transcendence, sifts through the storehouse of the past to create the patterns of relationships that establish the self. There are untapped resources available to memory, filtered images and selected events, that offer ways to transcend the operative patterns of the self. Imagination, the third mode of transcendence, responds to the infinity of possibilities and creates a future.

According to Suchocki, sin is the violation of any of these modes of transcendence, in their temporal modes of past, present, and future. Therefore, pride and hiding need not be identified as failures of trust that succumb to the anxiety produced by the tension of nature and spirit. Pride and hiding are a violation of empathy, distortions of the appropriate respect for self and other required by mutual relationships. Other sins result from the distortion of memory and imagination: the refusal to grow beyond painful and constricting memories, the laziness that cannot envision higher goals. Sin violates the potential of natural transcendence but is not primarily a vertical attack on God. Suchocki's "horizontal" view of transcendence emphasizes the social nature of the self and its shared vulnerability.

Developing a horizontal, or world-related, interpretation of human self-transcendence allows us to bring the social nature of the self into view, and through that social nature, to account for the vulnerability that allows us both richness and destructiveness of being. It brings creaturely interdependence and therefore creaturely obligation into view. The unnecessary violation of this interdependence and obligation is a direct sin against the well-being of creation. Sin, then, is rebellion against creation.[278]

Suchocki's assessment of the passivity of evasion as the sin of hiding provides criteria for judging certain sacrifices as sinful. Self-sacrifice may be sinful if it perpetuates the effects of past violence. Self-sacrifice fails to build Christian identity if it limits one's responsiveness to grace in the present. One who sacrifices excessively sins if he or she forfeits the fullness of the future by turning away from potential growth. Suchocki places limits on excessive types of sacrifice that would endanger someone's well-being by considering the integrated and interdependent nature of social existence, influenced by a process model of reality. The relational model depends upon the well-being of all. In a process view, loving oneself is not distinct from loving another.[279] Within this deeply relational worldview, diminishing the well-being of one compromises the well-being of all. Philippians 2:2 teaches that the love of all is embraced in the unity of Christ.

> If there is any encouragement in Christ, any incentive of love, any participation in the Spirit, any affection and sympathy, complete my joy by being of the same mind, having the same love, being in full accord and of one mind. (Phil. 2:1–2)

It is a false dichotomy that separates love of self from love of other. Self-sacrifice and self-realization are paradoxically united. These apparent opposites resolve in the unity of the love command.

If sacrifice is an image that originated in the Hebrew tradition as a saving process of reconciliation, sacrifice should still express salvation when used as a term for self-giving. Theories of atonement that express the efficacy of the Passion in terms of its moral influence and the subject's response teach that a response to the past event of the cross is experienced in the present. Likewise, self-giving sacrifice should make salvation actual, part of present salvation, the kingdom in our midst, the fullness of life found even in loss.

In his reflection on atonement as God's self-giving, Fiddes writes that pure self-giving is actually an impossibility, even for God. God freely chooses to be enriched by relationship with us.[280] Margaret Farley points to the subtlety in which receiving is as vulnerable an expression of one's personality as giving. Receiving and giving can both express other-centered love. The symbol of the Trinity grounds the work of many feminists who emphasize mutuality.[281] While there are limitations to an ethic of mutuality, the outpouring perichoresis of Trinitarian mutuality overflows any sense of rigid or legalistic reciprocity. I will explore Ricoeur's reflections on the expansive nature of the God-symbol that accents the spirit of generosity over equivalence in chapter 3.

## Assessment

Suchocki describes her own project as a "Christian natural theology," or a reflection on natural processes to discern aspects of life's mysteries (as opposed to building on a foundation of revelation alone). Her fundamental worldview adopts the process model and relational philosophy of Alfred North Whitehead to describe the "flux and continuity" of reality.[282] The influence of process thought yields a vision of the interdependent, temporal experience of reality. Process thought appreciates the potentialities in many relationships, past and present, and this fluidity generates a fruitful understanding of forgiveness. At the same time, her distinctive definition of divine transcendence and of human freedom causes some confusion, as the language of process thought does not always correspond to classical Christian understandings. Her horizontal view of "finite" transcendence, or the multiple options life presents, differs from a classic Christian perspective, which understands transcendence as a God-given potential to perceive God's holiness as a horizon for one's own self, and an experience of grace drawing one toward a faithful affirmation of holy mystery. Furthermore, it is not always clear in Suchocki's own constructive contributions where she is drawing on Whitehead or making a novel synthesis that incorporates Whiteheadian and traditional Christian categories.

At times the style of natural theology renders the Christian themes perhaps too "implicit."[283] One perceives a descriptive physiology of

sin rather than a kerygma to rouse the soul. The quality of change of
the organism is that of transformation — a term she uses frequently —
but not liberation. It is hard to hear Christ's call to sell all and follow.
Perhaps Bonhoeffer has rightly prophesied the dispiriting distraction
of analyses. Suchocki does speak of God's special mode of creation
through influence, but within her "implicit" theology this influence
appears more subtle than the initiative of grace which invites the
disciple into God's life.[284]

Her treatment of Niebuhr does not give him quite enough credit,
as he does account for an evasion-type of sin, which he labels "sensuality." However, Suchocki (as well as Saiving and Plaskow) charges
that Niebuhr does not treat the sin of sensuality as extensively as he
treats the sin of pride. They believe he overlooks the sin of hiding,
and its situation in social contexts, shaped by power inequities and
gender roles. Niebuhr does attend to sensuality in his discussion, if
not as centrally as the feminist authors.[285]

Suchocki recognizes that her model inverts the fundamental Christian understanding of sin as an offense against God, instead stating
that sin against creation is primarily against creation and secondarily
offends God. This connection, like her notion of natural transcendence, seems to be a way of recognizing the value and potential
of creation. Creation is then sinned against on its own terms, so to
speak. But from the perspective of Christian faith in God as Creator,
God is the transcendent source of all value that conveys value upon
creation. Sins against creation are not therefore "indirectly" received
by God; rather, wrongs against creation can be judged because God
establishes moral value in the first place. While Suchocki writes that
there is a "sense in which the violation of creation is also a violation
of God [that] has to do with the relational sense of God's involvement
with creation,"[286] her emphasis on creation's independent moral status, and its involvement with God, is confusing and distances God's
intimate concern for creation. Suchocki risks separating God from
the creature, which introduces a new distortion of love. To the believer, God is the transcendent source of the value of all creation. If
creation is loved "in God," it is not the less loved as itself. God is

the origin of love, and creation finds value in and through God. Any independence from God as the source of value is a hollow alienation which undermines the basis for its own existence. This need not be a criticism of secular ethics based on interdependence or nonviolence or the dignity of all life: it simply seems strange in a religious approach to creation.

At the same time, I approve her effort to recenter humanity within creation. By recontextualizing creation as the holistic framework of human action, she retrieves full attention to the suffering creation endures. She also envisions possibilities for transcendence in the rich variety of creation.[287] The possibilities for transcendence through memory, empathy, and imagination are manifold, offering a fruit-ful view of healing to guide decisions about self-giving sacrifice amid the challenges, limits, and violence of life. In terms of forging an authentic interpretation of the paradox between self-sacrifice and self-realization, Suchocki's work proposes "creative possibilities." In particular, the creative tapestry in which forgiveness weaves new pos-sibilities without discrediting past pain is very suggestive. Forgiveness is a rich and creative way to expand one's experience of life. The em-pathy that bonds self and other holds the distinctiveness of each self, prohibiting merger, absolutizing, and total self-loss. The contours of "life lived to the full" are open for imagination to dream and develop. In her vision, the self emerges in a deep ontological connection with all life. It is important to acknowledge the brutality of nature when pondering the interdependence of life. All consumption and survival means the inevitable destruction of life forms, and so the ambigu-ity of nature is unalterable. However, the interpreted transcendence of empathy and imagination permits conscious human choices about how to respond to the ambiguous situations we encounter.

Suchocki echoes the vision of Julian of Norwich, emphasizing that interrelation is the source of peace: universal well-being requires all to be well, for all to be well.[288] Indeed, self is discovered and created via myriad interactions with the other. There can be a productive tension between self-sacrifice and self-realization, having shown that

all sacrifice is not always virtuous, and that sacrifice that accepts violence or evades growth is sinful. Feminist and womanist critiques
of the cross critically — and loyally — evaluate sacrifice as a model
for discipleship. Suchocki, Andolsen, and Saiving showed that contrary to the assumptions of Nygren and Niebuhr, assertive self-love
does not inevitably seek to dominate others. They reframe the passivity of accepting unjust suffering as sinful, not as a special Christian
virtue. However, these caveats established by feminist theology are
not sufficient to guide Christian sacrifice. Nor is mutuality a sufficient criterion for healthy sacrifice. Opportunities for sacrifice will
emerge in the most mutually supportive relationships, posing problems that are not solved merely by empathy and consideration. The
necessary critique of excessive idealization of sacrifice does not exhaust the mystery posed in the gospel claim that one will save one's
life by losing it. How does sacrifice for the other contribute to the
realization of one's own self?

The complex role of sacrifice in realizing genuine Christian selfhood calls for a theory of self that incorporates the value of
wholeness, the reality of loss, and the paradox of their connection in
the depth of the self. The message of sacrifice contained within Jesus'
words and actions is complex, and subject to grave misinterpretation. The message of fulfillment and healing in the other pole of the
paradox, the pole of self-realization, also requires interpretation. The
scribe who asked Jesus who is his neighbor is told that the neighbor
is the one whom he tends. The Syro-Phoenician woman poses another question: Am I my own neighbor? Am I, myself, also an other?
The paradox of self-sacrifice and self-realization that forms Christian
identity suggests that salvation comes by loving the neighbor, that
one's life as a Christian is saved in the losing of it, but that one may
ask for salvation for oneself. For insight into the structures of the self
in relation to the other, I will turn to Paul Ricoeur's philosophy in
the next chapter.

## Chapter Three

# INTERPRETING SELFHOOD
# THROUGH GIVING TO THE OTHER

*Set me as a seal upon your heart, as a seal upon your arm, for*
*love is strong as death.* — Song of Solomon 8:6

Self-understanding is best understood as a dynamic process of interpreting one's actions toward other people in light of the guiding
symbols of one's culture, and sacrifice is a distinctive mode of Christian self-interpretation. This is the insight gained by reading sacrifice
with Paul Ricoeur. The feminist critique of the previous chapter
probed the gap between ideal and destructive forms of sacrifice,
but did not explicitly show how self-sacrifice should contribute to
self-realization. A more complete understanding of how self-sacrifice
and self-realization together answer the gospel promise of life to the
fullest develops from Paul Ricoeur's hermeneutic approach to intersubjectivity and identity. The advantage of engaging his philosophical
anthropology, as well as his hermeneutic method for interpreting religious symbols, is that an ontology of the self, or analysis of the
structures of identity, provides a firm ground for ethics that is able to
protect the integrity of the self. Assertions of equality and personal
freedom then flow from a coherently articulated philosophical framework of the structures of identity, which can more rigorously defend
these values than a merely "ethical" claim for personal integrity. The
strategy of this chapter is to align the problem of sacrifice and the self
with the challenge of interpreting one's religious and ethical identity

within the context of the other. How exactly does giving to the other contribute to self-realization?

The ethical relationship of the self and the other is the subject of Paul Ricoeur's major work *Oneself as Another* (1992), which follows his many earlier investigations of phenomenology, hermeneutics, and literary criticism. Ricoeur treats selfhood as a hermeneutical topic, meaning that self-understanding requires a reflective detour through interpretation and through experiences with other people. One's identity is not transparently self-evident, but is interpreted through the experience of living within multiple relationships. For Ricoeur, the fundamental intersubjectivity of human existence means that human persons always exist among others in ways that fundamentally shape one's identity. This relationality is not a decision or a choice, but an ever-present reality predating one's conscious awareness. One is intimately related to others at the heart of one's being. The need of others for one's concern, and even one's sacrifice, rests upon this basic interdependence. One exists as a being among other beings: given to them, and responsible to them. The reality of responding to otherness means "being enjoined as the structure of selfhood."[289]

Ricoeur's philosophy is a philosophical anthropology concerned with human capacity for responsible action. To exist is to act; human "being" *is* acting. His particular approach has been called "phenomenological hermeneutics," which combines reflection on human experience and the art of interpretation. During his prolific career, Ricoeur investigated many classic themes of philosophy and generated new approaches to the problems of meaning and understanding raised by contemporary discourse. The challenge of self-understanding and the nature of human willing continuously reappear in Ricoeur's study of different discourses — phenomenology, hermeneutics, literary criticism, psychoanalysis, structuralism, action theory, and narrative theory. Each investigation engages the cycle of criticism and renewed meaning in a new area of research: belief precedes criticism, suspicion yields to a restoration.[290]

Ricoeur's work is marked by an affirmative and hopeful attitude, despite the weight of negative experiences and the conflict of interpretations that confounds the attempt to find meaning. Even under the experience of negativity, we experience our frustrated desire to be. People tend to reach for new possibilities, affirming the hope to create new things. Imagination and language have the power to create and re-create reality. This is a form of poetics that crafts the art of life: the "creative act of configuration that is in fact a creative reconstruction of experience in a literary mode."[291] Reality is thus revealed in terms of potentialities. Ricoeur's positive sense of human potential, nuanced view of self-understanding within cultural contexts such as religious symbols, and method for critique are useful guides in the interpretation of sacrifice and Christian identity.

First, a brief sketch of Ricoeur's general theory of hermeneutics will provide the context for the ethical interpretation of identity and intersubjectivity. In *Oneself as Another* Ricoeur develops the central theme of otherness and ethical identity; the tenth chapter in particular presents Ricoeur's ontology of mutuality, exploring the constituent role of the other in one's selfhood. Otherness has multiple dimensions: the passivity of the body, encounters with other people, the strange authority of conscience. These present the occasion for the summons to sacrifice for the other. The universal summons to care has a distinct form in the Christian model of sacrifice, the vision of loving self-gift that guides the interpretation of Christian identity.

## I. Phenomenological Hermeneutics and the Hermeneutics of Self-Interpretation

Ricoeur grounds the journey of self-interpretation and its ethical implications on two principles: first, claims for the absolute nature of the self (such as Cartesian autofoundationalism) are false; and second, both self-constitution and textual interpretation are dynamic and intersubjective.[292] The positing of the self is the starting point for modern philosophy in the Cartesian tradition. However, the positing of the ego is "given neither in psychological evidence, nor in an intellectual intuition, nor in a mystical vision." The chief principle of Ricoeur's phenomenological hermeneutics is that consciousness is not universally or transcendentally structured, but is accessed through its cultural objectifications. The ego is an abstract statement that must be mediated by ideas, actions, and cultural objects, to "lose and find itself."[293] Human reflection and understanding depend on texts and signs that are interpreted not simply for knowledge's sake, but to convey self-knowledge. Such mediation is essential because self-knowledge is not immediately transparent without reflection; it is a task to be achieved. There is "no self-understanding that is not mediated by signs, symbols, and texts."[294] Artistic representations, actions, texts, and cultural institutions objectify one's experiences and make them concretely available to reflection. Self-understanding is interpreted by engaging the formative works of one's culture and by interacting with others — including sacrificing for them.

## The Hermeneutics of Symbols

Religious symbols are an important source among the cultural objects that guide the formation of identity, which Ricoeur acknowledges even as an officially secular philosopher. (Ricoeur was a devout Protestant in private life, although his ability to maintain a professional distinction was questioned by some.) As Mark I. Wallace observes,

> Thus consciousness is never independent or empty — a *tabula rasa* — but always already interpenetrated by the founding symbols and stories that constitute one's communal heritage. Thus the journey to selfhood commences with the exegesis of the imaginary symbols and stories constitutive of one's cultural inheritance in order to equip the subject to become an integrated self by means of appropriating the symbols and stories as her own.[295]

Ricoeur's method for interpreting symbols has been widely influential. His famous term "the hermeneutics of suspicion" has been adopted by feminists as well as liberation theologians as a method for critique.

First, symbols have a power that is not reducible to analytical statements. This recognition was a turning point in Ricoeur's method in

*The Symbolism of Evil,* as he begins to prioritize hermeneutics over phenomenology and delve into the power of symbols to convey meaning.[296] The philosophical rigor of thought only pursues secondarily what the symbol first reveals, especially in the case of evil, which is accessible to reflection only by way of symbols, myth, poetry, and narrative. At the conclusion of *The Symbolism of Evil,* Ricoeur confronts the failure of systematic philosophy to absorb the hermeneutics of myth. Philosophy remains dependent upon symbols, though both are necessary and different modes of reflection. "The symbol is the movement of the primary meaning which makes us participate in the latent meaning and thus assimilates us to that which is symbolized without our being able to master the similitudes intellectually."[297] A symbol's first primary literal meaning points analogically toward a second one. The new way of the symbol is "a creative interpretation of meeting, faithful to the impulsion, to the gift of meaning from the symbol, and faithful also to the philosopher's oath to seek understanding." This is the way by which "the symbol gives rise to thought."[298] Similarly, paradox offers a greater truth through the gift of the tension between meanings.[299]

Second, because thought always contains presuppositions, and because it risks systematic distortion, there is always the need to critique. Ricoeur delves deeper into the critical phase of interpretation in *Freud and Philosophy: An Essay on Interpretation* (1970). Psychoanalysis contributes to a more honest understanding of language and culture by providing a theory of disguised meaning. The double meaning within the symbol is not necessarily a simple relationship of analogy, but may be the product of distortion, dissimulation, and repression. "Thus we return to our notion of symbol as double meaning, with the question still undecided whether double meaning is a simulation or revelation, necessary lying or access to the sacred."[300]

Like the symbol, interpretation itself has an internal complexity. There is a conflict of intentions between the hermeneutics that attempts to restore and manifest the meaning of the symbol, and the hermeneutics that demystifies illusion to expose distortion. Marx, Nietzsche, and Freud are the masters of using suspicion to discipline interpretation as it seeks the demystification of religion, culture, and even the general problem of false consciousness.

> The philosopher trained in the school of Descartes knows that things are doubtful, that they are not such as they appear; but he does not doubt that consciousness is such as it appears to itself; in consciousness, meaning and consciousness of meaning coincide. Since Marx, Nietzsche, and Freud, this too has become doubtful. After the doubt about things, we have started to doubt consciousness.[301]

Third, symbols are a reservoir of meaning, a resource for self-interpretation that gives generously through expansion as well as critique. The disciplines of the school of suspicion do not constitute all understanding. Their reductive critiques in fact narrow the scope of experience to a particular aspect: economics, the will to power, or psychism. "But, in return, does not this discipline of the real, this ascesis of the necessary lack the grace of imagination, the upsurge of the possible? And does not this grace of imagination have something to do with the Word of Revelation?"[302]

Critical thinking is too narrow if it uses only the sterile tools of dissection and formalism, comparison and technical analysis. The formal and technical approach to language and being risks "emptying language." The philosopher should hope for more than analysis: "Beyond the desert of criticism, we wish to be called again."[303] A second wave of interpretation to restore meaning must follow upon criticism. There should be a mutual hospitality of symbol and criticism in the hermeneutical circle, a second naïveté in which the symbols can be heard again. "The circle can be stated bluntly: 'we must understand in order to believe, but we must believe in order to understand.' "[304]

As with textual interpretation, so with self-understanding: "Self-knowledge is a striving for truth by means of this inner contest between reductive and recollective interpretation."[305] Ricoeur proposes a marvelous image for this expansive power of symbols: a second Copernican revolution, decentering the self to reveal the wider surroundings. The symbols will guide the philosopher "out of the enchanted enclosure of consciousness of one's self."[306] To interpret the symbol is to hope for a hierophany, a revelation of human self-understanding in the presence of the sacred. The self discovers that its own being shares in the being mysteriously offered by the symbols. Narration is another theme in the interpretation of identity. After *Time and Narrative,* Ricoeur universalizes the role of narrative as a fundamental part of the emergence of the self.[307] The examined life is the narrated life. Narrative unites the various and changing elements of human experience to the integration of plots. Decisions provoked by life's vicissitudes and shaped by the stable ethics of character form meaningful connections. Narrative unites the actions of the subject, creating a role.

In summary, knowledge of the self is an interpretation, and narrative is a privileged mediation for interpretation among other signs and symbols.[308] The accounting of the self's possibilities begins with the interpretation of self and other, which Ricoeur addresses in *Oneself as Another,* the text which is the chief resource for this chapter.

## An Ontology of the Self Who Acts

*Oneself as Another* completes Ricoeur's phenomenological and hermeneutical work by providing an explicitly ethical study of the self as an actor among others. In the tenth chapter, after a series of preparatory investigations, Ricoeur arrives at the point of exploring the "ontological consequences of the hermeneutics of the self."[309] The investigation of otherness opens up a rich zone of contact between self and other that reveals the constituent relationship of otherness to selfhood. In this zone we discover both the intimate presence of the other in my existing as a self, in my understanding of this identity, and in calling for the responses that establish my identity. In approaching the theme of the ontology of the self, Ricoeur enters an ancient philosophical conversation, intending to deflect the trajectory of philosophical reflection from arriving at the self as its absolute foundation.[310] Instead, Ricoeur suggests a more modest form of knowing in the sense of confidence, rooted in testimony and attestation.

The themes of narration, mediation, action, and suffering are magnetic centers of gravity that draw the energy of his thought throughout the stages of the work. Ricoeur's concern for action and suffering qualifies his appropriation of major philosophical discourse in *Oneself as Another.* Ricoeur calls his backward cast through the high waters of philosophical anthropology a "Heideggerian reappropriation of Aristotle."[311] This means that in reflecting upon Aristotle's basic question about Being, Ricoeur asks what Being is. Like Aristotle and Heidegger, Ricoeur recognizes that Being has several meanings.[312] For Ricoeur, the *being* of the self (the ontology of selfhood) fundamentally depends on the ground of the self who *acts.* The power to act is recognized as belonging to a body — my body — which acts within the world and among other things.[313] Ricoeur emphasizes different themes than does Aristotle, and he also qualifies Heidegger's basic concepts in order to stress the acting subject. Ricoeur proposes action, instead of care, as the unifying ground for the analyses of philosophical anthropology. By adopting the notion of selfhood as a being-in-the-world which comes to self-apprehension through the mediation of the world, Ricoeur critically adapts Heidegger's notion of care and presence.[314] In sum, Ricoeur shifts the function of mediating self and world from Heidegger's care to action.

A more serious problem Ricoeur has with Heidegger's anthropology is Heidegger's exclusion of the other from my world.

> All of Ricoeur's reservations about Heidegger can be summarized as a criticism of his analytic of the human world, for giving no room for the other at the border of or outside the world which is mine. There is no place for the other — whether it is in my body as the other I am in an ambiguous way (to be body is indeed to take care of oneself as another), or the other here now, absent in the past or in the future to which I must describe his or her own world.[315]

Whether Ricoeur explicitly pursues this critique of Heidegger as severely as Heidegger deserves, Ricoeur in fact fully surveys this terrain Heidegger has left unexplored, making the role of otherness central to the interpretation of identity.

## Interpreting the Self via the Other

Ricoeur's hermeneutics of the self unfolds by examining the three problematics proposed in the introduction of *Oneself as Another*: analysis, sameness, and otherness. This triple mediation of analysis, sameness, and otherness provides a way of self-interpretation, guiding an ontological study that asks, "what sort of being is the self?"[316] First, interpreting the self takes an indirect route through theoretical analysis following the schools of Anglo-American or linguistic philosophy. This method focuses on the rules for describing speech and action; it provides certain insights, but needs to be enlarged by further attention to the acting subject.[317]

Second, the self can also be determined by its contrast with sameness. By examining a dialectic of selfhood and sameness, Ricoeur shows that selfhood, defined as constancy to one's decisions, grounds lasting identity, rather than the sameness of biological identity. Both selfhood and sameness refer to continuity over time, but in different senses. Ricoeur refers to the mode of identity characterized by sameness as *idem*-identity. Being the same in the sense of character means being exactly the same person, with a single identity and genetic fixity. Character refers to the involuntary aspects of human experience — one's birth, physically grounded capabilities, and perspective — which are unchosen and finite.[318] But the continuity of the self-as-the-same, while indeed inseparable from the acting-self, is not enough to guarantee the identity of the acting self. Sameness does not provide an avenue into the *acting* subject. The acting self decides and responds to changing circumstances, thereby creating an identity based on her promises. Ricoeur refers to chosen identity as *ipse-identity*, which achieves permanence in time by keeping one's word. It is the "capacity of the agent to initiate an imputable action."[319] This kind of identity is least dependent on the facets of sameness in character. *Ipse*-identity indicates the self-constancy of the subject's faithfulness to her actions over time. The selfhood of *ipse*-identity keeps promises despite the changes of time, and despite the circumstances that might make a promise-giver waver. Ricoeur thus sees the temporal criterion of constancy over time as the separation between *ipse*-identity and *idem*-identity.

Having taken analysis and sameness to the limits of their usefulness, the third dialectic of selfhood and otherness remains as the window into the ontology of the self. The dialectic of selfhood with otherness will provide a more integrated and profound point of entry into the structures of the self, and this investigation begins with the mystery of passivity.

Awareness of the other and awareness of being a self both arise from a basic experience of passivity. Fundamentally, passivity is a phenomenon of contact and receptivity. Passivity is the mode of experience that recognizes that one's being is constituted by others. Passivity means "encountering the other," but it is also a fundamental dialectic within selfhood that has an inner dimension as well. Otherness is a polysemic dimension of human experience that begins deep within the self. As Charles Reagan writes,

> Otherness does not come from outside selfhood, but is part of the meaning and the ontological constitution of selfhood. . . . The main point of this dialectic is to prevent the self from pretending to occupy the place of the foundation. Otherness is joined to selfhood.[320]

The self is not its own foundation. Nor is the self able to choose whether to receive the other. Ricoeur's phenomenological analysis of passivity is a fascinating and nuanced reflection upon the givenness of existing in one's own body, and upon recognizing the other as irreducible to my decision or preference. Passivity presents a fundamental and ambiguous source of contact with the other that is both a ground for acknowledgment and discernment, as well as the tragic conduit for victimization.

Here we see how two important aspects of otherness relate to sacrifice and identity. First, selfhood emerges via its encounters with otherness. The other extends a call for my response. This is the arena of self-realization through sacrifice (losing one's life to save it). Second, the manifestation of passivity within otherness encloses the potential dilemma of victimization inherent in sacrifice. Passivity leaves one vulnerable to the possibility of oppression.

Three dimensions of private passivity are implicit to a fundamental awareness of oneself and others. First, there is one's relationship to one's own body, which mediates one's being in the world.[321] One's own body is the locus for ascribing one's own action to oneself. Second, there is a passive relationship of the self to the foreign other through intersubjective relationships. Third, there is the passive relationship of the self to itself. This is the deep mode of passivity known as conscience. Through the categories of the body, other persons, and conscience, Ricoeur probes a rich metacategory of human experience of great complexity and "relational density."[322] Selfhood must fully engage these three dimensions of otherness: the otherness of one's own body, the otherness of other people, and the otherness of conscience.

The passivity of the body illuminates a basic principle in a hermeneutic of sacrifice. It suggests the limitations and givenness of the conditions and possibilities of action, one's finite circumstances and concrete burdens, the raw slag from which sacrificial actions are forged. Many sacrifices result not from victimization but the existential state of living among "natural" limitations and fragility. Fragility does not discriminate, but issues an equality among persons by reminding them of the weakness latent within all.[323] Finitude is the ultimate expression of corporeal passivity. It is the

> strangeness of human finiteness, insofar as it is sealed by embodiment, hence what we call here primary otherness, in order to distinguish it from the otherness of the foreign. One can even say that the link, in the same existentiale of state-of-mind, of the burdensome character of existence and of the task of having-to-be, expresses what is most crucial in the paradox of an otherness constitutive of the self and in this way reveals for the first time the full force of the expression "oneself as another."[324]

This is existential otherness, the experience of oneself as foreign, as puzzling, even — as Paul laments in Romans 7 — as resisting one's own best intentions. The mystery of existing as another extends to the encounter with circumstances and events not chosen or desired by the self. The vulnerability inherent in the passivity of the body makes a sense of one's own ethical otherness imperative. This is the recognition of my ethical status as if I were an other: in terms of claiming respect, I also am an other, also worthy of regard. Ricoeur introduces this mutually reflexive regard at a critical moment in his discussion, before turning to the passivity of other people, which contains the potential of harm.

The passivity of one's own body ceases to be private and becomes explicit in the experience of suffering. Suffering is the deepening of the passivity of one's own body by the overlay of an extreme passive experience of other people. Most pain is caused by other people. Victimization is thus the exploitation of passivity.

Passivity that takes the form of suffering can be described as the lessening of one's ability to act. If the self is the being who acts, a reduced power to act is a diminished existence. "With the decrease of the power of acting, experienced as a decrease of the effort of existing, the reign of suffering, properly speaking, commences."[325] Suffering begins where the power to act decreases. Such vitiation of agency is precisely the content of the concerns stated by Suchocki and Saiving, restated here in Ricoeur's phenomenological discourse.

The ever-present role of narrative in constructing and making meaning out of events in Ricoeur's work has a strangely poignant appearance in this reflection upon suffering. Narrative connects agents, and even passive participants, in its intertwined stories. When narrative is choked, it reveals a deeper form of passivity and suffering concealed in the stories untold. In Ricoeur's eloquent phrase, these "concealed forms of suffering" include "the incapacity to tell a story, the refusal to recount, the insistence of the untellable." Naming the oppression of silencing is a powerful response to an ideology of sacrifice that silences the recollection of sacrifice as suffering. Instead of co-opting narratives of exploitative sacrifice as tales of virtue and holiness, giving voice to victimization offers hope that a painful tale can be retold and healed in a new narrative.

Otherness goes beyond the corporal givenness of existence and the confrontation with the needs of other people. Ricoeur proposes also a third modality of otherness, the "original and originary character of . . . being enjoined as the structure of selfhood."[326] To be enjoined is to hear the call of another, a call that sounds in the court of conscience. However, the summons should not be uncritically — that is to say, passively — accepted. Conscience discerns whether a certain response is an ethically acceptable and authentic gift of sacrifice, or an excessive capitulation to the other. As such, conscience mediates the dialectic between selfhood and otherness; conscience is a depth dimension of self-other awareness.

Conscience pertains to the dialectic of otherness and selfhood as an existential experience of the phenomenon of strangeness. The inner mystery of conscience is experienced as an external voice.

> The point is that human being has no mastery over the inner, intimate certitude of existing as a self; this is something that comes to us, that comes upon us, like a gift, a grace, it is not at our disposal. This non-mastery of a voice that is more heard than spoken leaves intact the question of its origin. . . . The strangeness of the voice [of conscience] is no less than that of the flesh or that of other human beings.[327]

Both conscience and suspicion target illusions about the self. Both challenge and stretch the ethics of otherness beyond an easy accommodation to mutuality. One can give more than the comfortable and reciprocal expectations of mutuality, and can be asked to give too much. Conscience is the inner court that hears and judges the charge to respond to the other.

## II. Creation of Identity via Response to Otherness

The exploration of the phenomenon of passivity as a mode of human experience that brings self and other together is the foundation supporting an ontology of selfhood based in giving to the other. The three dimensions of passivity he identifies — one's finitude, others' needs, and the mediation of conscience — are the conditions of possibility for sacrifice. Passivity is also a source of the ambiguity in sacrifice, representing the unchosen aspects of relationships and decisions. Sacrifice establishes identity when formative commitments are chosen; sacrifice is nonetheless marked by ambiguity because of the painful consequences or circumstances that are unwilled — exactly the circumstances that render the act a sacrifice. The element of choice is decisive.

Traditionally, theologians have associated the act of willing with valuing and choosing the good. To value and will the good is a necessary element of a conscientious and deliberate act of virtue, and a cornerstone of identity.[328] Without decision, there is no genuine sacrifice, and so no possibility of the realization that emerges from this paradoxical action.

Sacrifice for the other creates self-realization by way of *responsibility* and *recognition,* through *promising* and with the consent of *conscience.* Ricoeur relates sacrifice to self-realization by demonstrating that self-conscious agency and identity are born through responding to the other. Responding to the other, in turn, realizes a capacity to act. Responsibility connects the past, present, and future self. One attests to being the same agent, interlinked by self-constancy.[329]

The self, as author of its actions, reflects upon them and discovers self-esteem and its capacity to act. Self-esteem thus develops via a reflective process of solicitude for the other. Self-realization, in other words, is discovered in the paradoxical process of surrender and self-creation involved in choosing to hear the summons of the other.

## Self Constituted Reflexively through Other

Recognition registers the plurality of self-constitution, acknowledging that interaction with the other creates self-esteem and solicitude. The other is part of the deep constitution of the self, intimately affecting one's own sense of self. To acknowledge oneself as the agent of action is tightly linked to the ascription of my actions to me by another. Ascribing action to oneself is a "reflexive recovery" of the ascription of which others speak. The other serves to mark the difference between "the ego that posits itself and the self that recognizes its self only through these very affections."[330]

> Self-esteem is not founded on accomplishment, but on capacity; the ability to judge (to esteem) is based on the ability to act (*le pouvoir-faire*). "The question is then whether the mediation of the other is not required along the route from capacity to realization" (181).[331]

The answer is yes: awareness is a reflexive phenomenon. One realizes a capacity to act with the mediation of the other.

The self as author of its actions interprets and evaluates them to find either self-esteem or regret. "On the ethical plane, self-interpretation becomes self-esteem."[332] Self-esteem accepts the confirmation of others that one is an agent, that one contributes to others by one's actions. Self-interpretation recovers "the joyous affirmation . . . of the effort to be . . . at the origin of ethics' very dynamic."[333]

Self-esteem thus also contains an expression of one's desire for the company of others; it is a reflexive moment of the wish for the "good life."[334] Self-esteem's social correlate is solicitude, the warm feeling of mutual concern for the good life shared with others. Solicitude depends upon self-esteem, by pointing to the insufficiency of persons to be a world unto themselves.

> Solicitude bespeaks a lack belonging to self-esteem, as the reflexive moment of the wish for the good life, constituted with a lack evolving with a need, a need for friends, and giving rise to the awareness of the self among others. Thus, it is seen that solicitude is not external to self-esteem, but is constituted as a moment of self-esteem in its lack and need.[335]

In solicitude, self-esteem is extended to the other, who finds value and worth in himself as do I. The movement also reverses: befriending oneself depends on having first shared friendship with others. Solitude mirrors esteem — you are as irreplaceable as I am.[336]

## The Promise

The promise is a particular example of the extension of the self that creates identity. As Reagan writes, "It is the 'you can count on me' of the promise that ties selfhood with the reciprocity for the other founded in solicitude."[337] Promising is a mode of self-creation in terms of the other: *I am the one you can count on.*

In some cases, promising may be too premature a foundation of identity. Helen Buss believes Ricoeur prematurely bypasses the feminist concern with achieving selfhood by an appeal to the general human quest for self-understanding.[338] Buss challenges Ricoeur's contention that self-dispossession is a key to belonging to oneself, and states that relationality need not be sacrificial. Since there are dynamics in the self-other relationship, especially in patriarchal structures, that can hinder the emergence of the self, she asks first: *How can I come to be the person on whom you can depend?*[339] Ricoeur acknowledges the "interference of outside powers capable of diminishing" one's ability to act. Not all interactions between the self and the other are unambiguously positive.

While the summons is a privileged experience of revelation, and an invitation to establish one's identity by committing to another, the decision to extend oneself rests upon free and conscientious decision. The other does not have unlimited power to determine what one gives or sacrifices. Ricoeur's response to Levinas provides a carefully nuanced exploration of the limits of the call from the other, a caution already stated by feminist scholars but developed specifically in Ricoeur's philosophy by showing how the freedom of conscience is essential to the formation of authentic identity as diagrammed in his philosophical anthropology. The shared concern is the potential for excessive sacrifices in which suffering has no meaning, and which obstruct the development of Christian identity.

## Conscience: The Tension of Response and Summons Mediated by Otherness

Conscience mediates the tension of summons and response between self and other, the subject of the well-known debate between Emanuel Levinas and Ricoeur about the total priority of the other. Levinas is known for insisting on the radical priority of the other. In works such as *Totality and Infinity: An Essay on Exteriority* and *Otherwise Than Being or Beyond Essence,* Levinas argues that the other confronts us as a face to whom we must reply. Levinas insists that radical alterity is the medium for the ethical command.[340] The experience of relationship is not a totalizing synthesis, but a face-to-face encounter. Persons are in fact opposed, as in a face-to-face meeting.[341] Strikingly, Levinas believes it is better not to notice the color of the eyes in the face. One gives because the other has a need, not because this particular other has a unique claim of affection or relation (or beauty).

Levinas sees self-imputation as having an exterior origin whose trajectory ends in me — but begins with the other. This insistence that the other originates the act of the responding self, by charging it to respond, strikes Ricoeur as deliberate hyperbole: "the systematic practice of excess in philosophical argumentation."[342] According to Ricoeur, Levinas's model makes the self excessively passive, minimizing the conscientious interaction between self and other that grounds moral action. Persistently refusing to choose a single focal point as the polestar for ethics, Ricoeur insists that *both* self and other have an unshakable *primacy.* The primacy of self-esteem balances the primacy of the call to justice from the other.[343] The basis for this mutual respect is the awareness of one's own dignity, which is extended to the other. The other is to be regarded as a subject on the analogy of my own experience of subjectivity.[344] The dialectic of self and other mediated by conscience, therefore, is ideally structured by equality, an encounter in which equals approach each other. Ricoeur summarizes the equal relationship between self and other as the "dual primacy of self and other." One's self is also worthy of respect and wholeness — oneself, in this sense also, is an other.[345]

For Ricoeur, the movement of the other toward the self crosses the movement from the self toward the other. The first is a gnoseological motion (the self comes to see the other as a subject); the second is experienced as the ethical dimension (the other has a claim on me). The ethical claim can be validated because the subjectivity of the other is predicated on one's own. The movement from self to other in awareness and commitment intersects with the movement from other to self in the other's cry for help. In this way one's response begins with the act of self-designation. One's own conviction affirms the command to respond.

If action derives from the command of the other alone and originates solely in the other, Ricoeur argues that one's moral agency is simplified, if not brutalized. The subject becomes a prisoner who cannot affirm any freedom or resistance against the summons. Furthermore, such a co-opted response reduces the self to a faceless slave, whose own unique way of giving and responding vanishes before the demand of the other.

> The assignment of responsibility, stemming from the summons by the Other and interpreted in terms of the most total passivity, is reversed in a show of abnegation in which the self attests to itself by the very movement with which it removes itself. Who, in fact, is obsessed by the Other? Who was hostage to the Other if not a Same no longer defined by separation but by its contrary, Substitution?[346]

When submitting to the other makes one a hostage, the self is obliterated: it has become the other.[347] By the same token, the other has accepted the powers of the executioner.

Without a conscientious response, one risks losing identity and forfeiting the creation of the self. Instead, Ricoeur believes one becomes a self by conscientiously responding to the other.

> Only a self — as the subject and object, in its conscience, of its own internal dialogue — can have an other-than-self rouse it to its responsibility. Only a self — insofar as it esteems itself as a

self capable of reason, and agency, and goodwill — can exercise solicitude for others.[348]

Ricoeur's view of dialogic selfhood corrects an excessive primacy of the other. It is precisely to counter the danger of ethical substitution that Ricoeur stresses an ontology of *mutuality* as the intersubjective basis of identity. By insisting on an ontological basis for ethics, he provides a firm ground that protects the integrity of the self in a philosophically sound view of personal identity. The absurdity of ethical substitution becomes self-evident against such an ontological framework.

Levinas's absolute responsibility proposes an absolute separation that is in fact illogical. It posits an unexplained capacity to respond to the other, but can neither explain nor validate the basis for this response.

> Now the theme of exteriority does not reach the end of its trajectory, namely, awakening a responsible response to the other's call, except by supposing a capacity of perception, of discrimination, and of recognition that, in my opinion, belongs to another philosophy of the Same than that to which the philosophy of the Other replies.... One has to grant a capacity of perception to the self that is the result of a reflective structure, better defined by its power of reconsidering pre-existing objectifications than by an initial separation.[349]

Ricoeur also insists that this capacity of reception contains the power of discernment. The acting self must be granted the capacities of recognition, perception, discrimination, and conviction. Otherwise, the voice of conscience is vetoed by the other, who may become not only a dictator but an executioner. The voice that declares my responsibility for ethical commitment must be echoed by my voice with its answering conviction.

Both Ricoeur and Levinas view selfhood as being summoned to responsibility. They share a critique of idealist phenomenology that traces the origin of or restricts all phenomena to a founding subjectivity. But Ricoeur and Levinas track different sources of non-absolute subjectivity; more specifically, Ricoeur allows for two centers. Bourgeois observes,

> The positive contribution of Ricoeur is that he expands Levinas in a needed direction to round out and render explicit the place in the subject for such a response as solicitude and self-esteem, as will be seen. These, however, from Levinas's point of view, remain within the context of totality of the subject. And likewise, Ricoeur's fundamental point in *Oneself as Another* presents a complex identity not found as such in Levinas, a point to which Ricoeur explicitly adverts in his comments on Levinas.[350]

Conscience must preserve the existence of the self lest the indwelling become colonization. Commanded by another, the self can only react. The commanding other gains power to define and control the one she commands. "Ricoeur stubbornly insists on preserving self-love and other-regard in a correlative tension that he argues is snapped by Levinas's one-sided emphasis on self-emptying obedience in the face of the summons of the other."[351] Here is the rediscovery of the paradox of losing and finding one's self — a tension between self-love and other-regard confirming the value of both.

If the other has absolute priority, the other is only deferring the time when another other will summon her, co-opt her self-determined power as an issuer of summonses, and conscript her into a silent reactant. The deferral of self-love in favor of other-regard sets in motion a cascade of infinite deferrals. The exclusion of the self from any claim to regard leaves no foundation on which to grant it permanently to the other. Concern for another shifts to *another* other who will issue the next summons. If regard is always for the other, it never really belongs to the other. Levinas's exaltation of the other as the only moral object paradoxically places the other in the same isolated position as Nygren's unlovable self, who knows agape as God's love for all, but is illogically excluded from offering it to itself.

It remains striking that the laudable moral purity, on which Levinas insists, is really an ethic for the offender who should be restrained but is most unlikely to listen to the summons of the other. Victims who are trampled by the heedless or cruelly powerful need hardly be exhorted to consider the other; they are prevented by an oppressive other from even protecting themselves. This morality has few resources for the victim, the silent faces behind the barbed wire who apparently inspire Levinas. But it does not seem that he has written an ethic for them. By insisting on the primacy of both self and other, and viewing ethical identity as an interpretive accomplishment based on confirming one's self-esteem through keeping promises to the other, Ricoeur's ethic more usefully guides a hermeneutic of sacrifice that tends to both sides of the paradox.

In summary, three themes — the constituent role of the other in one's selfhood, the equality and primacy of the self and other, and the fact of being summoned by the other — comprise the chief resources in Ricoeur's hermeneutical phenomenology of selfhood for the interpretation of sacrifice as a positive means of identity formation.[352]

## Critical Assessment

Ricoeur and Levinas can be compared on various terms: their contrasting use of similar philosophical influences; the priorities guiding their interpretations of selfhood; even stylistic choices. Part of their differences result from alternate reactions to Heidegger: Ricoeur's reflexive philosophical anthropology versus Levinas's radical ethical stance.[353] Ricoeur has his own idiosyncratic interpretation of Levinas — and would be the first to acknowledge that no reading of a text is absolute, including his own.[354] Ricoeur approves of Levinas's epiphany of the face that issues responsibility, admiring his strong evocation of the encounter of solitude with the transcendent other. "Each face is a Sinai that prohibits murder."[355] Each one is indeed confronted by the revelation of the other, whose transcendence cannot be reduced to a representation of mine. Even while critical of the hyperbolic extremes with which Levinas expresses his ethics, Ricoeur has affirmed "Levinas's positive statements about selfhood as 'unique and irreplaceable.' "[356]

Some of the difference amounts to a divergence in style. This does not suggest a superficial distinction but a profound complementarity of vision. Mark I. Wallace compares the biblical and philosophical approaches of Ricoeur and Levinas to the theme of selfhood as being summoned. Wallace demonstrates that "both Ricoeur and Levinas use the biblical texts to construe the project of selfhood in terms of being summoned — beyond one's choosing and willing — to take responsibility for the neighbor — even at great cost to oneself." Both see that the other awakens our sense of responsibility. However, they differ in their views of the self that is thus constructed and summoned, and in their hermeneutical method for interpreting the summons via the biblical texts.[357]

Ricoeur's ethics is grounded upon the freedom to affirm one's responses, and the freedom to choose the guiding aims that define the trajectory of the purposeful life. For Ricoeur, the experience of freedom affirms one's very being and is the condition for the flourishing of being. The freedom to be and to act enables one to respond to the summons of the other. In fact, the purpose of ethics is the freedom of the other. "The whole of ethics . . . is born from this redoubled task to make the freedom of the other person come to pass as similar to my own."[358]

The guide for such conscientiously chosen actions is not only a summons from the other, but one's personal aim or vision of life. The fundamentally narrative aspect of ethical identity is the purpose for acting and the story-vision of the world that encircles action. The meaning of one's being is made coherent through refiguration into a narrative unity.[359] Ricoeur's definition of ethics is "living well with and for others, in just institutions."[360] When questioned, Who are you? the responsible self answers, *Here I am, here for you.* This vision orients actions for the other, providing the narrative horizon for identity. Such an articulated vision of the good life unites individual actions into an integrated whole and provides a hermeneutical coherence to the narrative of one's life.

Morality is the imperative mode of this ideal.[361] The private nature of self-love and personal aims should not be an unrestrained guiding principle. Because the will is finite, and freedom is affected both by natural affection and evil, the restraint of the norm is necessary. Respect thus becomes "self-esteem that has passed through the sieve of the universal and constraining norm."[362] Embarking on a dialogue with Kant and Aristotle, Ricoeur establishes that the aim (a catchword for classic Aristotelian teleology) is prior to the norm (a shorthand for Kant's deontology), but the moral norm is a necessary corrective.[363] The universal norm does not merely correct one's potentially narrow views, but helps confirm the promises one has made: the other side of command is the self-imposed desire for constancy. The norm strengthens an inner wish for constancy to one's promises; it structures the desire for a unified and consistent will over the "intermittences of desire." This quality of endurance and coherence exists also in promises as a mode of self-commitment. "Man became the promise-making animal through the capacity to be able to count on himself in advance of himself, therefore giving himself the durée of a will within the temporal chaos of his desires."[364] The striving for moral norms occurs within the greater horizon of the aim of the good life because the ethical aim, or guiding vision of action, is the fundamental origin that orients action and identity. The combined application of aim and norm usefully guides a theory of sacrifice by focusing on the purpose of actions and offers objectivity to individuals struggling with personal conflicts. The norm's universalizing principle also judges what kind of sacrifices are acceptable or excessive, offering a criteria of justice for evaluating the sacrifices of others. The reciprocity of considering an action as normative for all produces two valuable questions: (1) What sacrifice that I might undertake is imaginable for another to do also? (2) What sacrifice may I ask the other to do for me?

## Constructive Conclusions

It is valuable to establish the centrality of the aim for a hermeneutics of sacrifice for several reasons. First, the aim orients the interpretation of narrative identity. The aim has a social basis and reflects Ricoeur's dialogic ethic. The aim guides hard choices where the norm is silent. The vision and aim is the creative source of ethics in unprecedented situations, not the deductions of formal method.

## The Tragic Defeat of the Aim

Tragedy is such a situation that does not provide solutions, or resolutions, but reveals the aporia where the norm fails and falls silent.[365] One must then dig to the ethical foundation of the guiding aim. Tragedy, in Nussbaum's view, is as much a quality of awareness in the mind of the subject as an objectively disastrous situation (though one's awareness is provoked by the actual situation). Tragic awareness confers a greater sensitivity to the lack of moral options. Tragic awareness, though painful, perceives the larger context and causes of difficult situations and may be able to find a creative resolution to conflict.[366]

Tragedy can spark a revelation of the larger aims of a community, as new forms of community adequate to a plurality of convictions and narrative identities are sought. The breadth of vision she urges recalls the integration of multiple aims Ricoeur saw as the foundation of narrative identity. We relate to others by enlarging our vision, adopting the aims of others, and expanding the shape of the common good. (One such large vision is the kingdom of God, which will be considered later.) Through critical appropriation of many narratives, the subject integrates them into his or her own narrative.[367] To return to the previous example, promising is a self-enlarging interpretation of self that integrates the aim of the other.[368] Self-constancy, therefore, also becomes fidelity to the aim of the other who is integrated into the self. Self-constancy reflects an other-constancy. By attending to a fuller view of the community and their firm attachment in the self via promising, practical wisdom enables greater mutual recognition.[369]

Sacrifice has this tragic element: the choice between not making the sacrifice (thus forsaking the goal or good it would bring) and making a sacrifice and accepting its cost. The tragic choice forces an individual "to depart from ... something that goes to the heart of that person's being."[370] Here is the connection between tragic choices, sacrificial choices, and personal identity. All persons have values, concerns, loves, and commitments on which they have set their hearts. The cost of fidelity, of keeping promises, becomes most sharply ironic in light of Ricoeur's belief that the purpose of keeping promises is to build identity. (*I am the one on whom you can depend.*) Tragic choices frustrate one's own desire for fidelity and self-attestation.

Life is endured, by consenting to its burdens. Necessity is lived and experienced as negativity, and even consent does not truly consent, or merge with necessity. As Muldoon writes, consent "does no more than identify the necessities which structure our willing."[371] Ricoeur states that "consent is the human but disquiet link between freedom and nature.... It represents converting, within myself, the hostility of nature into the freedom of necessity. Consent is the asymptotic progress of freedom towards necessity."[372]

Martyrdom is a paradigmatic Christian model of consent. For the martyr, the consequences are usually clear. Yet there is the distinction between the choice to witness to one's Christian identity, and the necessity of death forced by an evil situation or oppressor.[373]

Sacrifice that embodies a genuine decision may still be marked by suffering and endurance. The memory of the martyrs is sacrosanct in Christian tradition. Though compelled by their tormentors, the early Christian martyrs clearly saw themselves following the example of Jesus and actively willed to accept their fate with a profound sense of surrender. In most cases they did not directly will to die, but surrendered to martyrdom for the sake of preserving their faithful witness to their faith. Ignatius of Antioch, who spoke passionately about his hope for martyrdom, may not have been unique but nevertheless constitutes an exception that was not entirely endorsed by the church leaders of his time. Despite legitimate criticisms of glorified suffering, it is too soon to say that meaningful sacrifice has nothing to do with suffering. Such a statement is intuitively contrary to Christian wisdom. The role of potentially meaningful suffering in genuine sacrifice will be bracketed here. Further discussion of suffering must be deferred to a later chapter.

Tragedy reminds philosophy that the interaction of self and other is not pure and new each time, but exists in a tangled history. Freedom is an intersubjective exchange that participates fully in all the friction of human life.

> It is rather a question of the fact that the actualization of my freedom through your freedom and of your freedom through my freedom, has a specific history which is the history of slavery, of inequality, and of war.[374]

Because there is no neutral ground, the person who acts confronts the passive necessity of entering a given history of freedom and the counter-actions of others. One's actions are never purely conceived and executed with perfect freedom from all constraint. One does not act *ex nihilo*, as it were, but fashions decisions and implements them amid the raw material of situations and preconditions left behind by others.

> We now encounter a form of passivity which I will call the self-actualization of everyone by everyone else. By this I mean that we can only act through structures of interaction which are already there and which tend to unfold their own history which consists of inertias and innovations which themselves are sedimented in their turn.[375]

As Buss pointed out, there is ambiguity in self-realization via the other. The limit situations encountered in extremity and in tragedy upset the mutuality of self-esteem and solicitude. Such particular situations call for the risk and conviction of moral judgment.[376]

### Practical Criteria for a Hermeneutic of Sacrifice

Ricoeur's anthropology thus suggests a positive criterion: one's actions or sacrifices on behalf of the other should reflect and express deeply held values and personal aims. Sacrifice as fidelity should build identity. One should question sacrifice that subverts identity and agency, undermining personal integrity. The cost of sacrifice defeats the purpose of confirming discipleship if it threatens to undermine *ipse*-identity, that is, the conscious will to keep promises as an expression of one's core identity. On the other hand, resisting coercion is not the same thing as accepting danger if one judges that solidarity requires taking a risk. One can choose to lose one's self to preserve a greater integrity, as do the martyrs for the sake of their promises. At the same time, one may legitimately judge one's own life to be worth saving. Discernment means being aware that some responses are preferable to others. What cannot be surrendered is the discernment and reflection essential to conscience and genuinely responsible action.

The significance of his complex, multiply centered anthropology is that giving or sacrificing for the other has the potential to affirm subjectivity. Sacrifice creates an expanded self-understanding and enlarges the self because we are what we love. Ricoeur identifies the fundamental command of the other as a plea for love.

> There is a form of commandment that is not yet a law: the commandment, if it can be called such, can be heard in the tone of the Song of Songs, in the plea that the lover addressed to the beloved: "Thou, love me!" It is because violence taints all the relations of interaction, because of the power-over exerted by an agent on the patient of the action, that the commandment becomes law, and the law, prohibition: "Thou shalt not kill."[377]

The memory of the martyrs is precisely the memory of the strength of their commitment to their Christian identity amid the confusion and conflict of life. *Set me as a seal upon your heart, as a seal upon your arm, for love is as strong as death....* Free will oriented to the good in the classic sense of *libertas* is love embracing its ultimate aim. The scriptural reflections of the first chapter concluded that sacrifice is a response to God's gracious initiative, which inspires dedication to the other. A religious offering of sacrifice responding to grace includes the freedom to establish identity in order to give it away.

## III. An Ethics of Summons

### Scriptural Narratives of the Summoned Subject

Following this extended philosophical detour through the ontology of mutuality, which defends self-giving as a chosen gift or promise that establishes identity, we can now turn to Ricoeur's reflection upon the imitation of Christ, which takes the form of a meditation on the scriptural narratives of the summoned subject. God's abundant generosity sets a model for the disciple who interprets self-sacrifice under the rubric of the golden rule and the love command, a radically reinterpreted rule of equivalence. Sacrifice as a guiding aim has the potential to inspire a gospel flood of generosity.

The power of biblical texts to be the aim that inspires one's identity springs from their performative force. Such texts have the potential to enact a new reality in the mind of the reader; by suggesting a radical path of generosity and forgiveness, these possibilities are made present as new options. The biblical image or story reveals a new way of being and opens the reader to an encounter with God. It is the invitation to every reader to come, follow me, come and see, come take up your cross. The Scripture calls the reader to hear, accept, and imagine a new way of being — that of dedicated self-sacrifice as a way to salvation. The shock of this non-intuitive vision calls forth the work of questioning and imagining — the philosophy and critical reflection that is the secondary task. As Wallace says, "The journey to moral selfhood is made possible by the subject's willingness to receive new ways of being from its interactions with the biblical texts-worlds."[378]

Self-interpretation intersects with scriptural interpretation. Christian faith is the commitment that seeks and chooses Christian symbols as the structure of identity and conscience. In the final essays concluding the Gifford lectures that became *Oneself as Another,* Ricoeur places the voice of conscience in the voice of God. The theme of the final Gifford lectures is "the Christian is someone who discerns 'conformity to the image of Christ' in the call of conscience." Human conscience, now as the court of the Divine Other, encounters the ideal of radical love. The philosopher must be agnostic about the origin of conscience, but the theologian knows it to be the voice of God. "Indeed, conscience is now valorized as the inalienable contact point between the Word of God and human beings; it is the forum where divine forgiveness, care for oneself, and solicitude for others intersect."[379]

Ricoeur traces a lineage of figures that represents the summoned self within scripture. The prophets and their commission narratives are a paradigm for all biblical narratives that tell of a response to God. The Christ image is a very specific figure summoned both for suffering and for glory. Ricoeur points also to Augustine's figure of the inner teacher, who internalizes the call. Finally, conscience contains the ultimate intimacy uniting the caller and the call. In the court of conscience, the call is internal to the person summoned. At the same time, the call preserves its transcendent origin.

Charles Taylor masterfully narrates the modern Western tradition of the self and argues that the Western notion of self is itself an interpretation. He argues that our familiar sense of inwardness is not a universal sense of self but a historical mode of interpretation.[380] This notion places the validation of conscience, discernment, and subjectivity in a model of interiority. Augustine radicalizes Platonic knowing in his turn to interiority. Augustine wants to show that God is found not "outside," but within the depths of the human person. Augustine achieves this inner turn by developing the Christian figure of the Inner Teacher to which Ricoeur refers. In Taylor's terms, "God is to be found in the intimacy of self-presence."[381] Indeed, Augustine taught that humanity is most clearly the image of God through inner self-presence and self-love. In *The Trinity*, Augustine searched for the image of God within the human person, looking for an experience of transcendence marked by the same unity, equality, and distinction characterizing the life of the Trinity. With the "mental trinity" of memory, understanding, and will, Augustine first states confidently that he has found this image. "Here we are then with the mind remembering itself, understanding itself, loving itself. If we see this we see a trinity, not yet God of course, but already the image of God"

(XIV.11).[382] The dynamic understanding of self by the light of God that illumines memory and inner reflection is widened in Ricoeur's reflection upon the discovery of self through the other, both human and divine, and in loving response to both in sacrifice.

In the Christian narrative, the summoned self, following this interior call, finds a guide in the Gospels. Like tragedy, the Gospels offer a paradoxical ethic, posing unthinkable limit situations that disorient and destabilize. The Gospels pull our attention to moments that stretch conventions and call for imagination. The gospel ethic saves by liberating freedom, by regenerating and nourishing the freedom of the other.

> The ethical function of the gospel seems to me to be to restore the intending of the other person. It is the whole morality of the love of neighbor, an expression that signifies that the fundamental motivation of ethics is to make your freedom advance as mine does. The ethical process is unceasingly reborn from its origin in the mutuality of freedom.[383]

The Gospel presents radical choices that reorient human concerns. The world gains new possibilities.

> For Ricoeur, then, the specificity of Christian religious selfhood lies in the circumstance that in an important sense the textual "world" the Christian inhabits is a not a world of human possibility, at least not one of finite humanity. Rather, the Christian, whose "world" is the kingdom of God, hears conscience calling her to fulfill humanity in the kingdom of God, a call that is identical with the call to imitate Christ. In practice, this will entail reorienting human concern in the direction of a radical love for God and for others as God's creatures.[384]

The religious symbolism that imagines the world and guides human action is much richer than the symbols of sin and obligation. Ricoeur emphasizes the symbolism of dependence and creation — the economy of the gift, which re-centers the symbolism of sin and evil. Creation is a supra-ethical symbol for the relation of dependence and belonging within a supportive cosmos. Morality does not confront individuals in isolation, but within a system of nature embodying love of all creatures.

> The sense of radical dependence that is at stake here, insofar as it is attached to the symbolism of creation, does not leave us face-to-face with God; rather, it situates us within nature considered not as something to exploit but as an object of solicitude, of respect and admiration, as we hear in St. Francis's "Canto de [sic] Sole." The love of neighbor, in its extreme form of love for one's enemies, thus finds its first link to the economy of the gift in this hyperethical feeling of the dependence of the human creature, and our relation to the law and justification stems from this same economy.[385]

The symbol of creation is completed by hope for its final possibilities, the renewal of creation.[386]

Creation precedes and completes the symbols of judgment and punishment, especially satisfaction. Creation enriches the gift of Torah and the gift of forgiveness of sins; in the context of creation, the law and the cross belong to a relationship that is not simply judgmental. Religious symbolism is "polycentric," not limited to "moralizing reduction."[387]

## The Economy of the Gift: The Superabundant Measure

The scriptures offer a theology of generosity able to transform human action: the "economy of the gift." Conventionally human logic is logic of equality and equivalence. God's logic is of excess and superabundance. The logical punishment of the flood is countered by divine repentance.[388] Jesus responds to the rigid reciprocity of the *lex talionis* (an eye for an eye) with extreme examples such as turning the other cheek (although originally the restriction of vengeance to the same injury was a just development from unrestricted retaliation). The same logic of divine generosity pours out in the contrast Paul sets between the fault of one who brings death, and the grace of God which comes from Jesus. Here again the logic of generosity bursts the bounds of equivalence. Paul recognizes the generosity Jesus preached in Sermon on the Mount as Jesus himself, the gift of God.[389]

Ricoeur suggests these are not immediate rules of conduct, but provide a new pattern for action. The gospel does not provide moral norms or allow concrete precepts to be deduced from it. The extravagant recommendations serve to disorient one's imagination. The new pattern manifests an excess of giving, a logic of generosity to overturn the logic of equivalence.[390]

This fullest repertoire of symbols constitutes an economy of generosity. The gift of creation bridges the symbolism of God to affect the rules of human action. Because we have received life, we are beholden to accept the new command. The new command is therefore not limited by equivalence to what the neighbor has given me. It is grounded in the gift of the creator God.

> It is ethical, therefore, but also hyperethical in that this new commandment constitutes in a way the most adequate ethical projection of what transcends ethics, the economy of the gift. In this sense, an ethical approximation of this economy is set forth that may be summed up in the expression, "*Since* it has been given you, give...." According to this formula, and through the force of the "since," the gift turns out to be a source of obligation.[391]

As the symbol of creation completes the symbol of justice, the love command ("But I say to you that hear, Love your enemies, do good to those who hate you, bless those who curse you, pray for those who abuse you" [Luke 6:27–28]) completes the golden rule ("And as you wish that men would do to you, do so to them" [Luke 6:31]). The "conjugation" of these two rules expands the tension between equality and superabundance, which emerges in an ethics of self-interpretation as the distinction of mutuality and sacrifice. He asks, how is the golden rule reinterpreted in light of the economy of the gift in a religious perspective?

## Ethical Embrace of God's Generosity: Golden Rule or Love Command?

The love command is not reducible to the moral imperative, which trades in obligation, duty, and resistance, not the enchanted praise of the creature. Love as a command is the articulated invitation to encounter the creator. It is the poetic form of the imperative. From a literary perspective, the expression of love spills forth in praise, in terms of excess and contradiction, not the measured tones of justice. As such, love as praise resists analysis in the distant mode of justice.[392] The expansiveness of the economy of the gift creates a gap between the poetic and moral forms of the command. Love thus expresses and expands itself by the metaphorization of praise: this is love as eros.[393]

The command to love one's enemies is apparently closest to the economy of gift, even more so than the golden rule. The golden rule seems to express the logic of equivalence; it contains measure; the love command does away with it.[394] Therefore, the command to love one's enemies is best understood as a corrective to the golden rule. At the same time, there is great implicit generosity in the wishes that activate the golden rule. Under closer examination, the golden rule is marked not so much by measure, which in ordinary terms is limited, but by reciprocity. The apparent criticism of the golden rule as too narrow, by the greater generosity of the love command, applies only when the golden rule is wrongly identified with the *lex talionis*. "If you love those who love you, what credit is that to you?" (Luke 6:32).[395] In the *lex talionis,* a fixed content is exchanged; in contrast, the golden rule imagines hopes — what you wish others would do to you — moving both ways.

What more could one wish for than that one's enemy would surprisingly, inexplicably, love me? What more disorienting trans-formation could I imagine upturning my own attitude toward the enemy, who is also neighbor? The golden rule restates the love com-mand. Equivalence contains an economy of outpouring response, the irruption of generosity. The love command makes clearer the pos-sibility of overabundant generosity, enables us to dare to wish that

enemies may love us and that we may initiate this economy by loving
them. The love command dares one to dream that I might love the
enemy; conjoined to the golden rule, I may dream she might love me.
The golden rule does not restrict love, only violence. Its prescriptions
are reversible but not limitable. The reciprocity of the golden rule corrects the risk of the love command to suspend the ethical concern for
equal respect and self-protection.[396] The love command supplies the
imagination of an unlimited gift, and shows the expansive meaning
of measure in the economy of the gift. The love command contains a
radical order to turn and be struck again.

The golden rule should not be interpreted as *do ut des* (I give
in order that you will give), but reinterpreted as generosity.[397] A
verse from the Sermon "condenses" the paradox of measure and
overabundance. "Give and it will be given to you. A good measure,
pressed down, shaken together, running over, will be put into your
lap; for the measure you give will be the measure you get back"
(Luke 6:38). Equivalence is transfigured: "Superabundance becomes
the truth hidden in equivalence."[398] The superabundant measure is a
symbol of generosity in Jesus' teaching complemented by the sign of
the cost of such generosity to the finite human person: the symbol of
Jesus' cross.

The journey to the fullness of religious selfhood involves interpreting the images and symbolic possibilities of the call to discipleship.
The possibilities become real when they have been appropriated.[399]
In this way identity is not inevitably formed, but has the character
of earned discipleship. Such realization is not straightforward. The
road to realizing identity encounters obstacles and false starts. In
this way also, like interpretation itself, the path to sainthood is an
indirect route.

The judgment of conscience is a wager that risks an interpretation
of self-realization and self-sacrifice, in the hopes that the sacrificial
model of discipleship will prove fruitful. For this wager there is no
verification, only the weighing of the harvest. Wallace observes that
"the only verification of the truth of such choices is found, over the
course of one's existence, in the rich quality of a life well lived in

harmony with self and others."[400] This test also anticipates that a poorly placed wager will be revealed in the wasted ground of fruitless sacrifice.

Colored by the Christian narrative, there is a transition in the guiding aim: *I am the one who keeps my promise to you, despite the cost, so that we may live in friendship and a just society* shifts to *I am the one who keeps my promise to you, despite the sacrifice, so that we may live in the kingdom of God.*

The vision of living well has a special painful clarity when it is absent. It is the vision of the good life, and its threats, in a theological light, that I will take up in the next chapter, by bringing the question of sacrifice, self, and other to the theological vision of Edward Schillebeeckx.

Chapter Four

# SACRIFICE IN A
# CREATION CATECHISM

*I have calmed and quieted my soul... like a weaned child is my soul within me. O Israel, hope in the Lord from this time forth and forevermore.* —Psalm 131

The journey through feminist criticism and Ricoeur's anthropology has provided a basis for rejecting excessive sacrifice, as well as envisioning the constructive role of sacrifice in building identity and interpersonal relationships. Perhaps one might stop here. However, while Ricoeur offers a valuable philosophical framework for understanding the realization of identity through giving of oneself to the other, a retrieval of sacrificial language that adequately addresses feminist theological concerns requires an explicitly Christian theological interpretation of sacrifice. What is needed to complete an ethics of sacrifice and raise it to a theological hermeneutics of sacrifice? A theological hermeneutics of sacrifice calls for a religious view of salvation, suffering, and finitude, within the context of God's creation, with which to interpret the relationship of self-sacrifice and self-realization. The themes of creation and the reign of God express the theological dimensions of interdependence. Human fulfillment is then seen as part of a whole; self-realization is not measured by self-referential, autonomous completeness. Furthermore, the creaturely context of identity reminds the believer that there are natural limits inherent in created finitude that are not in themselves tragic. A religious view does not automatically endorse suffering and sacrifice. A religious view of salvation and sacrifice may interpret suffering and service critically because of the hope that the contrast experiences of suffering reveal God's desire that humankind and creation not suffer.

Ricoeur demonstrated how the symbol of creation establishes an economy of the gift. The response of gratitude for the gift of creation precedes all relationships to the other, breaking open the logic of equivalence, enabling generosity. Within the theology of Edward Schillebeeckx, creation is a central theme that illuminates his anthropology, Christology, doctrine of grace, and vision of human history anticipating the reign of God. Indeed, his work has been described as a "creation catechism" — a confession of faith in God the creator who wills to be for us and for our salvation, present in Jesus Christ and the church. Schillebeeckx's theological perspective enriches a study of Christian sacrifice because his immersion in the scholarship of New Testament literature has focused on the person of Jesus Christ and the interpretation of his death by the early communities. At the same time, far from isolating the meaning of Jesus' death or exaggerating the value of suffering for Jesus or his followers, Schillebeeckx is committed to the conviction of liberation theology that salvation includes earthly well-being. Schillebeeckx believes that finitude is a created good, despite its frailty, pain, and sinfulness. Nonetheless, he is acutely sensitive to the reality of suffering and the cost of solidarity with the oppressed of the earth. The potentially paradoxical juxtaposition of wholeness and suffering in Schillebeeckx's reflection make him a valuable conversation partner for this project.

For Schillebeeckx, humanity cannot be understood apart from God. God is the creator of human beings as finite creatures. The doctrine of creation thus grounds the theology of sacrificial discipleship: God entrusts creation to the autonomy of finite creatures, and wills for them to be the principle of its ongoing shaping. Because of the contingency and fallenness of this world, human history is a process full of suffering. Sacrifice is inevitable, whether part of a chosen vocation of discipleship or forced upon one by circumstances and oppression. However, Schillebeeckx believes God is present to this suffering and sacrifice, most vividly in Jesus Christ, who is the ground of hope for creation's fulfillment. Schillebeeckx's theory of salvation and suffering supports and validates the arguments against destructive sacrifice provided in the previous chapters from a theological perspective, while furthering an understanding of how the costs and suffering of sacrifice can nevertheless be integrated in Christian identity through hope for the reign of God. Schillebeeckx writes,

> On the basis of the Jesus event, we can say that Christianity is about love as the way to God, but a love that is not silent about the price, the cost of loving. The disciples of the risen crucified one were inculcated with this: the light appears in the darkness.[401]

Sacrificial action thus expresses a productive and critical creation faith, which accepts the responsibility and the cost of shaping the world. Sacrifice as an expression of productive creation faith also demonstrates that faith can be reconciled to finite creatureliness, but need not glorify suffering. The articles of Schillebeeckx's "creation catechism" develop this creed: God is Creator, for us and for our salvation, and present to suffering humanity, on the way to the reign of God. Subsequent exposition of Schillebeeckx's Christology spells out this premise, showing through the message of Jesus that indeed God wills our wholeness, not suffering. The negative contrast of the cross most dramatically challenges disciples to interpret suffering and assess their own choices for sacrifice in their creaturely task of bringing about the reign of God.

Section I presents Schillebeeckx's doctrine of creation. Section II shows how within this creation catechism, the person and message of Jesus Christ are an explicit sign of God's will for human wholeness and salvation. The cross is also God's witness to the cost of liberating practices in history. However, Schillebeeckx resists an understanding of Jesus' suffering as salvific in itself. The dissonance of these two themes — wholeness and suffering — generates insight into the paradox of self-sacrifice and self-realization. I will thus examine closely the good news that God wills wholeness for creation, and also focus on the meaning of the cross for the disciple who chooses to follow Jesus. Within the overarching context of God's creative and saving relationship to humanity, and Jesus Christ as the definitive message that God's cause is the human cause, in Section III I will explore the meaning that Schillebeeckx finds in the sacrificial suffering of discipleship. I will examine how his characteristic analysis of suffering as a negative contrast experience contributes to the understanding of suffering as a risk to the self examined in chapters 2 and 3. Section IV relates the inspiration and dedication that undertakes sacrifice to the acceptance of humanity's creaturely condition and commitment to take on God's cause, the healing of creation. Sacrifice is not a call for subservience to the other, but a radical invitation to work for the coming reign of God. First, a review of the developments in Schillebeeckx's long career will set his thought in context.

Schillebeeckx's exploration of diverse topics is unified by core concerns if not an overall systematic approach.[402] Among these core elements are the guiding questions: "What does it mean to be a Christian, a Christian community in the contemporary world?...How does being Christian relate to being human?"[403] Schillebeeckx employs hermeneutic and critical strategies to interpret religious themes and images anew in response to changing worldviews and current concerns. Rooted in the awareness of suffering, both hermeneutics and critical theory attempt new understandings that are liberative. Critical theory generates knowledge by negative contrasts, which reveal the gap between the distorted reality of the present and the anticipated *humanum* to come. Schillebeeckx's vision is thus characterized by liberative praxis, contemporary theoretical analyses, a this-worldly religious emphasis, and, above all, Christian hope.

Schillebeeckx consistently addresses three philosophical interests: (1) ontology and metaphysics, (2) epistemology, and (3) anthropology. These fundamental philosophical questions each relate to the central idea of creation. Creation is a unifying idea throughout his philosophical reflection on ontology and metaphysics, epistemology, and anthropology since the created human person comes to know

God through creation and in experiences of contingency.[404] Schillebeeckx's ontological reflections on reality as a divine creation proceed
from his faith convictions. His view of reality as a unity is also a philosophical assertion that both faith and philosophy address the same
reality. Schillebeeckx's consistent epistemological premise is that humans come to know God by way of creation. However, his early
writings emphasize the knowledge of God through the inner life
of grace through the concrete mediation of the world, whereas he
will later specify religious knowledge through the categories of social
action and praxis.

After joining the Dominican community in Ghent, Schillebeeckx
spent three years studying philosophy at Louvain. Dominic De Petter, a Dominican philosopher and spiritual director, encouraged
Schillebeeckx to read philosophers like Kant, Hegel, and Freud, and
promoted a phenomenological and sociological approach to human
nature. De Petter also emphasized the priority of grace in human
experience. Schillebeeckx also encountered the historical and psychological biblical interpretation of the German theologian Karl Adam
through De Petter. Schillebeeckx thus cultivated an interest in experience as the mode of encounter of the world and the medium of
transcendence.[405] Schillebeeckx's nuanced understanding of experience will help ground a view of sacrifice as an interpretive element
within certain experiences.

He lectured in dogmatic theology at Louvain until the end of the
Second World War. He then spent two years studying in Paris, officially at Le Saulchoir, the Dominican theological school near Paris.
He also attended lectures at the Sorbonne, where he heard Etienne
Gilson, Yves Congar, and most importantly, Marie-Dominique Chenu.
From Chenu Schillebeeckx learned the importance of attending to the
sources, appreciating the historical context, and understanding deeply
the particular moments within church tradition. "What struck Edward
most about Chenu was his combination of historical analysis and reconstruction of church tradition with involvement in the world."[406]
To Schillebeeckx, Chenu was a concrete model of the Dominican concern for God and the world, attuned to the problems of the world and

not just the church in a narrow sense. Schillebeeckx also met Marxist and atheist philosophers through circles at Le Saulchoir. Their commitments to the workers and critiques of bourgeois society impressed on Schillebeeckx the need for praxis that goes beyond piety.

A marked shift in Schillebeeckx's concerns and methods occurred in the mid-1960s. After the Second Vatican Council, Schillebeeckx shows a methodological turn to hermeneutics and critical theory in place of his earlier phenomenological Thomism. Schillebeeckx's thought shifted in the 1960s due to a new conviction that total meaning cannot be perceived and expressed cognitively or theoretically. How a particular and limited individual reaches the totality of truth, meaning, and God cannot be resolved via theory. It may only be partially grasped via praxis. Schillebeeckx concluded that theoretical frameworks are inadequate to the plural realities of modern society, and hold back responsiveness to the dynamism of the future. Schillebeeckx found a new way to speak of God as the future of humanity through the non-theoretical language of praxis based in suffering. The universal fact of suffering provides a common human basis for talking about God and faith. Suffering is common ground for discussion but also a call to political action.[407]

Through his visits to the United States Schillebeeckx encountered a secularized society that, unlike Holland, did not discuss theology as a "matter of general public concern."[408] Here, traditional language about God was no longer intelligible. This encounter drove his investigation of hermeneutics since if the perspectival nature of human understanding implies a correlation between human images for God, humanity, and the world, new anthropologies and new social orientations require coherent and correlated religious images. This study cemented the hermeneutic exigency within his theology — that faith, texts, and dogmas must be reinterpreted for each historical context.[409]

He was also dissatisfied with his own, more conservative earlier theology (Bowden notes that he once described this as "stale buns"!) "From now on we can see him moving increasingly away from the church towards the source of Christianity in Jesus and the reign of God and the needs of the modern world."[410] In this turn, around the

late 1960s, he begins to take up biblical scholarship and interpretation of the New Testament in a major way.[411] It is out of this work
that he will write *Jesus: An Experiment in Christology*. In Kennedy's
view, one of Schillebeeckx's most outstanding achievements is that
he was the first Roman Catholic dogmatic theologian thoroughly to
incorporate scientific exegesis of the New Testament. His movement
to the sources goes beyond the medieval theologians studied by the
*ressourcemont* scholars or the patristic writers that interested the
*nouvelle théologie* movement. Schillebeeckx moved to the roots of
Christian tradition itself in Jesus.[412]

Concern for justice marks Schillebeeckx as a liberation theologian.
For him, the "question of salvation and liberation and of a truly liv-
able humanity is, however, always asked within actual conditions of
disintegration, alienation and hurtful human encounters."[413] Common features of this method include a preferential option for the
poor, an emphasis on the relationship of theory and praxis, solidarity with suffering humanity as the primary theme of Christian praxis,
associating liberation with earthly salvation, and relying on the experience of the church community for theological reflection. Liberation
refuses to relinquish this-worldly well-being: it hopes for the present
realization of the fullness of life.

Schillebeeckx's critiques of modern society challenge the exploitative Western drive for self-realization, defined as living in any manner
that we choose, according to the liberal optimism of Renaissance humanism. In the first pages of *Church: The Human Story of God*,
Schillebeeckx recounts the reflections of Giovanni Pico della Mirandola at the beginning of the modern age, writing a new Genesis. In
this new creation story, God tells the person that:

> We have given you no particular dwelling, no face of your own,
> no special gift of one kind or another, O Adam (=man), so that
> you can have and possess any dwelling you like, any face you like
> and all the gifts that you could desire.... You shall determine
> your own nature yourself, in accordance with your own free
> will, and I have put your fate in your own hands.[414]

Five hundred years later, many persons on the crowded earth are discovering that the fantasy of unlimited possibilities and miraculous, technological solutions to civilization's problems is a contemporary re-emergence of the illusion of controlling our fate. Being finite, inter-subjective, and conditioned by history is a tale of accepting and transcending limitations rather than spontaneous self-creation. For Schillebeeckx, God is truly present to finite humanity as Creator; at the same time, the struggle for salvation cannot avoid all sacri-fice. That God wills to be creator for us, and wills human salvation, grounds the first premise of the paradox of sacrifice: self-realization is a holy task.

# I. God the Creator

## Being Creator Reveals God's Nature

The doctrine of creation is central to Schillebeeckx's thought. "I re-gard the creation as the foundation of all theology.... There is so much talk of the history of salvation that there is need to reflect anew on the concept of creation."[415] The ongoing importance of the doctrine of creation throughout Schillebeeckx's career goes back to Schillebeeckx's fundamental Thomistic orientation and early reflec-tion on creation in relation to metaphysical realism. Schillebeeckx's understanding of creation is also colored by existential reflection on finitude, inspired by Jean-Paul Sartre.[416]

Kennedy proposes that Schillebeeckx's thought coheres into a "Schillebeeckx catechism" that colors each question with creation. "What are human beings? They are creatures existing in a divine cre-ation."[417] At its core, the doctrine of creation is a revelation of who God is. Creation reveals a God who is pure positivity, absolute free-dom, adventurousness, and the presence of the future. Schillebeeckx's doctrine of creation is essentially traditional. In classic Thomistic fashion Schillebeeckx asserts that God is existence itself, not a being among other beings. Persons participate in God's pure existence. Schillebeeckx also shares with Aquinas a belief in the basic goodness and autonomy of creation. However, Schillebeeckx expresses the independent autonomy of creation using more daring language than does the medieval saint. Schillebeeckx speaks of creation as an adventure that makes God vulnerable and defenseless, willingly open to the unpredictable and uncontrollable outcomes that human freedom may wreak in history. By speaking of God as "defenseless," Schillebeeckx reinforces God's genuine permission for human free will. He does not seem to argue for God's passivity or diminished involvement with creation. Those options seem to be set aside by Schillebeeckx's insistence on God as pure positivity and rejection of the eternalization of suffering in response to Jürgen Moltmann. Schillebeeckx does not believe that God's compassion draws suffering into the eternal life of God.[418] The language is haunting, however — a rhetorical underscoring of the real autonomy granted to creation by God. Suffering and sinfulness are real options for finite creatures, whose independence God will not contradict.

Schillebeeckx's attention to experience in creation is a unique expression of the classic Thomistic teaching that while God's essence is not knowable, positive affirmations about God are possible through manifestations of the divine in creation. Kennedy characterizes Schillebeeckx's theology as a "vast excursus on a single text of St. Thomas" in which Thomas teaches that affirmations about the divine are possible because God is manifested in creation (*Summa Theologiae* I, q.1, a 7, ad. 1).[419]

Schillebeeckx's doctrine of creation has significant implications for his view of history and understanding of progress, attitude toward secular liberation, epistemology, and, most importantly for this project, his anthropology. In brief, regarding history, Schillebeeckx rejects using God as an explanation for human structures or culture in a way that exalts or ossifies them. Nor does he accept a liberal trust in the inevitable unfolding of "progress." Human history is a contingent, always changing result of human choices. Second, he applauds the engagement of secular agencies in the cause of human well-being. At the same time, he maintains there are inescapable dimensions of life that cry out for religious salvation, which are not healed by secular advancement alone. Third, his epistemology proceeds from his conviction that God is knowable in creation, but through contingent and historical processes that must be interpreted. God can be known, but only through the contingent experiences of history and the willful filter of human freedom. The question of how we know, especially how we can know the meaning of past events, has driven Schillebeeckx's historical studies, scriptural research, analysis of tradition, hermeneutical impulse, investigation of experience, and praxis. There are thus important and complex epistemological and historical implications of Schillebeeckx's doctrine of creation. The anthropological meaning of God as Creator begins with the inescapable finitude of creatures, but the inner truth of human freedom is always God's presence to the world.

## God Is for Us and for Our Salvation

Most importantly, for Schillebeeckx, God is *for* us. "The glory of God is the happiness of living humankind; the happiness of humankind is the living God."[420] Irenaeus's prayer of praise for the God who rejoices in creation inspires Schillebeeckx to meditate upon the creator who loves his creatures, and the human person who cannot be truly understood apart from God. Schillebeeckx takes Irenaeus's teaching as "the best definition of what creation means."[421] Creation faith is the belief that God has chosen to orient God's divine life for others. God has willed to be Creator, and to endow creation with the freedom to accept God. Creation is the decision of God to begin a relationship with finite humanity.

> Creation involves a divine action that simultaneously has two consequences. Creation is an action of God that (1) endows human beings with a finite, non-godly character; and (2) at the same time initiates a history of a human quest for salvation.[422]

Creation gives existence to finite beings, and offers them a covenant of grace. Creation is the beginning of a history of salvation as well as a continuing process. It is an ongoing expression of God's will to be "the origin, here and now, of the worldliness of the world and the humanity of man. He wills to be with us in and with our finite task in the world."[423] In creation God gives his creatures autonomy, and sets them toward salvation. The end, the aim, or the orientation for creation's friendship with God is implicit from its beginning.

The goodness of finite creatureliness is the core of Schillebeeckx's theological anthropology. He does not begin from the doctrines of sin or redemption, demean humanity, or identify finitude with sinfulness. God has created that which is not God and has made room for creatures to exist on their own terms. Humanity is truly set free. Although not-God, creation is good. To recognize honestly the uncertainty of finitude is not to condemn it. Human nature is not plagued by a deficiency that must be superseded by grace, or "saved" outside of nature. The opposite is true. Salvation does not overcome finitude, but brings the presence of limitless hope alongside our contingency.

> Finite beings are a mixture of solitude and presence, and therefore belief in the creator God does not remove the finitude and does not misunderstand it as sinfulness as fallenness, but makes it take up this finitude into God's presence, without removing finitude from the world and man or regarding these as hostile.[424]

Finitude belongs to the goodness of creation. Finitude is indeed a vehicle of grace, as the contrast that reveals God. Yet there is a fragility in finitude that calls for the comfort of religious trust in the Creator. Such trust is a necessary condition for the surrender of sacrifice. Being at peace with one's creaturely finitude enables a reinterpretation of wholeness that maintains the core of one's identity in relationship with God, but without requiring autonomous security, defiance, or power.

Being created means not being God. Finitude is the defining characteristic of humanity in the world. The experience of finite limitations and vulnerability presents all people with an interpretive opportunity and decision. Non-believers view their finitude as a void and a constriction. For the believer, contingency is received as a referent to the illimitability of God.[425] For this reason, finitude itself is a source of religious faith.

Humans are inescapably contingent, yet are given genuine autonomy. Finite humans are therefore indeed the agents of creation's ongoing history, for which we are responsible. If the history of suffering presents some with a theological problem of how to trust in God, Schillebeeckx explicitly refuses to attribute suffering caused by human sin to God. As a result of the turn to the subject, God can no longer be held responsible for all suffering (theodicy). Humanity produces its own history and must now acknowledge the accusations of "anthropodicy" — and confront the society it has created.[426] Humans are the principle of the world's history.

> If we are created (and for a Christian this means, if we are created in the image and likeness of God), then we must be something other than conservers, restorers or discoverers of what is already given. In that case, we ourselves become, rather, the principle of what we shall make of the world and society — and what could have not been and in fact is, by virtue of contingent free will. God creates human beings as the principle of their own human lives, so that human action has to develop and effectuate the world and its future in human solidarity, within contingent situations and given boundaries, and therefore with respect for both inanimate and animate nature.[427]

We are therefore responsible for the future of the world and cannot blame God for the current state of things. Bringing about a better future is the human task, to be addressed with all of the resources of science, technology, human wisdom, and creativity. While persons should not be reconciled to suffering caused by sin and oppression, which is the real possibility that finitude will influence evil, there is also creaturely finitude that is not meant to be overcome. Ricoeur expressed this as the passivity of one's body, of others who may oppress us even with their legitimate needs and demands, and the ultimate passivity of mortality. Many sacrifices result from the limits of natural finitude, not only the need to resist oppression and violence.

Reconciliation to this creaturely finitude grounds the willingness to accept the sacrifices made inevitable by finitude.[428]

Schillebeeckx's affirmation that God creates humanity in the first place and wills their salvation in the second place, has a third corollary: God is present to creation.[429] Creation is another way of saying that nothing comes between God and God's creatures. This can be interpreted either as a void, or as the absolute presence of God to the finite. Schillebeeckx expresses this presence-despite-radical-distance with his characteristic way of uniting paradoxes. "The boundary between God and us is our boundary, not that of God.... We recognize the divinity of God in the recognition and acceptance of our limits and those of nature and history."[430] The distance between God and the human is a boundary that exists only on our side. God who is pure positivity and sheer being is intimately alive within all creation. Yet finite humanity cannot escape its contingency, and so the limit is on our side. Nevertheless, God is always near.

The paradox of God's presence to finite creation means that God wills its autonomy, and does not contradict its freedom, but is nevertheless present in a saving way.

> God is also the Lord of our history. He is the one who began this adventure and so it is also close to his heart.... Creation is ultimately the meaning that God has wanted to give to his divine life. He wanted, freely, also to be God for others, and expected them, with their finite free will, which was also open to other possibilities, to accept this offer. Otherwise I do not understand at all why he, God, resolved to take the final precarious decision of creating human beings.[431]

The core of Schillebeeckx's doctrine of creation — which is inseparable from his anthropology — is that God is for our salvation. God wills human wholeness. At the same time humanity is finite and contingent in a broken world where sacrifice is unavoidable. Because Schillebeeckx defines salvation as wholeness, and because wholeness and sacrifice are in apparent contradiction to each other, further examination of his understanding of salvation is needed. In the next section I will explore the idea of salvation in Schillebeeckx's thought as vividly revealed in the person and message of Jesus Christ.

## II. Concentrated Creation: Christology

### God with Us

God is present to creation above all in Jesus Christ, who is the supreme sign and concentration of God's message. The life of Jesus reveals God's delight in his creation, expressed in the gladness of Jesus and his disciples, and their healing ministry that seeks to make others glad. Jesus is the most direct explanation of creation as the gift of salvation.

> For Schillebeeckx, Christology is a way of rendering belief in creation more intelligible, by explaining it in relation to human history in general and the story of Jesus' life in particular. If Christian belief regards creation as the beginning of salvation, then to speak of Christology as concentrated creation is to emphasize that the redemption offered by God the Creator is manifested, or condensed, in the man Jesus.[432]

Christology is a confirmation and advance sign of God's commitment to the final salvation of creation that has been entrusted to humanity. As such Jesus is the guarantor of God's unwavering relationship of creation. If in one sense creation means that finite humanity has been left to its own devices, as the genuinely autonomous principle of creation, in Jesus the reign of God can be anticipated. Jesus is

> the man in whom the task of creation has been successfully accomplished, albeit in conditions of the history of suffering. The consequence of this is that trust in this man is the specific form of belief in God, creator of heaven and earth, who reposes unconditional trust in man through his act of creation. Without this divine trust in man, creation would in fact make no sense!

This man Jesus makes it possible for us to believe that God indeed reposes his unconditional trust in man — whereas precisely
what happens in our history of suffering is for many people the
reason why they no longer believe in God.[433]

Jesus manifests both God's trust in creation, and humanity's response
to that trust. Jesus is the sign of the good news for the poor, in the
coming reign of God. Jesus' fellowship with the disciples and his healing praxis was an offer of the gift of salvation. The qualities of that
gift, including joy and liberation, remain decisive for the Christian
experience of salvation today.

The good news is a message of gladness, tidings of great joy. The
New Testament experience of salvation stems from the disciples'
shared experience of salvation in Jesus, expressed in various ways.[434]
The core tradition emerges from the personal fellowship of the disciples and centers on Jesus as the ultimate meaning of the disciples'
lives.[435] Schillebeeckx focuses on the spirit of gladness and celebration that permeated this fellowship.[436] He observes charmingly that
"sadness is an existential impossibility in Jesus' presence."[437] Disciples become his co-workers and share the ministry of preaching and
healing. Discipleship is seen as an imitation of Jesus — a trust that
exceeds the ethical fulfillment of the great commands: discipleship is
"conversion to Jesus."[438]

Schillebeeckx set out to find the "possible signs in the historical
Jesus that might direct the human quest for 'salvation' towards what
Christian faith proposes as a relevant answer."[439] That is, Jesus'
idea of wholeness must be the basis for a Christian answer about
the meaning of salvation. Very simply, God's cause is human salvation. God cares for humanity and Jesus looks after humanity as he is
"about God's business."[440] Jesus is the parable of God's care for us;
from his works we can determine God's concern.[441]

In his concern for man and his history of suffering, for publicans
and sinners, for the poor, the lame and the blind, the dispos-
sessed and those alienated from themselves by "evil spirits,"
Jesus is a living parable of God: this is the way in which God

looks on mankind. The story of God is told in the story of Jesus.[442]

Jesus thus works miracles to "make gladness something real for a lot of people."[443] These miracles are themselves a message of the gospel: "Jesus brings well-being, 'saving health,' because he is the Son filled with the Spirit (Mark 1:9–11)."[444]

Jesus' attitude toward the law shows that God is concerned for the well-being of humankind and does not wish to lay burdens upon them.[445] The stories in the Q tradition where Jesus critiques over-scrupulous ceremonial practice and radically interprets the law as love of one's enemies (Luke 11:46), as well as the Marcan accounts of healing and plucking corn on the Sabbath (Mark 2:23–28), demonstrate Jesus' concern for humanity as God's concern. The law and the Sabbath are not to be a burden, but a gift.[446] The Torah is proof of God's love for people, an expression of his concern for their salvation.

The originality in the New Testament presentation of his command is that the command comes from the authority of Jesus. For Luke, Jesus' new contribution to the great command to love God and the neighbor as oneself is to define the neighbor as any person in need.[447] Schillebeeckx takes the criterion for Jesus' message about the law to be his actual ministry. It does not matter whether or not Jesus specifically stated this principle about love of enemies as recorded in the New Testament. In practice, in fellowship, and in parables, Jesus in fact lived in this open way in order to proclaim the reign of God.[448]

This is Jesus' message of God's rule. For Jesus, God's rule is near. As God is merciful, so should the disciple be merciful. God's concern is for the well-being of humanity, so people are charged to love their neighbor and even their enemy. Jesus' critique of his contemporaries' interpretation of the law and the Sabbath observance springs from his conviction of God as "the 'God intent on humanity,' who does not will burdens for them, something on which Jesus' own praxis confers more and more historically substantive content."[449] In Jesus' praxis, then, we are invited to recognize God's no to suffering. In summary,

Jesus liberates the individual from an oppressive and narrow idea of God, by exposing the ideology as an orthodoxy that stood in a ruptured relationship to orthopraxis, and furthermore qua orthodoxy, had established an ethic as an independent screen between God and man, so that the relevance of the legal obligations to man's salvation had become totally obscured. The repercussion of Jesus' own message of God's rule on human ethics is therefore characterized as a factor of truly human liberation, thanks to his novel and original experience of God.[450]

## The Structure of Salvation Experienced in Jesus

Based on his study of Jesus' fellowship and ministry, Schillebeeckx concludes that Christian salvation relates to a person's experience of Jesus, and that Jesus interpreted salvation as wholeness and well-being from God. In Christian faith, salvation is offered as the early church's experience of Jesus, but the church then reinterprets that experience for today. This is necessary because one's expectation of salvation is affected by current worldviews and by one's interpretation of human nature. Therefore, consideration of historical context drives the major questions of *Christ,* Parts 2 and 3: how the basic experience of Jesus was shaped by the horizons of experience of the early church.[451]

Schillebeeckx identifies four principles that structure the experience of Christian salvation that is continuous with the early communities. These principles are: (*a*) God's history with humanity is God's cause; (*b*) salvation is centered in Jesus, who reveals the meaning of our lives; (*c*) the church community is the legacy and vital link to Jesus; disciples are related by the Spirit to Jesus and his mission; finally, (*d*) salvation has an eschatological fulfillment. Salvation is not the same as liberation understood on human terms, which will always be surpassed by the surprising nature of God's reign as anticipated by the gospel.[452]

*a.* The first principle means that God wills human salvation in spite of the threats in history. "So finding salvation in God coincides with finding our true selves. Salvation from God is concerned with human wholeness and happiness."[453] The first principle that structures the experience of grace also means that God acts in history. This premise founds Schillebeeckx's commitment to a liberative method.

> In the last resort — and at the same time that is "protologi-
> cal," from the beginning — God decides about the meaning and
> purpose of mankind, in man's favor. He does not leave this
> decision to the whim of cosmic and historical, chaotic and de-
> monic powers, on whose crooked lines he is able to write, indeed
> whose crooked lines he is able to straighten. As Creator, God is
> the author of good and the antagonist of evil, suffering and in-
> justice which throw men up against meaninglessness.... "I am
> concerned for you" (Exodus 3:16). God's name is "solidarity
> with my people."[454]

*b.* Salvation is an experience of Jesus. Schillebeeckx reckons that the ongoing flourishing of the Jesus movement in history is due to the sustaining presence of God within Jesus and within his church. The personal impact of a historical figure by itself is not likely to inspire the centuries of growth enjoyed by the church. Nor can Christian affirmation of Jesus' universal significance be an extended ideological abstraction across time and space, a cipher for God's universal love. The recognition of the presence of God in Jesus' humanity, rooted in the historical person of Jesus of Nazareth, is the core of Christian faith. Jesus' concrete humanity is the unique revelation for Christians; it precedes creedal statements. Whatever meaning Jesus has today must relate to his historical, original identity.[455]

*c.* The Christian today relates to the ongoing life of Jesus as medi-ated by the church. Christian praxis is the mediating link between the historical Jesus and his significance today.[456] As did Jesus, the church witnesses to the reign of God by

> doing for men and women here and now, in new situations (dif-
> ferent from those in Jesus' time), what Jesus did in his time:
> raising up for them the coming of the kingdom of God, opening

up communication among them, caring for the poor and outcast, establishing communal ties within the household of faith
and serving all men and women in solidarity.[457]

Therefore Schillebeeckx pictures the church's sustaining contact with
God as a horizontal, or contemporaneous, bond. It is not a vertical
relationship relying on memories of the past. That is, the church is
not just interacting with stories from the past, but constantly inter-
acts with a living reality. The experience of the church today is the
same as the New Testament church: all are in communion with God
through Jesus in the Spirit. That experience of God as a living reality
is the experience of salvation for those living now, mediated by the
church.

*d.* The fourth structural principle demonstrates that history is
marked by what Schillebeeckx terms an "eschatological proviso,"
the not yet realized or not yet fully grasped experience of salvation.
Though anticipatory signs of God's reign bring hope, salvation is not
identical with liberation. Definitive salvation is eschatological; liberation is always partial. This tension between salvation and liberation
is an important part of Schillebeeckx's view of salvation as wholeness and our incapacity to fully realize it. In response to criticism that
political liberation overshadowed mystical freedom in *Christ,* Schillebeeckx replies that while an indifferent mysticism bears false witness
to human reality, "a concern for liberation which has no mysticism is
equally only a partial expression of our humanity."[458] Human salvific
agencies are limited to "alienations which are basically the outcome
of physical, psychosomatic, psychic and social types of condition-
ing."[459] The more profound alienation of our finiteness cannot be
resolved by human effort and calls for religious salvation. Humanity
is caught in the tension between experiencing finitude as an alienation
that calls for salvation, and hearing the exhortation of faith to accept
this finite state. Paradoxically, finitude appears as a need that humans
cannot fill, but one that must be accepted at the same time. Schillebeeckx's interest in contemplation suggests that in the very acceptance
of finitude through religious faith there lies a means of resolving this

tension. The quest for wholeness arising from suffering, because of its very depths and disorientation, has always had a religious dimension. The church cannot be replaced by secular liberating activity, because only religious salvation addresses itself to human finitude. A distinction always remains between the political commitment of a critical community and the distinctively Christian memory and celebration of the promise of the reign of God. The former community is "in danger of becoming a purely political cell without evangelical inspiration — one of the very many useful and indeed necessary political pressure groups, but not an *ecclesia Christi*."[460] What religions and churches offer is the living memory of God's universal will to salvation. Though we may experience only fragments of salvation, these nevertheless contain God's promises and offer hope.

Despite the disjunctures and nonsense of suffering, people can and must dialogue with each other, and in this way we can speak of the hope for one history. Because God's redemption occurs in history along with history's suffering, it is felt to be fragmentary and passing. Yet salvation does occur here in our earthly history — mediated immediacy touches this world.[461] The human family, at least potentially, is one. "The real history of human beings occurs where sense and non-sense lie side by side and one upon the other, are commingled where there is joy and suffering, laughter and lamentation, in short: finitude."[462]

## God with Us unto Death: The Ultimate Contrast of the Cross

The memory of Jesus' healing praxis and the good news of forgiveness combine with the cruel event of the cross and the complexity of sacrificial images surrounding his death to yield a true paradox. The disciple hears the message that God desires the salvation of humankind, juxtaposed against the reality of suffering. Indeed, in some way these two seemingly contrary realities are aligned. *One must lose one's life to save it.* The life and death of Jesus together present the core justification and challenge to sacrifice as a model for holy living, a life that seeks salvation for one's self and others. How is the Christian to interpret the suffering of Jesus and emulate his sacrifice as a model for discipleship?

## No Alleluia Christianity

Against the good news, Jesus' announcement that he will suffer is a shock. Bewildering as it seemed to Peter, their fellowship does not mean "alleluia, we are freed. No more suffering and oppression. Goodbye to all tears, goodbye to all slavery!"[463] On the contrary, the death of Jesus gains meaning from the world's opposition to his radical message. His death is not merely a tragedy or a misunderstanding. The cross witnesses to the radicalness of Jesus' message, and the radical violence that opposed it. Without seeing this meaning in Jesus' death, we run the risk of owning a "sheer earthly alleluia Christianity."[464] Christians partake of suffering because they proclaim God's reign. As did the messiah, the messianic community will also suffer.

Schillebeeckx elucidates from the life and death of Jesus a theological understanding of the suffering that results from liberating action for others. In other words, by making sense of the suffering Jesus experienced as a consequence of his concern for others, there may be principles to guide chosen acts of sacrifice as Christian disciples who nonetheless seek wholeness or salvation, for themselves and others. That is, how will the disciple who sacrifices interpret the consequent suffering?

Suffering constitutes the major source of friction in a hermeneutic of sacrifice, and it is accessible to analysis on multiple levels. Chapter 1 analyzed the death of Jesus as open to sacrificial and non-sacrificial interpretations. I then concluded that it is not necessary to interpret Jesus' death as a cultic sacrifice, while that is a legitimate and culturally appropriate expression that recognizes Jesus — like the cult — as a gift from God for reconciliation. The core meaning of sacrifice was taken to be dedication, which often has a cost. Similarly, chapter 2 analyzed models of atonement theory to show that the suffering that accompanied Jesus' death is not salvific in and of itself. This reflects the observation made in chapter 1 that the death of a sacrificial victim is not significant in itself. This distinction is important lest suffering itself be taken by the believer — especially the marginalized and disempowered believer — as an acceptable and virtuous experience. Even though giving to the other is fundamentally constitutive of identity, Ricoeur searched for the point at which the suffering of being-commanded becomes a loss of agency and identity. For Schillebeeckx, the paradox of self-sacrifice and self-realization means the collision of Jesus' preaching of the coming rule of God and God's concern for the well-being and wholeness of humanity, and the inevitable suffering inherent in the sacrifices that at times face the Christian disciple. There is a dissonance between seeking wholeness and accepting the cost of sacrifice that may not find resolution. Therefore one particular resource in Schillebeeckx's doctrine of creation, Christology, theological anthropology, and view of salvation is his characteristic resistance to suffering while acknowledging the difficulty and necessity of the struggle for liberation.

Schillebeeckx does not acknowledge Jesus' death as meaningful in itself. His view of Jesus' suffering contains three points. (1) Suffering is not glorified. God says no to suffering, including the suffering of Jesus. (2) Jesus' life is inseparable from an interpretation of Jesus' death, and vice versa. (3) The enclosure of death within Jesus' life of ministry enables the interpretation of his death as service. Even though suffering does not provide the core meaning of Jesus' life and death, Jesus' suffering nevertheless reflects onto the disciple's self-understanding of suffering.

## Suffering Is Not Glorified

For Jesus to share in our humanity means to share in human suffering. Schillebeeckx does not interpret suffering as meaningful in itself, however, and has made strong critiques of the glorification of suffering. Schillebeeckx interprets the meaning of Jesus' death as a consequence of his life and as a final act of service.

According to John Galvin, Schillebeeckx's story leaves open what exact meaning Jesus may have made of his own death, but finds the key in his steadfast continuation of ministry despite opposition. At some point public reaction became divisive to the point of violence.

> Aware of this reaction and conscious as well of the tension between his approaching execution and his message of God's kingdom, Jesus must have pondered the meaning of the death he was to undergo. In view of the situation, it is possible and legitimate to ask if Jesus not only accepted his death freely, but also provided for his disciples an advance interpretation of its significance.... On the other hand, holding that we have no certainly authentic passage in which Jesus ascribes salvific value to his death, Schillebeeckx suggests that Jesus left his death as a final prophetic sign for others to interpret on the basis of his life. In any case, Jesus' fidelity, in life and death, to his gospel of salvation far surpasses in importance any reconciliation of his message and his fate on the level of theory.[465]

Jesus most likely consciously accepted the consequence of conflict, aware of the provocative effect of his actions upon Herod, the Pharisees, the Sadducees, and the Romans. Schillebeeckx believed he "must have rationally come to terms with the possibility ... of a fatal outcome."[466] Mark 10:45 shows that he at least anticipated his own vindication.

There are disputes over Schillebeeckx's view of Jesus' death. In the end, Schillebeeckx himself insists that the rejection and death are not in themselves meaningful, at least not in a purely expiatory sense. Bowden observes that Schillebeeckx's extensive study of the reign of God and its importance to Jesus does not devote great attention to Jesus' death. Schillebeeckx identified three ways of organizing interpretations of Jesus' death (addressed in chapter 1): the prophet-martyr, the salvation-history context, and the atoning-death interpretation. Galvin believes Schillebeeckx finds that the prophet-martyr and righteous sufferer cohere more deeply with Jesus' historical life and are more free from conscious theoretical shaping than are presentations of his death as atonement. But the saving significance of Jesus' death is not of central concern for Schillebeeckx.

As Bowden expresses it, it is "as though Jesus' death has to be seen as an inevitable consequence of his lifestyle and as a prelude to his resurrection."[467]

Schillebeeckx meditates on the mystery of the violent death of Jesus as revealing both the potential for cruelty and injustice in human history, and the desire of God to be present to that history. Indeed, God participates in history directly through Jesus — but not to employ this injustice in an instrumental way, such that Jesus' death is necessary, desirable, or glorious. Yet through it God transcends our history by overcoming the negativity of suffering by the victory of the resurrection. The Christian will not "blasphemously claim that God himself required the death of Jesus as compensation for what *we* make of our history. . . . Therefore, first of all, we have to say that we are not redeemed *thanks to* the death of Jesus but *despite* it."[468] At the same time, the significance of Jesus' death is not cast aside by this "despite" because of the very will of God to transcend its negativity.

> On the other side, however, this "despite" is so transcended by God, not because he permits it in condescension but because through the resurrection of Jesus from the dead he conquers suffering and evil and undoes them, that the expression "despite the death" in fact does not say enough.[469]

Our history of unrighteousness is weaker than the mystery of God's mercy. Nor can we force a theoretical reconciliation of injustice and mercy, to make suffering splendid or necessary, so that its absurdity not offend our need for logic. Schillebeeckx refuses to allow the death of Jesus to be made into a justification for violence.

> If men think in a purely human way about God, this can result in bizarre and humanly degrading theories and practices. Men have often enough made human sacrifices in their attempt to honour God. This occurred frequently in the past, but is it any different now? Does not the absence of liberation and the presence of so much suffering reveal itself again and again in the contemporary world under the banner of God and religion? Has not at least

one Christology made Jesus into a God who does not show mercy until the blood of the one who is greatly loved flows? Jesus, however, said: "if you are conscious of God's approach, do not be afraid (see Mark 4:35, etc.). God is above all a God of the people. He is a God who thinks of human sacrifice as an abomination" (see Lev. 18:21–30; 20:1–5). God is a fire, certainly, but he is a fire that burnt the bush without consuming it (Exod. 3:2).[470]

According to Galvin, in contrast to theological views of Jesus' death as a final act of freedom, Schillebeeckx's reflection on the crucifixion

> stresses the passive character of death and its negative dimension...while speaking at times of the value inherent in Jesus' death, Schillebeeckx's usual procedure is to locate the meaning elsewhere, either in Jesus' free acceptance of death (as distinct from death itself) or in divine conferral of value on Jesus' death through the resurrection.[471]

The reign of God is the key to Jesus' view of his mission as well as its failure: a failure common to the prophets, who looked for the future coming of God.[472]

### Interpreting Jesus' Death in Continuity with His Life

While whatever meaning Jesus may have given to his own death and shared with his disciples is not certainly knowable, the best clue to that meaning is the purpose that drove his life. "Jesus' whole life is the hermeneusis of his death. The very substance of salvation is sufficiently present in it, which could be and was in fact articulated later on in various ways through faith in him."[473] Both his life and death express his ministry for sinners. Jesus was sent to sinners, his message concerned their forgiveness, his concrete practice led him to many encounters with sinners, he offered them fellowship, he invited them to conversion, he made disciples of them — in short, Jesus presented sinners with the reign of God in actuality. Solidarity with sinners marks

Jesus' practice from beginning to end. And in the end, it means being delivered into the hands of sinners.

> Solidarity of that kind, mingling with sinners, is for their salvation: Jesus means in that way to open up communication; his being delivered into the hands of sinners (Mark 9:31 with 14:41) is for Mark at the same time the real import of Jesus' death: the "saving gift" to sinners, so to "mix with sinners" that in the end he himself goes to the wall.[474]

Despite Schillebeeckx's own statement about the meaning of the cross "despite" Jesus' death, Schillebeeckx does not read Jesus' death as a parenthetical exception to his life. His death is not merely the "notwithstanding," or the act "despite which" God has acted in history. By this Schillebeeckx means that interpreters cannot simply lift up the healing acts of Jesus' ministry, point to the fidelity that brought him to a final and fatal confrontation with the authorities, and discard his death as insignificant, something "despite which" God sought to reveal God's saving plan in Jesus. Even his death reveals something of God's loving will for people. This is the key to accepting a meaning in death, or any suffering that is consequent on dedication to the cause of others. It is indeed through a final action of suffering that Jesus lived his last moments. Jesus' death as the culmination of a life of service means his death is also to be understood as service.

## Jesus' Death as Service

Schillebeeckx notes that in the process of reflection and interconnection, the New Testament has combined the themes of serving and dying. This is paradigmatically evident in the Last Supper tradition (Mark 10:45). Presiding at the meal, Jesus acts as host. This is the role he has taken throughout his ministry to outcasts and sinners. As host, he has also fed the poor and the crowds with miraculously multiplying bread. His service at the Last Supper recapitulates the hospitality conducted throughout his life. Such service is also reflected in the washing of the feet. Through theological reflection on the Last Supper as service, the death that followed the Last Supper is conjoined to the service. Serving becomes the ethical paradigm that frames the Last Supper and the passion. As such, Jesus' very death is itself a service.

> Serving, service performed of love, thus becomes the final stamp set upon the life of Jesus; it is carried over from a historical event to the Lord who is to come.... That death was an act of loving service performed by Jesus for his own, for which they are made a "new fellowship": a "new covenant."[475]

The cross is a seal, an indelible mark of identity — a confirmation of the message of God's love, in which Jesus trusted until the end. Jesus' followers also acknowledge that persecution is a possible fate for them, one that may challenge the depth of their previous lives. *Whoever will save his life will lose it.* Schillebeeckx interprets this passage as the loss of finality that comes from evading the test. "Without Jesus' violent death there would have been no special seal on his message, his life-style and his person, and nothing would have been known of his Galilean mission." Jesus' last prophetic sign is his death as being for others to interpret. The death of Jesus is a question to God, but the answer is not God's complicity with the cross.

> Can we suppose that it was actually God himself who set him through his trial and execution among the oppressed and outcast, thus to make his solidarity with the oppressed a de facto identification? Or is such a view not rather a blasphemy, in that it ascribes to God what the course of human wrong and injustice did to Jesus?[476]

The cross is the definitive sign of God's solidarity with humanity, together with the resurrection. God judges suffering and affirms the life of Jesus by his resurrection. God has "the last word. There is V-Day, God's third day."[477]

The risk of persevering in one's mission can be undertaken only through trust in God. Our protest against suffering is not able to force a fissure between suffering and the sacrificial act of dedication which occasions it. It is part of a religious hermeneutic grounded in trust — the eyes of faith — to see these together. The disciples take up this vision, with their eyes fixed on the hope of continued fellowship with Jesus. Nevertheless, there is a refractory element in suffering that resists analysis. This is true when reacting to the suffering of others as well as our own.

## The Opacity of Jesus' Suffering

Of suffering, Schillebeeckx writes, "the only adequate response is via a practical exercise of resistance to evil, not a theory about it."[478] The need for practical action connects with the even more pressing need for purpose and direction, found in narrative vision. "People do not argue against suffering, but tell a story."[479] Schillebeeckx thus decides to ground his Christology neither in the Chalcedonian formula of Christ's human and divine natures nor on soteriological doctrines about Christ's atonement. The starting point for his Christology is the universal problem of suffering, which can be approached only through symbols and stories attempting to grasp these intractable realities. As Galvin observes, "Fully aware of how hard it is to tell a story well, yet firmly oriented on the narrative form of the Gospels, Schillebeeckx attempts to retell the life story of Jesus as a liberating story of God."[480]

> Faith in Jesus as Christ is an "answer" without arguments: a "nevertheless." Christianity does not give any explanation for suffering, but demonstrates a way of life. Suffering is destructively real, but it does not have the last word. Christianity seeks to hang on to both elements: not dualism, not dolorism, no theories about illusion — suffering is suffering and inhuman — however, there is more, namely God, as he shows himself in Jesus Christ.[481]

Schillebeeckx began *Jesus* with a story of the lame man waiting by the Temple to be healed. Another man's faith illustrates the intuition of something "more" amid unacceptable suffering. Bent over by a disability, I see him wait in the last pew of the church. A woman with him props up his sagging shoulder and chin. Every Sunday, the priest and minister of the cup bring the bread and wine to his pew, and the priest always pauses to place a hand on his forehead in blessing. Each week the hunched man lifts his hand and rests it on the forehead of the priest in return.

In the next section, I will turn to Schillebeeckx's treatment of how suffering functions in the integration of sacrifice and Christian identity. Here I will begin to integrate the theory of suffering and salvation into Christian discipleship. Suffering clearly marks Christian identity through the imitation of Christ. Suffering for others takes on a special meaning when it becomes service. But in response to the feminist critique presented in the second chapter, which objected to a simplistic or idealized portrait of suffering discipleship, this section views this ideal critically, attempting to reconsider the ideal of sacrificial discipleship with a second naïveté. Ricoeur emphasized the constructive role of chosen sacrifice for identity. Within the paradoxical relationship of sacrifice and self-realization, Schillebeeckx considers the interpretive value of suffering.

## III. Integrating Accepted Suffering into Christian Discipleship as Sacrifice

In Schillebeeckx's view, suffering, and specifically the subset of chosen acts of sacrifice on which this project is focused, functions in the interpretation of Christian identity as a negative contrast with productive, cognitive value. I am not concerned with the entire fabric of human suffering, the whole history of suffering, which is a central theme for Schillebeeckx, but only the heuristic and interpretive function of suffering in relationship to sacrifice. By definition, sacrifice necessarily implies an acceptance of hardship and suffering. However, the act of willing self-gift does not require the unquestioned subjugation of self to other, and in fact resists it for the sake of the *humanum*. Belief in God as pure positivity means "by nature God promotes good and opposes evil, injustice and suffering."[482]

Suffering at times presents an overwhelming experience that defies meaning. But in extreme cases, chosen sacrificial actions serve as a seal on one's willed identity. One may choose to make one's own meaning, and extend one's self in vulnerable love. Yet even so, self-giving is not unquestioned surrender, but an action requiring discernment in light of the reign of God. Schillebeeckx shows how sacrifice contributes positively to Christian identity, beyond marking the boundaries of suffering that are purely negative. The core of identity is what one sets one's heart on; it is closely linked to the old sense of belief. In Schillebeeckx's words,

> Human beings have no other choice than to set their hearts on something. . . . The question as to which God you worship has to do with whether your heart is focused on the destruction of others, or on peace and freedom for each person; on solidarity, justice, and love; in friendship, gift of self, and the loss of self in the service of others, if necessary.[483]

## The Interpretation of Suffering

Schillebeeckx's treatment of suffering combines his characteristic interest in experience and interpretation, his concern for those who suffer, and his conviction that God wills human wholeness. Influenced by the critical theory of the Frankfurt school, he argues that the meaning of human wholeness can be revealed by means of negative contrast experiences. Suffering contrasts with humanity's desire for wholeness. Suffering is spontaneously resisted, and this resistance awakens a revelation of God's no: God is against this suffering. God's no is the foundation of the negative contrast method.

### Negative Contrast Experiences

Through the concept of negative contrast experiences, Schillebeeckx examines the cognitive, revelatory, and productive dimensions of suffering. Suffering is an inevitable human experience, a threat to salvation, and as common as dirt. As such, suffering is a unifying experience among the world's people: Christians and those of other traditions, poor, voiceless, democratic, technocratic, secular, and atheist. Life is marked by suffering, evil, and meaninglessness.

But the very experience of resistance to such pain, and the hope that better times will come, are contrasts that bring insight. In Schillebeeckx's words, negative contrast experiences "form a basic human experience which as such I regard as being a pre-religious experience and thus a basic experience accessible to all human beings, namely, that of a 'no' to the world as it is."[484] The very fact of registering injustice as such generates a sense of protest and indignation. This protest is possible because of an inner conviction that suffering is unacceptable. Mary Catherine Hilkert writes, "in radically negative situations, human persons spontaneously protest."[485] The pain and protest exist together because one feels that better ways are possible. As painful as suffering is, there is nevertheless a revelation to be found in misery and oppression: the revelation that God rejects suffering.

> The fundamental human "no" to evil therefore discloses an unfulfilled and thus "open yes" which is as intractable as the human "no," indeed even stronger, because the "open yes" is the basis of that opposition and makes it possible.... Those who believe in God fill out the one two-sided basic experience in religious terms.[486]

For religious persons, then, a negative contrast experience is an experience of suffering which contains an indirect revelation of the presence of God, a recognition of God's will for our salvation. God can be found in human experience dialectically — in suffering.[487] Negative contrast experiences are a form of religious knowledge containing the consciousness of pain as well as a vision of human possibility that protests in indignation. This dual dimension hones the prophetic character of suffering and enables faith to serve a critical role for society, to challenge and inspire more humane conditions. Faith maintains this critical role, though it has been supplanted by science for so many other functions.

> The sense of indignation is associated with an incipient awareness of hope which prompts a prophetic protest against the

causes of suffering. And so, a negative contrast experience militates against what should not be, on the basis of a hope in what should be.[488]

What specifically is the suffering in this human history to which God is opposed, according to Schillebeeckx? Grace is a specific experience of liberation from concrete evils. It is not a vague, general awareness of "freedom" or "well-being." Through grace, humanity is freed from:

> sin and guilt; from all kinds of existential anxieties, which men of antiquity experienced above all as the fear of demons, the grip of fate or *heimarmene*, a complex of anxieties which are concentrated around the problem of death, "to deliver all those who through fear of death were subject to lifelong bondage" (Heb. 2:15); freed also from existential cares and all kinds of everyday concerns (Matt. 6:19–34); from sorrow, despair and hopelessness, from dissatisfaction with fellow men and with God; from a lack of freedom, from unrighteousness; from oppressive and alienating ties; from lovelessness, arbitrariness and egotism; from credulity (Mark 13:5–7; Luke 17:22–37); from exploitation of credibility (Mark 9:42; Luke 17:1–3a; Matt. 18:6f); from merciless condemnation of others (Matt. 7:1–5); from concern over problems of reputation, trying to be someone or to cut a good figure (Mark 10:35–45); from panic and absence of pleasure; to be freed from a life like that of men "who have no hope" (1 Thess. 4:13), etc.[489]

Suffering in our "un-meaningful history" includes "violence, lust for power, coveting at the expense of others, enslavement and oppression — there is Auschwitz, and goodness knows what else in the private sphere and in our own personal life." Suffering and evil permeate history as "a permanently thriving parasitical 'epiphenomenon' of our localized freedom." This suffering is brought about "by nature, by persons and by structures."[490]

The revelation of negative contrast experiences illuminates humanity's hope for wholeness despite its constant experience of suffering
throughout history. Human nature, or the *humanum,* is thus interpreted by suffering, as by a silhouette of our needs and relationships
that are denied or distorted. "Man does not yet know who he is,
but he can, alienated as he is from himself, know who he is certainly not, and therefore who he, in this alienated state, will not and
may not remain."[491] Such reflection anticipates the negative shape of
salvation — the outline of what is lacking. The entire interpretation
of suffering itself serves as a contrast to salvation and defines the
contours of wholeness.

Schillebeeckx's insight that there is something productive about
negativity recalls Martha Nussbaum's reflection on the generative
potential of tragedy. Tragic awareness does not resolve a problem
but may offer a broader perspective and drive the search for repara-
tions and prevention. Negative contrast experiences have their own
cognitive value and indeed challenge both contemplative and controlling forms of knowledge. The passive contrast experience leads
to a contemplative awareness of reality and God's will that goes beyond the "positive joyousness of contemplative, ludic and aesthetic
experiences." Suffering has an "implicit ethical demand" which im-
pulsively seeks a new kind of praxis. Suffering contributes a particular
critical analysis of both contemplative and "controlling" forms of
knowledge (that is, scientific and technical knowledge through which
persons may claim to be the controlling subjects who can manipulate the world based on rational systems).[492] Critical theory engages
the power of suffering to analyze social conditions, criticize their oppressive structures, and suggest methods to overcome such structural
injustice.[493] The cognitive effect of suffering sharpens one's desire
for happiness and articulates the goals for the future for which one
demands.[494]

The final word for Schillebeeckx is that suffering *reveals* God.[495]
Suffering reveals God's care for humanity by what is lacking. Suffering itself has no redeeming value. In chapter 2 I argued that suffering

does not make a sacrifice automatically virtuous; much suffering results from exploitation. At the same time, the presence of suffering
does not automatically render a sacrifice unhealthy. Suffering is often
a part of the struggle for wholeness, a process in which persons may
choose to persevere and accept the costs in hope of a greater good.
Such suffering is still negative, but instead of being glorified as endurance for endurance's sake, it is resisted and judged, only accepted
as part of the refractory reality one labors to change. Schillebeeckx's
attention to the contemplative dimension of suffering is important because it highlights how suffering functions as an interpretive tool. The
cognitive dimension of suffering may discern "right sacrifice" from
victimization by distinguishing between the idealization of suffering
and protests which look for a new way.

## Interpretation as an Element within Experience

The interpretive power of negative contrast experiences can be understood through Schillebeeckx's view of experience in general. For
Schillebeeckx, experience is an inseparable mélange of reality and
interpretation, of encounter and expectation. Experience has both
objective and subjective sides. An experience occurs as the encounter
between "objective reality" — that which is contacted by a person —
and the person's subjective capacity to receive that reality. Experience
is transformed and shaped by the nature of the one experiencing it.
Experience, in a sense, is a given-as-received. The interpretation with
which one receives an event is a description that is inextricable from
the experience of the event itself; interpretation is an inner element
of the encounter. Therefore, interpretation is an element within experience. Experience has a depth dimension, which often brings a
surprising new recognition of reality, or even a conversion. There is
a quality of revelation in any limit experience that overflows with
meaning. The receptive framework is itself part of the experience.
This theoretical view of interpretation is important since it indicates
how the experience of sacrifice is shaped by the Christian interpretation of grace. Having an interpretive framework attuned to suffering
that can accompany the path to salvation — "having this mind in

you" (Phil. 2:5) — alters the reception and interpretation of suffering as sacrifice. Attuned to the grace in sacrifice, the history of suffering and the history of salvation may cohere in this concrete, particular moment. "An experience of a historical failure and at the same time a passionate faith in God's future for man is for the religious person no contradiction, but a mystery eluding every attempt at theoretical or rational accommodation."[496]

If God does not will suffering, suffering can have meaning only when it is inextricably connected to serving for a cause — in short, as a purposeful sacrifice. Such cases demonstrate vividly this theory of experience and interpretation, which explains how an interpretation of purpose fuses with action. Otherwise, suffering, which in Schillebeeckx's view is a surd in history resisting explanation and justification, becomes an ideology. In the Middle Ages Jesus is represented as the one who bears the suffering of humankind, representing all the suffering people of this time.

> However authentic this experience may be, here the Christian interpretation of suffering enters a phase in which the symbol of the cross becomes a disguised legitimation of social abuses, albeit to begin with still unconsciously....This opened a way to concentration on one's own suffering, detached from suffering for a cause; in this way a cult of suffering could arise, detached from the critical and productive force of suffering. The suffering and death of Jesus were at the same time detached from the historical circumstances that brought him suffering and death. "Suffering in itself," no longer suffering through and for others, took on a mystical and positive significance, so that instead of having a critical power it really acquired a reactionary significance. Suffering in itself became a "symbol."[497]

The inspiration for suffering is thus deeper than one's self; it takes up God's concern. God wants courage and commitment that will bear God's cause for humanity; such endurance is favored.[498] But God does not want deliberate asceticism.

In this kind of suffering man is not concentrated on himself, nor on his own suffering, but on the cause which he takes up. All this is equally true of religious sacrifice. Such sacrifice is experienced as sacrificial love: for Christians that means "participating in the suffering of Jesus Christ" (2 Cor. 1:5). Despite all these considerations, however, there is an excess of suffering and evil in our history. There is a barbarous excess, for all the explanation and interpretations. There is too much unmerited and senseless suffering for us to be able to give an ethical, hermeneutical and ontological analysis of our disaster. There is suffering which is not even suffering "for a good cause," but suffering in which men, without finding meaning for themselves, are simply made victims of an evil cause which serves others.[499]

## The Suffering of the Disciple

Suffering is resisted as a contrast to salvation but cannot be dismissed. It is too easy to fall into an "alleluia Christianity." Again, there is the constant back-and-forth between Schillebeeckx's warnings away from and resignation to suffering. Schillebeeckx's reading of the exhortation to persevere despite persecution in 1 Peter and Hebrews acknowledges the reality of suffering in Christian discipleship, but maintains a space for critique of passive piety and the glorification of suffering. Though the disciple is called to act in solidarity with the oppressed, this is not an invitation to self-destruct for the other, as we will see in his dialogue with Levinas below.

A decision for discipleship following Jesus means the readiness to suffer, since preaching the reign of God meets opposition. This suffering is given a post-Easter Christological expression as a targeted warning coming to the individual as if directly from Jesus: "if any man would come after me, let him deny himself and take up his cross and follow me" (Mark 8:34, Matt. 10:38, Luke 14:27, Matt. 16:24). Those who served with Jesus experienced this fellowship and suffering most intensely. The offer of discipleship continues to be an offer of salvation with implications for the identity of the disciples and their suffering in the image of Jesus.[500]

By grace, the Christian is given a new identity in Christ that is a new mode of existence. As existence in grace, Christian life is patterned after God's unconditional love as manifested in Jesus' person, message, and praxis of the Kingdom even unto death. This way of life is a new alternative for human living that is made possible through a share in the relationship that binds Jesus to the Father through the Spirit. Thus, the New Testament understanding of grace has both a mystical and an ethical dimension.[501]

The gift of this grace comes from our participation in Christ's death and resurrection. The call to service, like the Last Supper, is expressed with a Christological emphasis on the cross.

The Letter to the Hebrews proclaims that salvation flows from the kerygma but also from the historical witness of the Christian community, including their suffering and their hope for the future. The community is an example to the world and an imitator of Christ in his patient suffering. The community is holy; it serves the world in a priestly role by suffering for others, by being the Temple for the world. Such spiritual sacrifices are acceptable. "1 Peter shares with Hebrews and much of the rest of the New Testament God's predilection for the suffering, afflicted and oppressed righteous."[502]

> In a way reminiscent of the Gospel of Mark, the ideas of the "necessity" and yet the freedom of suffering for others, bringing salvation and opening up the future, and the disarming and yet vulnerable and wounded "defenseless love," run through both writings like a golden thread. *For this very reason* one author — Hebrews — calls Jesus the *high priest,* and the other author — 1 Peter — deliberately speaks of the Christian community as a *priestly* people of God. What was once a cultic sacrifice is replaced by this "spiritual sacrifice" of solidarity with the suffering of others.[503]

Innocent suffering, reminiscent of Isaiah 53, is acceptable. It benefits others and leads them to convert. However, the expression of the experience of suffering for others functions differently in 1 Peter from Hebrews.

> The great difference between 1 Peter and Hebrews, which is so closely related to it ..., is that while 1 Peter interprets suffering for others as an expiatory sacrifice, it does not understand it in a cultic sense (*sacrificium propitiatorium*). It sees it as an *invitation,* to vulnerable love for others.[504]

Christian vulnerability flows from Christian hope, for which they must be able to account to others. This is the purpose of the "invitation."

> This is a hope which is grounded in suffering for others, so that these others may be led to reflection and even to be converted, "to be brought to God" (3:18), just as through the suffering of Jesus, Christians and sinners are brought closer together.[505]

This may appear to be an ethic for the hopeful victim, in the style of Levinas. An invitation to suffering appears close to an invitation to accept abuse, the destructive idealization of suffering of which the feminist scholars warned. Brown and Parker specifically denounced the instrumentalizing of the oppressed, so that by their suffering the powerful may be moved. Is 1 Peter an ethic of subservience to un-merited suffering? Schillebeeckx believes that although 1 Peter refers to suffering for God as a grace (using the Greek term *charis*), here grace is really meant in the sense of the Hebrew term *hen. Hen* im-plies favor in terms of that which merits favor; the qualities or reasons why someone is favored.[506] Suffering itself is not considered the gift of God, but a quality in the sufferer which God regards with favor. It is not grace as the gift of God, but grace as favor seen in the human person. "Unmerited suffering with God in view is acceptable to him and is looked upon by him with favor — which indicates a very different attitude toward this suffering from the one that is con-demned as being negative."[507] In other words, the suffering of Jesus was condemned and perpetrators are judged. For Jesus and also for the disciple, God "only allows" this suffering. God's condemnation will come upon those who work evil. Those who do right will trust in God. "Therefore let those who suffer according to God's will do right and entrust their souls to a faithful Creator" (1 Pet. 4:19). The attitude of trust in God as the sovereign creator (4:19b) is an acceptable attitude, even if the suffering itself is not a gift from God.

The resignation to the secular structures of the world outside the church expressed by 1 Peter belonged to its historically conditioned situation. Schillebeeckx preserves for the church in other times and circumstances the possibility of actualizing other options.[508] Christians who seek liberation in the concrete conditions of the present day may interpret the duty to respond to suffering differently than did the early church. The modern church will not escape suffering for its prophetic stance, but it need not adopt a passive role in the face of suffering.

In conclusion, the meaning of suffering centers in the dedication to a chosen value that steadfastly persists despite suffering. Suffering can become meaningful if given direction and committed to fruitfulness, as a seed dying for future growth. Faith in Jesus affirms the history of suffering and the history of salvation by taking God as trustworthy because of Jesus' certainty unto death.[509]

In Schillebeeckx's phrase, "The ideas of the '*necessity*' and yet the *freedom* of suffering *for* others... bringing salvation..." (emphasis added), there echo themes raised by Ricoeur: suffering in the face of necessity, freely acting as subject for others amid the passive experience of life's difficulties. Schillebeeckx's term, "solidarity," echoes the fidelity and the self-constancy emphasized by Ricoeur that keep promises and ground identity. A freely chosen commitment to solidarity and fidelity reflects the aim and identity of the Christian community.

### Sacrifice in Extreme Cases as a Seal on Identity

Nevertheless, Schillebeeckx continues to preach that suffering is overvalued, and necessary only in extraordinary circumstances.[510] The tension between self-sacrifice and self-realization pulls constantly from one pole to the other. Solidarity may foresee, acknowledge, and still persist in a dangerous commitment, thus consenting to an out-come of suffering. This action requires a radical confidence in God, despite all circumstances. To recognize, foresee, and stand firm upon a course that suddenly changes from rewarding liberative action to costly sacrifice can only be grounded upon a religious attitude of trust. In such cases, one does lose oneself in the process of trying to save one's commitment to a treasured value or relationship. I have proposed "dedication" as the core meaning of sacrifice. When the cost of sacrifice threatens personal security, the decisive quality of dedication is heightened as dedication in the sense of trust, which perseveres despite loss.

Disciples must take up the cross: "these words are basic to our being Christian." At the same time, Schillebeeckx warns, they

> have often been *devalued* in ascetic terms and at the same time have been *over-valued:*...exegesis has drawn a veil of dull-ness and sobriety over Christianity, a dark cloud of penance, sacrifice and the inflicting of pain, even of self-contempt and self-depreciation. Christianity is said to be at its best when blood flows and people have to suffer under a harsh yoke — at least that is what certain Christians said who themselves happened to experience neither pain or yoke. This interpretation completely forgets the context in which the New Testament...speaks about the "messianic need to suffer."[511]

This context is the situation of persecution and trial. The context for suffering is the extreme case threatening torture and death: "situa-tions which occur only exceptionally in someone's life." This is the case of the rare, decisive challenge to acknowledge finally the faith by which one has lived. In such extreme cases, sacrificial actions serve as a seal on identity.

## The Opacity of Human Suffering

In spite of the tendency for discussions of brave endurance and resis-tance to cast a heroic light upon the stalwart sufferers, it is difficult to theorize about suffering. There are overwhelming experiences of the opacity of suffering that defy meaning. True stories forbid the romanticizing of suffering: such as the story of a woman with three children who have muscular dystrophy. The wasting disease, which ends in death as the heart and lungs weaken fatally, is caused by a recessive gene. The mother could hope in the mathematical odds for conceiving healthy children, a hope that failed and failed again after the first discovery of her and her spouse's genetic heritage. Her story is a black contrast experience, which, like finitude, can be open to interpretations of either atheism or trust. Such suffering demonstrates the refractory dimension of reality, resisting all reason.[512] Like evil, which Ricoeur could approach only indirectly, via the fecund depths of the symbol, suffering resists justification even in a cruciform ethic. Like the stain that symbolizes sin but evades thought, suffering hinders brisk moral recommendations with the weight of its pain. It is difficult, if not impossible, to incorporate suffering rationally into a model of discipleship or a measured ethic.

Schillebeeckx's phenomenological and hermeneutic approach to recognizing meaning as inseparable from experience means that in the end, suffering and death can be, in themselves, services for others. This does not abstract suffering from a history of absurdity and violence. But as an offering of service, such suffering is formally an act of hope, rather than an act of passive endurance. In such an act, the history of salvation and the history of suffering are brought together and occupy the same moment. Ricoeur's theory of experience also enables a reading of the suffering within sacrifice as another dimension of the otherness passively given to existence and human encounter. Like bodiliness, conscience, and other people, suffering is a phenomenon that is given, not under our control. Suffering is *other* than our aim. Suffering is a consequence of dedication, the otherness hidden in sacrificial action, an element open to interpretation as either acceptable or insupportable. An action may be experienced as futile pain or purposeful sacrifice reflecting the individual's interpretive framework. Similarly, as Suchocki expressed with her view of the transcendence of memory, interpretation may transform past incidents into meaningful events.

While in response to unwanted causes of suffering one may choose to act in ways that recover one's purpose and mend relationships in the best way possible, suffering itself cannot be rationalized. Suffering can be resisted only by action so that history may perhaps be otherwise. Passivity turns to action with the "sensible resolution": "let us try and make history with more meaning to it!" Although total meaning is reserved for the future, the present is the time to hope and to criticize.[513] One's present choice is to undertake service with the spirit of creation faith, discerning action that will bring in the reign of God.

Grace enables the self-emptying and selfless action of transformation and conversion.

> Receiving grace always involves complete self-denial, openness to others, availability and readiness to learn, in joy at the value of the treasure that has been found, a pearl (the Eastern symbol for the mystery of life for which man surrenders everything else; Matt. 13:44).[514]

> Again, the kingdom of heaven is like a merchant in search of fine pearls, who, on finding one pearl of great value, went and sold all that he had and bought it. (Matt. 13:45)

The pearl itself is a symbol of transformation, born out of the suffering that is imposed on the oyster in the shape of the foreign, immovable rock. Yet through an accepting response the invading dirt becomes luminous, a sea change creating something much bigger than it was before. There is also transformation in the interpretation of suffering as graced sacrifice.

## Service under the Proviso of the Reign of God

If suffering is not willed by God, but is a seal of discipleship under extreme circumstances, sacrifice and discipleship are linked by three principles: (1) Suffering is integrated into Christian discipleship through a mystical and political spirituality. (2) Those who follow Jesus will serve the other seeing that person as a revelation of God.

Finally, (3) one's service in sacrifice is oriented to the reign of God as the ultimate priority, even surpassing service to the other.

## Mystical and Political Spirituality

Janet O'Meara defines the mystical and political dimensions of faith as marked by both positive and negative disclosure experiences. Both passive receptivity (a mystical experience) and "critical negativity" (a judgment that leads to action) contain positive and negative elements. Mystical awareness of God's presence and the goodness of life form the positive pole of mystic belief; there is also profound recognition of negative knowledge about God in the apophatic traditions of spirituality. Critical negativity stems from moments of despair and oppression, but contains a positive impulse toward a way out of the suffering. Mysticism and critical suffering are creative because the passivity of contemplation is a womb of new awareness. Contemplation grasps for insights into new possibilities of living the struggle.

> On the one hand, although in the form of negative experience, suffering comes upon one in a way that is similar to the passive structure of positive contemplative experiences. On the other hand, under the aspect of critical negativity, the reality of suffering resists the passivity of the contemplative dimension in a way that leads to possible action that will overcome both suffering and its causes.[515]

Sacrifice which seeks the transformation of unjust conditions expresses a political spirituality. By trusting in God despite opposition, political action is also a mystic act of reconciliation with finitude.[516] It is through the interpretation of suffering with a mystical and political spirit that one finds the gift of transforming suffering into sacrifice. Such action persists in creating Christian identity. Ricoeur spoke of selfhood as an indirect interpretation, taken as an indirect route through culture, texts, and other people. Sacrifice is the ultimate indirect route to salvation.

## Priority of the Reign of God

The suffering of sacrifice is oriented finally toward the reign of God. Schillebeeckx's response to Levinas demonstrates this nuanced apprehension of service to the other.[517] He agrees that the other is a privileged place for the experience of God. The other can make ethical commands that are in no way derived from my moral claims, or deduced from a shared acceptance of communal rights and expectations. The presence of the other is a claim upon me that manifests transcendent otherness.

But, lest the other appear supremely privileged in this relationship, Schillebeeckx judges that the absolute right of the other is hedged by the proviso of the reign of God, the definitive aim orienting action and subjectivity. The other is indeed an end in himself but not the final end for me. Human beings cannot be the ultimate source of ethics for two reasons. First, the other may be a source of violence to me or I to him. This affirms Ricoeur's reservations about the excessive priority of the other. Second, there is a religious proviso that prevents the ethical response to the other from being the fundamental and final religious duty. The other is a means to the experience of God, not the end of the revelation itself. While the other is a revelation and invitation that is *tremendum et fascinans,* the other is not to be idolized.

Identifying the aporia in Levinas's absolute ethical foundation leads Schillebeeckx to analyze the modes of hope that ground service and surmount victimization. Even if the ethical demand is accepted out of fidelity, hope that sacrifice will bear fruit arises not from human beings, but from hope in God.[518] The other is neither a ground for hope, nor the ultimate source of the command. It is God who calls the disciple to unconditional service. Heeding God's call surmounts all other obligations; those whom Jesus called were summoned in the midst of their daily work. The call presents the disciple with an open, enlarging, disorienting aim, much like the tragic conflicts that Ricoeur pondered.

It shatters every frame of the "master-disciple" relationship, because it is a conclusive, latter-day act on the part of the eschatological prophet; it serves to condense his call to metanoia

into an eschatological metanoia as a disciple of Jesus, a vocation to total commitment, burning all one's boats in the service
of the kingdom. To associate oneself with Jesus like that is
to put oneself unconditionally at the service of the kingdom
of God.[519]

The reign of God is the ultimate call.

Schillebeeckx connects the broken circuit in Levinas's ethical telos,
which ends in the other, by realigning the orientation of sacrificial
action to God. This move parallels the response by which Ricoeur
extricated himself from the potentially constricting circuit of Kant's
universal maxim. As Ricoeur concluded, when the norm fails, return
to the teleological aim. Responding to the other as the principle of
ethics may reach a dead end if the other becomes an oppressor, or if
the reciprocity of conventional aims proves insufficient to exceptional
circumstances, special needs, or tragic cases. There must always be
a deeper and ultimate orienting aim — which exists in God the creator and origin of history. Within Schillebeeckx's Christic theology
of discipleship, that aim is found in the reign of God.

Both philosophical and religious views of ethical identity may affirm that the subject inscribes her identity through a commitment to
promises made for the sake of a greater vision or aim. What is unique
about the Christian willingness to accept the cost of sacrifice is not
merely a desire to remain faithful to promises, and to confirm one's
identity by so doing, even at great cost with possibly futile outcomes.
This type of courage and constancy can be shared by humanists, exis-
tentialists, or persons of other faiths. The uniquely Christian element
in the sacrificial hermeneutics of identity is that Christians accept suffering that may be an inevitable part of keeping certain promises with
the hope founded in trusting Jesus that their suffering will be healed,
and that their aim to bring good to another will be fulfilled in the
kingdom of God.

Jesus offers healing to those who follow him, yet warns that to
keep one's connection to the kingdom of God, one might have to
leave family behind, suffer the costs of discipleship, or pluck out

an offending eye. This is a paradoxical kind of wholeness. A similar tension pervades the relationship to the other. The balance of self-sacrifice and self-realization is not numerical equality but paradoxical balance. Christian sacrifice is defined in relation to God and the community under God's care. These relationships are guided by equality without reducing it to numerical sameness or identical effort. Sacrifice is measured according to the scales of the kingdom of God, a "good measure" that overflows. The reign of God thus acts as an orienting aim for Christian sacrifice, representing the genuine wholeness sought by all and measuring our acts of sacrifice. Sacrifice aims to bring about the new creation.

## IV. Creation Faith

### Grace and New Being

A Christian view of suffering and hope for wholeness is appropriately grounded in the doctrine of creation. Creation faith judges suffering while acknowledging the cost of discipleship, thus preserving the tension in the paradox of self-sacrifice and self-realization. Creation faith has a critical force that participates in the transformation of the world. Creation faith enables the confident, "mystic" trust in the God of Mary, as well as the engaged mysticism of Martha, actively concerned for other people. With the Holy Spirit, the disciples are made children of God and sent out to the world to bring about the reign of God.[520] The basic new way of life of the disciple in grace is expressed as adoption or birth from God, two concepts that "express that the Christian has a share in the particular relationship that binds the man Jesus, as the Son, through the Spirit with the Father — three concepts (Father, Son and Spirit), which in the New Testament point to God, but *in* his attitude towards man."[521]

Grace is fundamentally an experience of being the child of God. The grace of baptism gives the believer the gift of the Holy Spirit, bringing forgiveness of sins and new identity.[522] The effect is an experience that transforms and confirms one's identity in relationship to God. This new life brings a sharing in the communion of God the

Father and Jesus. Grace conforms the believer to Jesus Christ, so that he or she cares for others with his brotherly love. Grace places the believer between the confirmed experience of the transforming presence of God, which is already real in the life of faith, and the not yet realized fulfillment of her hope to live wholly in the reign of God.

The connection between sacrificial identity and a new relationship to God was noted in chapter 1. The effect of grace thus parallels the function of cultic sacrifice as well as existential sacrifice defined as dedication to God. Like the Hebrew cult, grace is God's gift, it confers new identity, it brings liberation and fullness of life, and it is a means of communion with the divine.[523]

God's grace enables a new way of being, a renewed discipleship characterized by hope for God's coming reign. It is God, in this sense, who gives the sacrifice. This life is appropriated by faith in Jesus, through which humanity comes to live by God's righteousness. Grace is the transformation to living in the kingdom, and participating in God's mercy. Because it is God's mercy that sustains the sacrificing disciple, hope is possible. Schillebeeckx meditates upon the communion between human and divine that is also a blending of suffering and hope.

> Abide in love, even if this love does not seem to get anywhere and is vain: believe in this vain love and existing for others. Christian ethics has a Christological and an eschatological foundation: because of this it comes under the perspective of effective hope, "of faith which is at work in the love of neighbor" (Gal. 5:6).[524]

Responsibility for creation is a charge given to the human person who is naturally related to the wider web of all life. Salvation is a cosmic hope, deeply rooted in scriptural visions of the redemption of the whole creation.

> Faith in God the Creator is not simply a question of another interpretation or another theory without any relevance for praxis. As I have said, God's glory is human happiness. But this happiness is not simply an individual concern. Of course individual

action is in no way socially neutral or politically innocent, above all in modern conditions (as J. B. Metz, among others, is accustomed to say). That means that the believer's concern for God's honor is also a struggle for more justice in the world, a commitment to a new earth and an environment in which human beings can live fuller lives. ... Christian salvation is not simply the salvation of souls but the healing, making whole, wholeness, of the whole person, the individual and society, in a natural world which is not abused.[525]

Schillebeeckx developed a model of human nature in relation to the whole cosmos with his system of anthropological constants. The dimensions of the self are outer, inner, social, political, historical, and ecological, as seen through the unifying theological lens of creation faith. Human communion allows us to share ourselves with others and be confirmed in our existence and personhood by others.[526] We are essentially related to others. The very outward presentation of every human face indicates one's orientation toward others. Human identity is structured by the authorization by others to be a personal and responsible self. Being oneself is not the achievement of an isolated self: a full and mature sense of identity requires the support of one's individuality by many others. One's own limitations are transcended by loving relationships, which in turn help fulfill personal identity. Because all persons are encountered as an end in themselves, well-being and wholeness must apply to every individual. This healing applies not only to personal relationships but also to social connections, the institutional and social dimensions implied by the third person. The category for a distinctive experience of grace that Schillebeeckx labels "J" speaks of "Being redeemed for community" and category "K" refers to the experience of "Being freed for brotherly love." "Redemption is freedom for self-surrender in love for fellow men; that is abiding in God. Ethics, and above all love of one's neighbor, is the public manifestation of the state of being redeemed."[527]

For Schillebeeckx, salvation is the fullness of human life in friendship with God, solidarity with others, including the sustaining and co-suffering network of ecological relationships. Salvation is the wholeness of each; the mutual integrity of all. Religious faith in creation and eschatology orients the origins and goal of earthly history. Sacrifice thus seeks to bring about an inclusive and wide view of salvation, taking up the cause of the creator for creation.

There is an "inexhaustible potential for expectation and inspiration to be found in belief in creation."[528] Human dignity and hope for progress can always be secularized into a benevolent humanism. Then the finite limits of humanity always remain such. Creation faith acknowledges God's presence alongside human finitude, providing an endless source of creativity and hope.

> Finitude or secularity will continually point to the source and ground, inspiration and orientation, transcending all secularity, which believers call the Living God and which is not capable of any secularization. Precisely for that reason belief in creation is also the foundation of prayer and mysticism.... Therefore the fullness of salvation, too, cannot be reduced to what people themselves achieve. The salvation of mankind is God himself, as its wholeness.[529]

God's possibilities exceed our limited expectations of salvation. Authentic creation faith has an endlessly "critical, productive and liberating power ... [which] above all is realized in the proclamation and praxis of Jesus of Nazareth."[530] Our limited values will always be surpassed by the inspiration coming from faith in God the creator. At the same time, it is being endowed with the autonomy of authentic creatureliness that enables humanity truly to express creativity and care of this world. Because God has made room, humanity may sow its own seeds and hope for harvest. Because God is present, there are grounds for hope that the harvest will be rich.

## Reconciliation to Finitude

A separate important element of accepting many inevitable sacrifices is a trusting resignation to the limited conditions of finite humanity.

When interpreted with faith in God, contingency presents an invitation to accept one's finitude — to be reconciled as a creature to the Creator.

In relation to sacrifice, Schillebeeckx's emphasis on grace as mystical and political permits an understanding of the grace of sacrifice as an act of reconciliation with finitude and with the costs that compassion will experience by undertaking sacrifice. This reconciliation participates in the creative liberation of human history, even while acknowledging the eschatological deferral of true wholeness for the earth community. In this ethical manner, as in its original cultic formulation, sacrifice is a gift of God for reconciling finite beings to their creator. Such sacrifice can be seen as reconciliation of humanity to finitude, and to the Creator as a creature.

The yes to sacrificial discipleship is an affirmation of one's Christian identity. God's no resists suffering per se. The Christian transformation of an ethic of self-giving into the religious witness of sacrifice thus builds upon the yes and the no, revealing its special form of identity as citizenship in the kingdom of God. The fullness of life known in God's reign acknowledges a paradoxical form of wholeness, one that need not be challenged by certain accepted losses.

One category of grace Schillebeeckx identifies (category N) refers to grace as "life in fullness" — a theme that has been central in the paradoxical opposition of sacrificial living and discipleship as the call to the fullness of life. It is here that we see a resolution of the paradoxical conflict. The life of grace persists despite suffering, because the believer is always in communion with God through grace. This is a source of constant comfort, rooted in hope. It explains the joyful nature of discipleship, even through sacrifice and suffering. This again is the result of a reframing of the paradigm of suffering. It is not the dilemma of innocent suffering versus guilty suffering. Suffering exists whether one is the innocent passive victim, or the active, sacrificing subject. This gift, grounded upon the freedom of the disciple, as an experience of grace, enables trust in God, and resolves the conflict between sacrifice and suffering.

In the Tanach righteousness always has an intrinsic connection with a flourishing and happy life...[that] led to a crisis
which is expressed above all in Job. However, Job continued
to believe in the mystery of God and in the mutual interconnection between life in accordance with God's will and the
human concern for happiness and fulfillment. The New Testament knows a similar intrinsic connection, but makes it between
the life of grace and human life so that *suffering and misery in
themselves need not contradict this connection; indeed in the
context of grace they can even acquire a new significance.* However, communion with God in grace implies that in the last
result nothing can separate us from God...this has eschatological consequences for human nature itself: eternal life, physical
resurrection, and "a new heaven and a new earth" with just
conditions, a life without alienation, without suffering and tears
[emphasis added].[531]

Sacrifice is a profound experience of humanity's not yet realized
wholeness. The need for sacrifice concretely confirms the reality of
human limitations, pains, and sinful failings, which still cry out for
redemption. Those who sacrifice indeed experience suffering in the
present moment; at the same time, their actions testify to inspiration
felt in this present moment that hopes for the eschatological future.
Schillebeeckx's view of history as a dynamic process means that the
Kingdom is not expected through God's sudden disclosure upon a
static world. The kingdom arises as if through a process of ongoing
leavening.

The eschatological proviso thus reserves sovereignty over the future to God, but does not remove the human responsibility to work
and transform society. The peace of the kingdom is anticipated, experienced in fragments, and furthered by human ethical action. The
eschatological proviso prevents us from identifying salvation with
our work. Hope is based on God's creativity and on the resurrection.
Human responsibility is marked by an eschatological dialectic in that
people must work to bring in the kingdom of God — but their work

rests upon hope in God. The resurrection grounds the knowledge that God is with us in the worst.

> Jesus' suffering and death in solidarity with the rejected and broken of the world give unconditional validity to his message and praxis: God is irrevocably present as salvation for men and women, even in situations of extreme negativity. The notion of God's saving immediacy in the mediation of extreme negativity is central to Schillebeeckx's understanding of the saving significance of the death of Jesus. The redemptive force of this death does not lie with suffering and the negativity of failure as such, but with unbroken communion and solidarity to the point of death.[532]

Salvation is still offered despite human rejection and the cross. "The living God who is the future of human history is in the risen Jesus, the presence of the future." The good news is that God's "nevertheless" has the last word. God remembers past acts in new saving grace in the present. Our limited acts of liberation have a future. Sacrifice thus discloses the eschatological nature of reality; it is a praxis that struggles despite the cost to bring in a new future.

## A Trinitarian Definition of Sacrificial Discipleship

A final definition concludes the theological hermeneutics of sacrifice drawn from Schillebeeckx's catechism of creation. My presentation of Schillebeeckx's creation creed through the articles of faith in God the Creator, Christ the parable of God's concern for human salvation, and the challenge of discipleship inspired by the Spirit, provides grounds for inscribing sacrifice within this creation catechism. The creation creed establishes a Trinitarian context for a theology of sacrificial discipleship which understands sacrifice as an expression of creation faith in God the Creator, Son, and Holy Spirit.

Sacrificial discipleship reflects the vulnerable adventurousness of the Creator, who makes space for the other, accepting a risk of unintended consequences in the process. God remains pure positivity.

For the disciple, the cost may be great or small, but one's Christian identity is not surrendered.

Sacrificial discipleship lives in the Spirit of transforming community, seeking justice, encouraging the particularity and survival of its full diversity. This spirit fosters the life of all creation, enabling difference to thrive, sustaining fragile life forms. It does not impose a totalizing sameness. A discipleship inspired by the Spirit imaginatively brings in the future. There is an ascetic imagination that envisions true humanity in its interdependence and mutual well-being, able to overcome the insecurity of contingency and relinquish excess material consumption.

Sacrifice is thus creative as God is creative, and embraces our task of creation. Sacrifice that promotes wholeness is indeed a creative action. The last chapter turns to God the Creator as the deepest symbol of creative sacrifice.

Chapter Five

# SACRIFICE IN
# THE IMAGE OF GOD

*For God created all things that they might exist, and the*
*generative forces of the world are wholesome.*
> — Wisdom of Solomon 1:13–14

The theme of divine creativity, which framed the discussion of Edward Schillebeeckx's work in the last chapter, now becomes the point
of entry for a deeper assessment of Christian sacrifice in the light of
God's creativity. Four main sources — scriptural analyses, feminist
scholarship, the philosophical anthropology of Paul Ricoeur, and the
liberation theology of Edward Schillebeeckx — have been consulted
for insight into the paradoxical relationship between self-sacrifice and
self-realization in the formation of Christian identity as mediated by
relationships with the other. Each suggests important values to be
maintained in a retrieval of the symbolism of sacrifice to inspire Christian discipleship. By looking back on how each source approaches the
paradox of self-sacrifice and self-realization, we can then look to a
new way of imagining Christian sacrifice. Here a new context for the
question of Christian self-giving is sought in the proposals of contemporary theologians for how self-giving and self-limitation shape
divine creativity. To ground the idea of self-giving sacrifice in the aim
of creativity renews the symbol of sacrifice and helps restore the balance between self-sacrifice and self-realization. First, a review of the
means for navigating the challenge of interpreting sacrifice suggested
by the analyses of the previous chapters.

## I. Retrospective Assessment of the Sources

### The Complexity of the Symbol

The dangerous ambiguity within the complex symbol and practice of sacrifice was the initial justification for this project. Ricoeur proposes a method to navigate such complexity — the hermeneutics of suspicion that uncovers ideological distortion in a text, tradition, or symbol. Ricoeur explores how the symbol serves as a bearer of meaning that is not finally determined; there are possibilities to be uncovered within the symbol via interpretation. The corollary of this is that a symbol can be made to function *differently*.

This phenomenon was also indicated by scripture scholarship, which indicated the many ways sacrificial images convey meaning. That is, there is diversity in the antecedent practices of Hebrew monotheism, as well as in the varied interpretations of Jesus in relationship to sacrificial themes within the New Testament texts. Even within a religious community of shared heritage like early Christianity the repertoire of sacrificial symbols shifts in meaningful ways. Because any given symbol contains possibilities of meaning, the external form of the symbol is not as important as the way it is used, and how it is interpreted. The scriptural exegeses presented in chapter 1 collectively indicate the purposeful reshaping of sacrificial imagery by the early Christians. Even the underlying logic of sacrificial atonement is explained in diverse ways: as a cultic ritual with its own efficacy (as in the Letter to the Hebrews), or as a legal procedure in which an adversary is defeated by one's advocate (John A. T. Robinson's interpretation of Romans).

Schillebeeckx reminds us that cultural documents are an expression of community faith, rooted in the language and worldview of a particular community yet passing on a common hope. Recall that in his interpretation of the Letter to the Hebrews, priesthood means a brotherly intercession, standing between God and suffering humanity.[533] Only close attention to how the writer employs references to priesthood would suggest that Hebrews is a *non*-cultic, or demythologized, view of sacrifice. It is a badge of compassion and solidarity, not a mark of cultic divisions among people. Sacrifice can then be interpreted as a choice that expresses compassion and one's relationship to others. Sacrifice does not validate suffering for its own sake or for the sake of a pious passivity.

The lack of a single model for sacrifice in relationship to Jesus and the absence of a dominant interpretation of how sacrifice functions suggest that the fluidity of sacrificial images in itself is meaningful. The fluidity of the models is itself significant because it reveals the centrality of models of sacrifice for Judaism and early Christianity — the image and process are not easily discarded. Yet the very variety of its expressions shows the distinctiveness of the Christian vision, which wrought from the heritage of sacrificial themes a variety of symbolic expressions to convey the excess of meaning celebrated in the event of Jesus Christ. That event naturally found expression in sacrificial categories to signify the disciples' connection to the deep tradition of Hebrew faith and practice, in which sacrifice is a significant form of religious experience. Jesus' life and death is naturally interpreted in continuity with that tradition because his disciples perceived his dedication to God and to themselves, a religious attitude connected with offering sacrifice. The sacrificial symbols within Jewish faith are not simple or monolithic themselves. The surplus of meaning contained in the disciples' experience of Jesus evoked further expression of the many ways to experience salvation in Jesus and to describe some of these in sacrificial terms.

The possibilities are not unlimited, however. Such expansiveness would finally render the symbol meaningless. Furthermore, some possible interpretations are harmful. It is necessary to judge which among the plurality of sacrificial interpretations express the gospel authentically by ascertaining the central meaning of Christian sacrifice, or that which Tracy called a "core metaphor."[534] I have argued that for Christian sacrifice, that core meaning is *dedication*. Faithfulness to the tradition includes the full narrative of Jesus' life and ministry. Judgments about dangerous sacrificial interpretations will assess whether such a reading focuses narrowly on the suffering of the

Passion to the exclusion of Jesus' fellowship, or even more narrowly, on bloodshed instead of undying commitment.

## Balancing Sacrifice and the Self

Feminist scholars warned that the rhetoric of sacrifice may encourage persons to accept suffering, exploitation, and even violence, believing that such endurance is a Christian virtue. They observed the devaluation of self-love in some theological traditions and the tendency for some persons to be more comfortable with a self-denying role than justified assertiveness or even mutuality. All of these factors weaken one's agency, prevent the full expression of one's gifts, and minimize contributions that might be made to society according to one's unique capacities. Ricoeur spoke of failed agency and lost authenticity. When the call of the other is unconditionally prioritized and treated as an inexorable duty, there is no opportunity for the self to discern whether a response is appropriate. Under such conditions the self cannot be truly said to be acting in a way that expresses one's own values and identity. Schillebeeckx also acknowledged the risk of violence to oneself. He does not allow that the other has the final say on one's energies and talents; in the end, the aim of Christian action should be the furtherance of the reign of God.

The exposition of feminist scholarship in chapter 2 indicated the problems and ambiguities created by some interpretations, with potentially dangerous implications for the reader who encounters the text. The scholars I have reviewed, including Joanne Carlson Brown, Rebecca Parker, Barbara Hilkert Andolsen, Valerie Saiving, and Marjorie Hewitt Suchocki, highlight the value of alternate visions contained in scripture, theological traditions, and models of anthropology. Their work clarifies that preaching, healing, and remaining faithful to a message of forgiveness is the substance of Jesus' saving work, not simply his physical expiration on the cross. The legitimate place of self-love in that gospel message is reclaimed and detached from anthropologies that assume self-love must be unsound, aggressive, and narrowly self-serving. Sin is reconsidered from a feminist view, which perceives that some tendencies to accept a sacrificial and passive role amount to a sinful evasion of responsibility.

Feminists demonstrate that it is necessary to cut through the ideological or simply anachronistic accretions of models from past centuries in order to retrieve meaning from the Gospels for today — or, in reverse, it is appropriate to propose truly novel interpretations.[535] The early church's acceptance of the power of sacrifice does not easily translate into a contemporary worldview. In addition, the very durability of tradition preserves patriarchal and even misogynist language and beliefs (for example, that all women deserve punishment because of the sin of Eve).[536] Even among societies and congregations for whom this sexist worldview is largely discredited, traces are preserved in well-known texts and liturgical language, perpetuating such notions with the authority of tradition. If such models become unintelligible to a new generation, they will at best thwart understanding. At worst they function in intelligible, deliberate, and dangerous ways as noted above to oppress vulnerable persons who are compelled into subservient and sacrificial situations.

By drawing on experience which affirms the goodness of the self, this style of theology uncovers the equivocal nature of some interpretations of suffering and retrieves the gospel message of Jesus' will to heal. Suffering, as shown by critiques of atonement theories, is often a cipher for something else and its value exaggerated or misjudged as a result. The suffering of sacrifice can be identified equivocally with virtue; the intrinsic value of self-denial can be overemphasized; the simplification of sin as pride can overlook failures to invest fully one's God-given talents; and self-love can be distorted into egoism and aggression. It becomes necessary to examine and judge biases that unduly emphasize passivity or the role of the victim.

The affirmation of self-love as a positive duty compatible with Christian discipleship is a central constructive contribution of feminist scholarship to the question of sacrifice. This affirmation calls for an adequate treatment of self-realization to balance self-sacrifice. The retrieval of scriptural themes of healing and fellowship is one way to balance an emphasis on suffering. Precisely because Jesus' ministry affirmed women, the poor, the lowly, and the sick, and called them to share in the good news of healing and fellowship, interpreting the gospel invitation to "lose one's life to save it" requires special care. Feminist scholars insist that one should neither hide one's full growth because of a false ideal of abnegating service, nor endanger oneself through excessive denial or accepting violence. Womanist theology in a particular way claims survival as a goal on the journey to healing. Suffering is not idealized, but resisted: "with God's help, black women...will make a way out of no way."[537]

There remains the tension between self-sacrifice and self-realization at its core: how does sacrifice positively contribute to Christian identity? Mutuality is a meaningful guide in questions of justice but is a narrow measure for love relationships if construed as strict reciprocity. The first chapter noted a pattern of ritual prophylactic sacrifice that attempts to manipulate the deity or obtain gain from the transaction. Such careful equivalence contradicts the spirit of communion and generosity in what Turner called the sacrifice of abandonment. There is a similar contrast between caution and generosity in the interpersonal patterns Ricoeur expressed as equivalence versus abundance. If the gospel stories with their own logic of outpouring generosity capture one's imagination, then conventional human logic based on equivalence may be transformed. Schillebeeckx also finds questions of equivalence somewhat beside the point. His emphasis on social and global conditions of suffering sets the problem of injustice, misery, and torture on a larger scale: "Christians are led to bear witness to Jesus Christ and thus to spread the gospel, because they want to further God's kingdom of justice and love throughout the world."[538]

## Interpreting Self in Relation to Other via Sacrifice

The work of Ricoeur and Schillebeeckx suggests ways to interpret one's ethical identity through analyzing the intersubjective or social dimensions of the self, and the concomitant call to responsibility, solidarity, and sympathy. Both Schillebeeckx and Ricoeur demonstrate that identity is realized through self-giving, which is explicitly described as Christian sacrifice by Schillebeeckx. Both are willing to criticize the excessive priority of the other and to reject suffering as a good in itself. Both acknowledge principles that mediate between self and other: Ricoeur stresses the equality and primacy of both oneself and the other, and Schillebeeckx emphasizes that faith directs one's actions first to the reign of God.

For Schillebeeckx, sacrifice is a charism of Christian identity. Discipleship is a new way of living, an offer of salvation that is patterned on the praxis of Jesus Christ, his healing ministry, and preaching of the kingdom.[539] Jesus' life of service extends to and includes his death as a sign of sacrificial dedication, though his saving message is not made dependent on his death. Schillebeeckx acknowledges the reality of suffering in Christian discipleship, since those who preach the gospel will find opposition. There is no "alleluia Christianity."[540] The special emphasis on perseverance demonstrates the challenges that call for sacrifice and recalls Ricoeur's attention to keeping promises as the means of maintaining identity. Sacrifice is never a goal in itself and is rightly approached with suspicion. One accepts the cost for the sake of integrity. If identity is based on commitments, maintaining integrity requires honoring such commitments. *I am the one who keeps my promise to you, despite the cost.* Through consenting to a commitment — with its consequences — the agent remains in that sense the subject of her actions. However, Ricoeur's insistence on the tension between the primacy of self and other maintains a window for the revision of promises that become destructive. Among the complex of aims within an individual's life story, some may become impossible to keep without threatening other, more fundamental aims. There is a creative balance to be maintained.

In Schillebeeckx's terms, the disciple accepts the costly route of solidarity as part of discipleship. Though Schillebeeckx denounces the idealization of suffering as an ideology in which suffering acquires its own value, he nevertheless shows that sacrifice contributes positively to Christian identity. The core of identity is that on which one's heart is set. Sacrifice is a seal of identity. In Schillebeeckx's words,

> Human beings have no other choice than to set their hearts on something.... The question as to which God you worship has to do with whether your heart is focused on the destruction of others, or on peace and freedom for each person; on solidarity, justice, and love; in friendship, gift of self, and the loss of self in the service of others, if necessary.[541]

The ancient prophets saw clearly the centrality of inner disposition behind an act of sacrifice — one's heart is revealed by how one sacrifices. For both Ricoeur and Schillebeeckx, sacrifice itself is not the aim of action. Sacrifice at times becomes necessary to preserve commitments fundamental to one's ethical aim or Christian values.

### The Interdependence of Finite Creatures

Schillebeeckx's creation catechism provided a vision that orients sacrifice by the Christian revelation of God in Jesus and by faith in God as creator. Christian sacrifice thus expresses a charism of sacrifice colored by Christianity's particular orienting values. The disciple who participates in the Spirit shares in the self-offering service that marked the life of Jesus. Discipleship also partakes of Jesus' spirit of gladness. Christian sacrifice continues Jesus' healing, inclusion, fidelity, and acceptance of finitude. Schillebeeckx also draws our attention to the suffering of the poor in the most inclusive and vulnerable sense. In our times, the earth is recognized as the new poor.

> Not only human beings but also the "image of God" are sullied: the *ecce homo* on the cross, and on the many crosses which have been erected and continue to be erected, and also the *ecce natura* as the polluted world of creation — in animals and plants and the basic elements of life.[542]

The earthly community has finite resources and is fragile. The planet's many ecologies also participate in humanity's interdependent communion, whose members must sacrifice for each other.

The theme of finitude influences Schillebeeckx's beliefs about humankind as mortal beings who share in each other's sorrows and salvation. Schillebeeckx emphasizes that life is intersubjective; humans depend upon each other. Finitude will require sacrifice apart from any question of sinfulness or human injustice. Time and resources are limited in a shared community. Indeed, even self-understanding is profoundly linked to life with others and shaped by participation in a particular place and time. The interdependence Ricoeur described by way of reflexive self-knowledge is paralleled by Schillebeeckx's anthropological constants: the outer world intersects the inner. Sacrifices often result from these overlapping and demanding relationships. Many sacrifices are the result of sin and violence, but not all. Simply as finite creatures, humankind will experience more demands than can be met, more needs than can be satisfied, conflicts of preferences that are equally valid, and infirmities of sickness and disability that resist healing. Part of the task of humanity, precisely as finite creatures given autonomous responsibility for history, is to respond creatively to conflicting needs. Sacrificial choices will be part of the creative strategies that seek to meet the most pressing needs. Sacrificial decisions will reveal what are an individual or community's guiding values.

In summary, one finds one's self by giving to the other through promises that establish one's core identity, and through fidelity to those promises over time and despite hardship. Such faithful solidarity demonstrates that on which one's heart is set, through the "gift of self, and the loss of self . . . if necessary."

## II. A New Foundation for Sacrifice in Creation Faith

In pursuit of an understanding of the paradox of sacrifice and Christian identity, the previous four chapters have arrived at a model of sacrificial discipleship as a seal of identity and an expression of Christian love, corrected by the feminist caveat against destructive self-abnegation. At this point there remains to renew the symbolic expression of Christian identity in terms of realization and sacrifice by looking beyond the symbol of the cross for its source.

How does reflection on the Creator inspire sacrifice, or shed light on the paradox of self-sacrifice and self-realization? Analyzing the ways God's creativity can be expressed via self-giving or self-limitation provides a deeper theological ground of Christian sacrifice. To read God's self-giving as creative — that is, as a source of new life — provides a profound and positive model and foundation for the sacrifice of Christians. Interpreting God's creativity as kenotic grounds a view of human self-giving as holy, as a reflection of God's self-giving holiness. God's creativity provides a new orienting value for a hermeneutics of sacrificial discipleship. Sharing in the triune dynamic of self-giving, orienting sacrifice to the new creation (the reign of God), and attending to the context of the earthly creation — these are the orienting values of sacrifice in a creation catechism.

## Theological Ground of Christian Sacrifice in God's Creativity

The model of sacrifice so far has been based on a single image, discipleship in *imago Christi*. The ethical exigency of Christian sacrifice is usually shaped specifically by the memory of Jesus Christ, while theological anthropology does traditionally acknowledge two sources: Christology or the Genesis symbol of humankind as the image of God. These two sources, Christic and properly theological, are linked because the life and death of Jesus provide an interpretive key for the love of God. The link is made explicit through the idea of kenosis, or self-emptying, which offers a specific Christological interpretation of divine self-presence in Christ. Jesus is an expression of the love of God, the love demonstrated throughout salvation history beginning with the story of creation. In contemporary doctrines of God, the New Testament references to divine kenosis in Christ have been extended to kenotic language about God's creative activity. The search for a deeper theological meaning of self-gift therefore finds rich resources in the idea of kenosis. Through kenosis, God's creative and self-giving love becomes a model for sacrifice.

Contemporary scholarship of creation in dialogue with science has reflected on the idea of kenosis as part of the ongoing process of creation.[543] Kenosis is seen as a dynamic of creation that gives concrete articulation to the love of God. This connection has at times excited controversy, especially when linked with ideas about God's suffering.[544] However, the idea of divine creativity as an expression of self-emptying love may be fruitful for the understanding of sacrifice, by implying that creativity and self-giving have a natural relationship. The way in which God's kenotic love makes space for the free flourishing and independent unfolding of the world's processes then has implications for human efforts to love genuinely and to frame the self-other relationship.

The traditional use of the symbol of the *imago Dei* as an interpretive key for understanding the nature of human being can therefore be focused by the self-emptying, kenotic, or sacrificial dimensions of divine creativity. Reflection on the theological depth of sacrifice will propose a new criterion for right sacrifice — the criterion of creativity. As I will indicate below, sacrifice and kenosis are not synonyms. However, both express a pattern of divine self-giving that can serve as an analogy and inspiration for human self-giving. The analogical comparison between God's creativity and human self-giving provides a way to envision sacrifice as nurturing the integrity of the individual and of the community to which he or she is integrally connected. The Creator is thus the fundamental model and most vivid image of creative sacrifice. Therefore, Christians who sacrifice are both in *imago Christi* and in *imago Dei*.

As a foil to the Christological focus of the previous chapters, reflection on the creative self-giving life of the Trinity explores how being the image of God is a task for us. God's creativity is the origin of life. Human creativity participates in this process in a limited way, not only in the gift of birth but through exploration, intellectual discovery, art, friendship, the new creation of hope and freedom by means of forgiveness, and by empowering others to experience their creativity also. To the extent that these creative processes involve self-limitation, discipline, forbearance, bearing burdens, and other pains, they are sacrificial. To illustrate the connection between kenosis and creativity, I will draw on the interpretations of God's creativity as sacrificial or kenotic by Arthur Peacocke and John Haught. Their proposals offer an "interpretive commitment": a proposition about one way to explain creativity, with the potential to symbolize the creative purpose and potential of sacrifice in a new way.[545]

## Kenotic Theologies

In Catholic theology, sacrifice traditionally refers to the cross and the Eucharist; kenosis to the Incarnation. Both constitute similar patterns in the self-emptying life of Christ and offer an interpretive lens for the life of the Creator. References to divine self-limiting as a method of creation often employ the term *kenosis* rather than "sacrifice," although some authors use both. Sarah Coakley, a British feminist and patristic scholar, has explored the fluid vocabulary of *kenosis* and demonstrates its connections to sacrifice and creation. Coakley observes that with this term, theologians are

> dealing here with a sliding scale of uses that move us around the terrain of systematic theology in intriguing ways, from the doctrine of Christ, to the doctrine of the Trinity, to the doctrine of providence, to the doctrine of creation. And the matter does not stop there . . . we see that this theme of kenosis has profound importance for how we perceive the *humanum* — how we think of the nature of human freedom and of the willed (and graced) response to God.[546]

Arthur Peacocke has created a zone of communication between theology and science, testing the exchange of vocabulary and concepts between these worldviews. "Emptying" acquires a technical form meaning self-limitation, or as God's relinquishing of control to chance. Peacocke analyzes the role of chance and uncertainty in the functioning of the world and speaks of God as having a "self-limited omnipotence and omniscience." He characterizes this self-limited omnipotence further aided by the revelation of Jesus as "vulnerable, self-emptying and self-giving love." Creation involves self-limitation because God has "allowed his inherent omnipotence and omniscience to be modified, restricted and curtailed by the very open-endedness that he has bestowed upon creation."[547] Such limitation is love:

> Thus it is that we come to a recognition that in creating the world continuously God has allowed himself not to have over-riding power over all that happens nor complete knowledge of the direction events will take. The self-limitation is the pre-condition for the coming into existence of free self-conscious human beings, that is, of human experience as such. This act of self-limitation on behalf of the good and well-being, indeed the existence, of another being can properly be designated as being consistent with, and still exemplifying the ultimate character of *God as "Love."* For human life — and it can only be a human analogy — love is supremely manifest in self-limiting, costly action on behalf of the good and existence of another.... Such reflections leading to the notion of God's self-limitation of his omnipotence and omniscience at least render it meaningful to speak of the *vulnerability of God,* indeed the *self-emptying* (kenosis) and *self-giving of God* in creation.[548]

To endow creation with freedom is risky.

> The cost to God, if we may dare so to speak, was in that active self-limitation, of *kenosis,* which constitutes God's creative action — a self-inflicted vulnerability to the very processes God had himself created in order to achieve an overriding purpose, the emergence of free persons.[549]

The continuity of Jesus' kenosis with the vulnerability of God includes the dimension of presence to the world, openness to its unpredictable events, and willingness to risk in order to bring about a greater love and deeper communion. Jesus "risked his all on the faithfulness of God in the hazardous events of his times" in his commitment to God's cause as his own, bringing about the reign of God.[550] Jesus, as the self-expression of God in one particular human, is the self-limitation of God. Jesus is the explicit revelation of the sacrificial love of God.

> So the eventual self-expression of God, in "the fullness of time," in the restricted human person of Jesus can be seen as an explicit manifestation and revelation of that perennial (self-limiting, self-emptying, self-giving) relation of God to the created world which was up until then only implicit in him.... *Because sacrificial, self-limiting, self-giving action on behalf of the good of others is, in human life, the hallmark of love, those who believe in Jesus the Christ as the self-expression of God's own self have come to see his life is the ultimate warrant for asserting that God is essentially "love,"* insofar as any one word can actually refer to God's nature.[551] (emphasis added)

Peacocke interprets the cross as an act of love that has a transforming effect on the beloved. The Holy Spirit fills our hearts with the love of God as we contemplate Jesus and brings us to at-one-ment. We are brought into that same self-offering love for God, by responding to Jesus. This occurs not merely by following the example of Jesus, but by experiencing the power of divine love to create love within our hearts.[552]

Peacocke's understanding of God's self-limitation is one model of divine kenosis. A second figure that addresses the paradigm of power, its relinquishment, and divine creativity, is John Haught. Haught also avoids treating the self-abandonment and self-emptying of God as powerlessness. Instead, he frames this as defenselessness or vulnerability, attributes which have the power to disarm evil. Power is thus redefined as the ability to transform and bring about change. For Haught,

> The image of the self-emptying God lies at the heart of Christian revelation and the doctrine of the Trinity. And it is just this surprising portrait of the divine mystery that allows us to situate intelligibly the process of the world's creation and evolution.[553]

The essence of kenosis in creation is to permit creation's genuine autonomy. Love does not coerce: therefore the loving God will not compel creation's direction, or overwhelm it by God's annihilating presence.

> Indeed, an infinite love must in some sense "absent" or "restrain itself," precisely in order to give the world the "space" in which to become something distinct from the creative love that constitutes it as "other."[554]

God's creative power must involve a certain "self-concealment." As Creator, God acts to preserve the otherness of creation. A paradoxical self-distancing enables this intimate communication with the world *as other.* God's absence, which permits freedom, is precisely how God is present.[555] The idea of empowering freedom recalls Ricoeur's statement that gospel ethics intends the freedom of the other. "It is the whole morality of the love of neighbor, an expression that signifies that the fundamental motivation of ethics is to make your freedom advance as mine does."[556] That God restrains God's power and accepts a vulnerable openness to the outcomes of creation's autonomous processes bears an analogical relationship to human sacrificial restraint that respects the other. God's restraint is not powerlessness; indeed, as Haught shows, it is the very essence of power understood as influence or creative empowerment. To intend the freedom of the other often calls for sacrificial restraint of one's own needs, sacrificial giving to support what another needs to realize his freedom, and not least the sacrifice of withholding one's own opinions to enable the other to discover her own. In conclusion, these examples of kenotic theology show that creativity is a divine method of expressing love that involves self-limitation, risk-taking, and vulnerability to suffering.

## Participation in a Sacrificial Sacramental Economy

If, as these kenotic interpretations of the doctrine of God suggest, God's very being involves self-giving, the mystery of participating in God's life through the sacraments means sharing in a self-giving life.

The sacrificial life of the Christian unfolds within the entire sacramental economy and the mystery of creation. Kevin Seasoltz shows
how the paschal mystery reveals God's way of being, marked by
sacrificial love and giving. It is God's very nature "to give, to be a
for-giving God." Through baptism the believer shares in this mystery,
and likewise expresses the inner disposition of love through concrete
giving.

> Hence our Christian lives always involve us in a participation
> in the dying and rising of Christ which means that they must be
> grounded in the fundamental principles of sacrificial love and
> self-giving. The fullness of God's revelation has taken place in
> the humanity of Jesus, but it is still in the process of being real-
> ized in his church. *The way of God is the way of sacrifice; our
> way to God is the way of self-sacrifice.*[557] (emphasis added)

Furthermore, the self-giving way of holy sacrifice directly relates to
Christian identity. This experience of salvation in accepting the gift
of God's communion conveys new identity upon the human person
and initiates a gift economy. "The human response is described as an
offering of self in the sense that one freely opens oneself to the gift
and embraces the gift, so that one ultimately receives the meaning of
one's life from God."[558]

David Power describes sharing in Christ's self-gift and self-emptying
as a "gift economy."[559] The "embodied gift" of loving service is another way to express what Robert Daly called the "incarnational
spiritualization of sacrifice." The self-emptying gift economy expresses
the mutuality of giving that originates with God in creation, appears in
the Incarnation which renews creation, continues in the sacramental
communion, and gives us hope for the new creation. Human giving
follows from the grace to share God's giving and imitate the praxis
of Jesus.

Self-emptying is thus a mode of divine life to be imitated by the
church, in prayer, in worship, and in charitable action. Coakley offers an interesting interpretation of prayer as a human experience of
kenosis, a further suggestion of how self-giving has a creative and

enlarging effect upon one's religious identity. She considers contemplative prayer as an example of divine empowerment occurring in the form of human vulnerability. She suggests that ultimately we may identify the spiritual practice of wordless prayer as the human mode of kenosis, as love-in-vulnerability.

> This is to take a few leaps beyond the notion of kenosis as a speculative Christological theory about the incarnate life of Jesus; but if the majority of New Testament commentators are correct, then the "hymn" of Philippians 2 was, from the start, an invitation to enter into Christ's extended life in the church, not just to speculate dispassionately on his nature. The "spiritual" extension of Christic kenosis, then ... involves an ascetical commitment of some subtlety, a regular and willed *practice* of ceding and responding to the divine. ... In prayer ... it is "internalized" over time in a peculiarly demanding and transformative fashion. ... What I have elsewhere called the "paradox of power and vulnerability" is I believe uniquely focused in this act of silent waiting on the divine in prayer. This is because we can only be properly "empowered" here if we cease to set the agenda, if we "make space" for God to be God.[560]

Coakley suggests that in dying to self, or in ceding one's usual limits in prayer, one discovers a paradoxical affirmation of the depth of one's own self. Such sacrifice is not reductive; rather, it expands the self. Again, the theme of sacrifice as creating space, or as a setting aside, hearkens to the etymological roots of sacrifice as "making sacred," to set aside for God. The openness to divine depths via the emptiness of prayer is akin to the possibilities Suchocki finds in the transient finitude of creation. Setting aside space for the other reflects God's creativity. Paradoxically, emptiness and fullness are in harmony. Emptiness by its very freedom permits the promise of growth not yet seen. The space of listening can be as vital to the discerning soul as an empty moment in the rhythm of music, or a heartbeat, a pause and a new pulse of life.

There is a consistent revelation of God's self-giving way of being, in Jesus' historical life, in a sacrificial theology of the Trinity and creation, and in the sacramental life of the church. Through the sacramental economy, the believer is empowered to participate in God's giving by communion with Christ, which frees and renews human giving.[561] To participate in that economy is the graced living out of the human identity as *imago Dei*.

### Being the Image as a Task Oriented to Earthly Creation

To be the image of God as a reflection of God's dynamic self-giving and creativity expresses the challenge of Christian identity as an unfolding vocation. Christians seek to realize a community of love and justice because of faith that God has endowed all persons with dignity as created in the image of God. Being the image is a starting point that inspires Christian self-interpretation, and is also an ongoing guiding aim for ethical action. David Tracy connects the interpretive and ethical tasks of Christian theological anthropology by recognizing how the symbol of creation in the image of God challenges and guides ethical action.

> Christians continue to believe that all human beings are made in the image and likeness of God. They have become far more sensitive, however, to the fact that this theological indicative, in the present world, must also function as an imperative. The task of human beings, on this newer reading, is to actualize what they are potentially, and to actualize that reality in the struggle for a *not-yet* acknowledged dignity of every human person: for the need, in sum, for human rights in their full social, economic, cultural, political, civic, and religious dimensions.[562]

Mary Catherine Hilkert draws a striking conclusion from theological reflection on the image of God in light of the Trinity that underscores the communal dimensions of anthropology expressed by Ricoeur's intersubjective anthropology, Tracy's call to honor human rights in all their dimensions, and Schillebeeckx's attention to social and ecological justice. If God is a triune, relational mystery of love, then "human persons do not image God primarily as individuals, but rather in right relationship with one another. The image of God is reflected most clearly in communities characterized by equality, respect for difference and uniqueness, and mutual love."[563] These are precisely the conditions that support a right understanding of sacrifice. Ironically, until conditions of greater equality and justice are more fully realized, sacrifice under harsh circumstances is often needed to bring about such community.

References to humanity as the image of God recall the Edenic creation of all creatures, intended for a Sabbath harmony. The symbol thus represents the ideal of a peaceful earthly community. However, as Hilkert states, in reality widespread violence and exploitation exposes the image of God as a desecrated image. The suffering person is the threatened image, the crucified face of Jesus today.[564] Indeed, the image of God transcends the humanity of all persons: Schillebeeckx identifies the suffering image of God in crucified nature.[565] Through the contrast between the ideal and humanity's present state, the symbol expresses an obligation to overcome the violence and misery that threatens the poor and the earth itself. The symbol has the power to envision humanity as belonging to a sacred creation. That religious vision is essential in the movement to capture people's imaginations and consciences for the transformation of our social and ecological practices. Being the image is a call for just relations among human communities and their extended natural family, the earth's interdependent ecologies. By acknowledging that the dignity and harmony of the creation community is not yet realized, Tracy points also to the eschatological nature of the hermeneutics of sacrifice. Being the image is an indicative that must become an imperative: a challenge to work toward, but one that is not yet realized. Being the image is a task set before humanity. The struggle to realize humanity's potential reaches for what Tracy called above "a *not-yet* acknowledged dignity." To recognize that dignity spurs liberative action so that all may more fully experience being what they already are, but have not yet fully realized. Being the image is a creative task.

## III. *Renewing the Symbol of Sacrifice*

The cross of Jesus Christ and God's creativity are fundamentally related as expressions of God's self-giving love; together the symbols
establish a foundation for sacrifice in Christian discipleship. To recover the creation-based symbol of the *imago Dei* as the human
reflection of God's sacrificial love connects to the deep mystery of divine life behind all giving, places sacrifice in the creation community,
and highlights the creative purpose of sacrifice, oriented to the new
creation. Divine creativity thus provides the criterion, context, and
aim for sacrifice. Creativity is a criterion for sacrifice such that sacrifice should envision the fullest possibilities for the global community
becoming a new creation. Even when accepted for this purpose, sacrifice itself is not the goal, but a means to fulfill an aim. Our earthly
creation is the context: a suffering macrocosm of suffering persons,
unjust structures, and oppressed ecologies crying out for the sacrificial self-limitation of humankind. The new creation and the reign of
God are orienting aims for sacrifice.

The symbol of sacrifice functions in relation to Christian identity and action; both the symbol as a revealer of reality, and ethical
practice are at stake. The fundamental values of self-sacrifice and
self-realization are complementary impulses within sacrifice, and not
centrifugal forces that oppose sacrifice to realization. Tracy's analysis
of the polarity of participation and distance in both religious symbols
and sensibilities provides a theoretical framework with which to analyze and integrate the values contained in the paradox of self-sacrifice
and self-realization.

David Tracy observes that the most basic polarity of religion is

between those religious forms which heighten an awareness of
human participation in whatever powerful reality is construed
to be the Whole or the Ultimate as distinct from those religious forms which heighten a sense of human distance from that
same reality (e.g., the utterly transcendent God of monotheism).
In the life of most traditions both these religious sensibilities

are present to some extent but almost always one sensibility (participation or distance) dominates.[566]

Tracy has analyzed the basic polarity of religious sensibilities marked by participation and distance as part of his theory of religious experience, interpreted as a classic event containing an excess of meaning. "Any classic will produce its meaning through the related strategies of intensification of particularity and intensification of distanciation in expression."[567] The religious experience of radical mystery encounters mystery as both disclosed and concealed. While there are parallels between the paradigm of participation and distance that Tracy outlines and the poles of self-sacrifice and self-realization that this project describes, my main purpose is not to explicate those thematic connections, but to present Tracy's paradigm in support of the claim that a full understanding of sacrifice requires integrating both polarities.

Tracy's description of both religious sensibilities amplifies the polarity hitherto called the paradox of self-realization and self-sacrifice. A sense of radical participation emphasizes the experience of the whole, the *plenum,* the sacred that fills one's world and grounds the felt synthesis of "cosmos-person-God."[568] The contrasting sensibility is a powerful awareness of distance, an unworthiness and separation from the utterly transcendent God. Religious forms express the two radical religious sensibilities in the shape of rituals, symbols, myths, theologies, and institutions. Manifestation classically appears in preverbal symbols and rituals, verbal myths, and religious manifestations of sacred space. Manifestation expresses a sacred time of origins and creation, in rituals and forms that express again and again the overcoming of chaos. Proclamation "initially ruptures the realm of manifestation" by the power of the disruptive word. In the historical time of proclamation, persons confront and reveal the power of God through the word.[569]

All images of this transcendent God — even icons — are now named mere idols unable to honor the transcendence of God and the ethical-political-religious human sense of responsibility toward the Other and all others. Responsibility to the neighbor, not merely the friend, emerges in history as one of the greatest achievements of the prophetic biblical traditions.[570]

Tracy draws these contrasts strongly but urges that they be taken not as dialectical opposites, forcing an exclusive choice, but as a polarity. The religious sensibilities of participation and distance imply each other. "The forms of manifestation and proclamation are not binary opposites. They are polarities whose dialectic is one where each primary emphasis implies and never rejects the other in order to posit itself."[571] To sustain both polarities is to gain a richer understanding of the variety of religious apprehensions of God and diverse forms of human response.

Tracy provides an example from the Catholic tradition of how a religious perception of humanity maintains both polarities, and at the same time returns us to considering the person as being in the image of God:

> The greatest strength of the Catholic ethical vision is its insistence, in its ethics, on the religious polarity of manifestation and proclamation: the relational person, not the modern purely autonomous individual; rights with the vision of the Good including always the common good; ecological theologies with justice for the poor, oppressed, marginalized — who in fact suffer most from ecological devastation; love and justice; liturgical awareness and the struggle for social justice; Franciscan spirituality and Jesuit spirituality; the responsibility of the human in history and the participation of the human (as micro-cosmos; as *imago dei* in nature).[572]

A *participatory* sensibility enlarges the aim guiding an individual's action by enhancing the experience of what Tracy calls the felt synthesis of the cosmos and the person. A religious sensibility marked by a sense of participation in the whole enables self-understanding, commitment, love, and union, in terms of the other. A sense of participation grounds our awareness of intersubjective dependence on other

people and the sustaining environment. A religious sense of participation also implies an awareness of belonging to the creation as a
beloved creature, called to loving self-giving. In the felt synthesis one's
connection to others and to the earth is embraced, and known as an
inner relation. The horizon of ethical duty expands. Suddenly there
are more neighbors. This expansion complements the enlargement of
aims by tragic awareness explored by Ricoeur (chapter 3), and the
disorienting, surprising revelation in the gospel parables examined by
Schillebeeckx (chapter 4).

A *proclamatory* ethical sensibility testifies to a religious judgment
upon the sinful distance between the ideal of justice and community
and actual circumstances in which persons harm and exploit each
other and the earth. Awareness of one's connections to the whole
does not thereby confer unlimited responsibility. Ethical duty implies
heeding anew the call of the other, and also honoring one's commitments to oneself. The norm does not merely impose the rights
of the other over against a presumed selfishness but challenges the
individual to include one's own aims when forming a reciprocal, mutual, self-inclusive ethic. The norm thus expresses two duties, the
constancy owed to the other, and also the care owed to the self, as
an authentic response to Jesus' message of God's forgiveness and desire for human well-being. The ethical proclamation also denounces
idealized suffering, glorified death, and endurance. The religious attitude that acknowledges the distance between the transcendent other
and the limited and sinful self indeed urges one's duty to the other,
but paradoxically also affirms the claim of the self against those
who would stifle it. The religious sensibility that Tracy describes as
strongly aware of ethical obligations extends the range of obligation,
thereby enhancing the religious sensibility of participation in the fullness of being. The prophetic proclamation that God requires justice
can also herald a new, historic, ecological consciousness.[573]

The theme of creation and its anthropological symbol, the person
created in the image of God, manifest a religious sensibility of participation in the whole. This participatory, relational identity intersects
with the proclamatory expression of distance and ethical obligation

(signified by the cross) precisely at the symbol of sacrifice. Becoming the image calls for critical, justice-oriented, and self-affirming sacrificial action expressing both the sensibilities of participation and distance.

The tradition will continue to have living relevance for the contemporary situation if theology engages in critical reflection on the actual situation and on liberating praxis, and if communities reflect upon the tradition with fidelity and retrieve overlooked resources.[574] A hermeneutics of sacrifice seeks to examine the tension of self-sacrifice and self-realization in a way that is faithful to contemporary experience and Christian tradition. The reader is called into the desert of criticism, and beyond again to seek the fullest meanings of the symbol. Additional symbolic possibilities for sacrifice as a manifestation of Christian love exist in the deeper origins of the manifestation of divine self-giving on the cross through kenotic interpretations of God's creativity as self-giving. This restoration of the symbol of sacrifice has also been suggested by retrieving the theme of self-realization and wholeness in the gospel message as a necessary context for the interpretation of sacrifice. This journey of criticism and renewal has depended on the wager that the polarity of self-giving responsibility and self-affirmation as part of the whole will empower a theology of sacrifice. A theology of sacrifice is not complete if it attends only to "losing one's life." Restoring the symbol makes explicit the complementarity of new life with loss and change, as polarities in the process of *sacrificial creativity*. Both dimensions are needed. They are not opposites, but paradoxically enrich each other. An integrated symbol of sacrifice seeks the resolution of the paradox of self-sacrifice and self-realization by suggesting the fruitfulness of *creative sacrifice*. The term "sacrifice" points to the losses incurred in self-giving under finite, oppressive, and even tragic situations; the modifier "creative" eschews defining sacrifice by suffering or loss alone. "Creative sacrifice" points to the realization of a new and fuller reality or identity by means of self-gift that seeks the well-being of self and other.

The story of creation in the Book of Genesis acknowledges that chaos precedes creation. Though God may be credited with creation *ex nihilo* in subsequent theological reflection, human attempts at creativity do in fact emerge out of chaos, the present situation with its challenges, painful memories, hostilities, and sheer resistance to the novelties and discomfort of change. Tracy offers an intriguing comparison of chaos and creation at the human level in the ritual of an initiate undertaking the painful transition to a new identity. This is a "willingness to enter chaos on behalf of a manifesting cosmos: thus the often frightening negative liminal experience of the rituals of initiation (pain, terror, solitude, nudity) before any *communitas,* much less any restored cosmos, is possible."[575] For humankind, sacrificial creativity can often only be envisaged in terms of the loss we experience. Chaos exists before community is built; identity is shaped by the sometimes painful commitments one makes; even prayer embraces a kind of loss or vulnerability. For God, space-making, freedom-making, even time-making, is a generativity without loss. For finite persons, loss is a constant reality and the hope for which we sacrifice is at times seen only through a glass darkly.

The mystery of self-realizing sacrifice partakes of the ethical paradox of solidarity with the neighbor — to love the neighbor as one's self. Such sacrifice is holy if it seeks wholeness for the self and the other. It is a means to salvation but remains marked by the contingencies of human life, both the simply finite and sinfully oppressive burdens. Christian sacrifice is an offering of self to show love of God and neighbor, in response to the experience of God's love, that reflects the sacrifice of Jesus Christ on the cross and God's kenosis in creation. Being the image of God implies that our self-giving should reflect God's creative self-giving. It is God's way of being as Creator that renews the idea of sacrifice as creative self-giving. Christian sacrifice realizes one's identity as the image of the sacrificing God.

# STUDY GUIDE

## Chapter One / The Sacrificial Nature of Christian Life

• The ethical meaning of sacrifice as self-giving represents an evolution from ritual or cultic sacrifice in a history-of-religions sense. How does the Hebrew insight about the true meaning of inner sacrifice play into the Christian "spiritualization" of sacrifice? For example, how are the themes of justice and interiority employed by the prophets in their own critique of sacrifice?

• Christian interpretation of Jesus' death as a sacrifice relied on many images from the Hebrew Scriptures. What major sacrificial themes and images did the evangelists retrieve? In what way might early Christian and first-century Jewish ideas about sacrifice have influenced each other? What does the continued use of sacrificial images, although in new and flexible ways, suggest about the significance of sacrifice in the religious heritage of the early Christians?

• Discuss how sacrifice is or is not an essential interpretation of the death of Jesus.

• Reflect on the core meaning of discipleship. Is such a meaning possible? On what should it be based?

• How is the word "sacrifice" generally employed in theological, biblical, ecclesial, and pastoral contexts? In your experience, do these usages express a tension between self-denial and self-discovery?

## Chapter Two / The Feminist Critique of a Distorted Ideal of Sacrifice

+ List several concrete examples of actions that are commonly asked of women that intuitively seem to be a negative experience of sacrifice.

+ In general Christian practice and understanding, in your view, are there readily identifiable ways to draw distinctions between inappropriate sacrifice and genuine self-giving? What gives these approaches validity?

+ What factors affect the way a Christian understanding of sacrifice changes over time, especially in terms of terminology? What cultural, pastoral, and social contexts are most significant for interpreting sacrifice today? How is the traditional meaning both changed and preserved in contemporary reflection? Give examples. In your view, is tradition helped or hindered by interpretation?

+ How are suffering and passivity treated in different atonement theories? Are these themes essentially related to sacrifice as an ideal form of Christian love?

+ How have feminists and womanists argued that the cross encourages victimization? What aspect of their critiques do you find insightful?

+ What is the role of self-love in Christian life? Does self-love function in the discernment of how to give and relate to others? How is this message conveyed in scripture, church teaching, or prayer traditions?

+ How is the experience of self-love complicated by gender, class, or other social traits?

+ Is it appropriate to view some sacrifice as sinful?

## Chapter Three / Interpreting Selfhood through Giving to the Other

+ What is the role of the other in the development of one's identity? Is this a conscious process?

- In what way is it useful to explain the self in terms of promises rather than "stable" characteristics such as genetic inheritance, social background, and basis aspects of personality?

- Is it adequate to define one's identity as "I am the one who will be there for you...? act in these ways for you?" What prior bases of identity exist — and can these be considered apart from other relationships?

- Is it easier to be guided by a vision or aim of the good life, rather than by explicit rules and norms? How might this play out in terms of a guiding ideal of sacrificial love?

- Is total giving of oneself to the other ideal, risky, legitimate? What does it mean for Ricoeur to call this illogical?

- What are the limits of requests that another can make of me? Do these limits change if the other is a family member? Elderly? Sick? An abstract good like a cause of social justice or the environment?

## Chapter Four / Sacrifice in a Creation Catechism

- Why does Schillebeeckx insist that finitude is good? Do you agree?

- Are humans destined to limitations and to sacrifice? Is this fair? If sacrifice is inevitable, can it be virtuous?

- Is it reasonable to interpret an action, especially an extreme one, in light of the rest of a life?

- How does Schillebeeckx's discussion of the cross occurring "despite" God's will relate to your own understanding of the crucifixion?

## Chapter Five / Sacrifice in the Image of God

- How do the cross and Creation both express similar themes of the love of God?

- How does this affect your view of the Trinity or the Incarnation?

- How might one judge a sacrifice as creative? What future criteria would you employ?

# NOTES

## Introduction

1. Paul Ricoeur, *Figuring the Sacred: Religion, Narrative, and Imagination,* trans. David Pellauer, ed. Mark I. Wallace (Minneapolis: Fortress Press, 1995), 284–87.

2. Oliver O'Donovan, *The Problem of Self-Love in St. Augustine* (New Haven, CT: Yale University Press, 1980), 1.

3. David Tracy, *The Analogical Imagination: Christian Theology and the Culture of Pluralism* (New York: Crossroad, 1981), 236.

4. Augustine, *The City of God,* trans. Marcus Dods (New York: Modern Library, 1993), Book X.1.

5. This and subsequent quotations by Augustine are from *City of God,* X.3

6. See O'Donovan's analysis of Augustine's views on self-love; O'Donovan, 1. Augustine addresses self-love as part of the inner image of God in *The Trinity,* 5, ed. John E. Rotelle, OSA, trans. Edmund Hill, OP, *The Works of Saint Augustine: A Translation for the 21st Century* (Brooklyn: New City Press, 1991), XIV.11.

7. *Towards a Global Ethic: An Initial Declaration, 1993 Parliament of the World's Religions* (Chicago: Council for a Parliament of the World's Religions, 1993). John Paul II, "The Ecological Crisis: A Common Responsibility. Message of His Holiness Pope John Paul II for the Celebration of the World Day of Peace, January 1, 1990," in *And God Saw That It Was Good: Catholic Theology and the Environment,* ed. Walter Grazer and Drew Christiansen (Washington, DC: United States Catholic Conference, 1996). Benedict XVI, "The Human Person, the Heart of Peace," Message of His Holiness Pope Benedict XVI for the Celebration of the World Day of Peace," January 1, 2007.

## Chapter One / The Sacrificial Nature of Christian Life

8. "The Kutadanta Sutta," in *The Long Discourses of the Buddha: A Translation of the Digha Nikaya* (Boston: Wisdom Publications, 1995).

9. Frances M. Young, *Sacrifice and the Death of Christ* (London: SPCK, 1975), 9.

10. Robert J. Daly, *The Origins of the Christian Doctrine of Sacrifice* (Philadelphia: Fortress Press, 1978), 138.

11. See Jon Douglas Levenson, *The Death and Resurrection of the Beloved Son: The Transformation of Child Sacrifice in Judaism and Christianity* (New Haven, CT: Yale University Press, 1993), 200.

12. Conversation with Ewert Cousins, October 11, 2003.

238 *Notes*

13. Turner, "Sacrifice as Quintessential Process," 90.

14. Ibid., 111.

15. Henri Hubert and Marcel Mauss, "Essai sur la nature et la fonction du sacrifice," *L'Année Sociologique* 2 (1899); English translation: *Sacrifice: Its Nature and Function* (Chicago: University of Chicago Press, 1964); Victor Turner, "Sacrifice as Quintessential Process: Prophylaxis or Abandonment?" in *Blazing the Trail: Way Marks in the Exploration of Symbols,* ed. Edith Turner, Anthropology of Form and Meaning series (Tucson: University of Arizona Press, 1992); and René Girard, *Violence and the Sacred,* trans. Patrick Gregory (Baltimore: Johns Hopkins University Press, 1977).

16. Turner, "Sacrifice as Quintessential Process," 99.

17. Daly, *The Origins of the Christian Doctrine of Sacrifice,* 5.

18. Joseph Henninger, "Sacrifice," in *The Encyclopedia of Religion,* ed. Mircea Eliade (New York: Macmillan, 1987), 544.

19. Daly, *The Origins of the Christian Doctrine of Sacrifice,* 32.

20. Joseph A. Fitzmyer, *Pauline Theology: A Brief Sketch* (Englewood Cliffs, NJ: Prentice-Hall, 1967), 47.

21. Young, *Sacrifice and the Death of Christ,* 25, 28, and 73.

22. One may also become the victim of another's sacrifice. History is full of the chronicles of genocide, ghettos, and witchhunts, in which bloody sacrifice emerges from social crises. René Girard argues that this pattern runs through mythology and the deepest levels of culture. Girard's theory of sacrifice and culture is an important critique of a social dynamic whereby violence and its ritual replication in sacrifice are used to release tension and channel human aggression. According to Girard, this pattern is based on mimetic rivalry, the imitation of the desires of another that accelerates into contagious violence and targets a surrogate victim to release this violence. By showing that the gospel rejects violence and does not acclaim the act of crucifixion, Girard makes it possible to reclaim a notion of sacrifice that is free of the taints of sacralized violence. This is a more positive view of Christian sacrifice and a development from his earlier work. His conviction that biblical religion stands with history's victims buttresses the spiritualization of sacrifice as an ethical action in Hebrew and Christian religious thought. His larger concern with mimetic rivalry and violence as the fundamental dynamic of human relationships and the source of culture is tangential to this work. Nonetheless, he anticipates the important distinction between a passive victim of sacrifice and an agent who chooses sacrifice as a willed expression of dedication to the divine. This question of passive versus active sacrifice will recur in chapters 2 and 3. René Girard, *I See Satan Fall Like Lightning,* trans. James G. Williams (Maryknoll, NY: Orbis Books, 2001), 147.

23. Hubert and Mauss, "Essai sur la nature et la fonction du sacrifice," 51.

24. Turner, "Sacrifice as Quintessential Process," 97.

25. Hubert and Mauss, "Essai sur la nature et la fonction du sacrifice," 98–100.

26. Ibid., 61.

27. Young, *Sacrifice and the Death of Christ,* 22.

28. Turner attributes Hubert and Mauss's reductive strategy to the school of Émile Durkheim (Turner, "Sacrifice as Quintessential Process," 109). According to this view, the sacral world is projected by society; the god is the idealized society.

Through sacrifice, the individual recognizes and responds to the collective forces of society, represented as gods. Henninger notes that this theory has been criticized for drawing universal conclusions from exceptionally developed sacrificial systems, like the Hebrew and Vedic societies Hubert and Mauss analyzed, which may not apply to more "primitive" societies (Henninger, "Sacrifice," 551).

29. Turner disagrees with Hubert and Mauss's view of sacrifice that supernatural forces are conferred upon the sacrifier through the victim. The killing and consuming of the victim enable unity with the god. Turner, "Sacrifice as Quintessential Process," 58.

30. Ibid., 95. Turner's study of the Ndembu community demonstrates that they symbolically sacrifice themselves in order to restore community life for everyone. Sacrifice is not experienced as an impersonal structured flow of divine force. Sacrifice transforms the community, inspiring harmony, rather than attempting to hide or justify its failings.

31. Ibid., 89.

32. Ibid., 111.

33. Ibid., 112.

34. Ibid., 111–12.

35. Abraham J. Heschel, *The Prophets* (New York: Jewish Publication Society of America, 1962), 196.

36. Ibid., 200.

37. Ibid., 219.

38. Ibid., 210.

39. Daly, *The Origins of the Christian Doctrine of Sacrifice*, 21.

40. Texts criticizing cultic formalism include Amos 5:21–27, Hosea 6:6 (cf. Matthew 9:13, 12:7), Isaiah 1:10–17, Isaiah 29:13 (cf. Mark 7:6–7, Matthew 15:8–9), Jeremiah 7:1–28, Micah 6:6–8, Psalms 50:12–15, 51:18–19, and Sirach 34:24–35.4.

41. Young, *Sacrifice and the Death of Christ*, 33.

42. Ibid., 31.

43. Jon Levenson, "Sacrifice as the Basis of Worship: An Overlooked Commonality of Judaism and Catholicism," Annual Driscoll Lecture in Jewish-Catholic Studies, Iona College, New Rochelle, NY, March 11, 2003.

44. Paula Fredriksen notes the distinction between sacrifices that achieve purity and sacrifices that atone for sins. Levitical impurity, such as contact with the dead or sexual activity, is cleansed by immersion or sprinkling with water, and waiting until the passing of a liminal time (a sunset, a week). Moral impurity resulted from voluntary actions that were sinful and defiling. These include adultery, ritual infanticide, and idolatry. These sins were purged by blood sacrifice on the holy day of Yom Kippur. Atonement for sin called for sacrifice when practical, she argues, but if not possible (as in the case of thousands of Diaspora Jews who could not come to the Temple), their inner repentance was understood as a petition for the atoning effect of sacrifice. Paula Fredriksen, *Jesus of Nazareth, King of the Jews: A Jewish Life and the Emergence of Christianity* (New York: Alfred A. Knopf, 1999), 68.

45. Daly, *The Origins of the Christian Doctrine of Sacrifice*, 24.

46. Young, *Sacrifice and the Death of Christ*, 39.

47. Louis-Marie Chauvet, *Symbol and Sacrament: A Sacramental Reinterpretation of Christian Existence,* trans. Patrick Madigan and Madeleine Beaumont (Collegeville, MN: Liturgical Press, 1995), 241.

48. Ibid., 33–34.

49. Ibid., 56.

50. This is the sacrifice of praise cited in Hebrews 13:15, which quotes Psalm 50:23 (He who sacrifices thank offerings honors me), and Hosea 14:2 (that we may offer the fruit of our lips). Chauvet argues that the *todah,* a type of communion sacrifice, represents a precedent for the Christian meal. Ibid., 243–44.

51. Daly, *The Origins of the Christian Doctrine of Sacrifice,* 48. See also Jon Douglas Levenson, *The Death and Resurrection of the Beloved Son: The Transformation of Child Sacrifice in Judaism and Christianity* (New Haven, CT: Yale University Press, 1993), 209.

52. Regarding the extension of expiatory significance to all sacrifices, Grigsby cites especially Ex. R. xv.12: "I mercifully take pity on you by means of the Paschal Blood and the blood of circumcision, and I propitiate your souls." Bruce H. Grigsby, "The Cross as an Expiatory Sacrifice in the Fourth Gospel," *Journal for the Study of the New Testament* 15 (1982): 66, n. 22.

53. Daly takes a strong view of the influence of the *Aqedah* on the evangelists. In his view, while the actual relationships between the themes of the *Aqedah* and New Testament texts must be taken as provisional, "the sacrificial soteriology of the New Testament can no longer be adequately discussed apart from the *Aqedah.* Daly, *The Origins of the Christian Doctrine of Sacrifice,* 52. In contrast, Brown does not feel that this tradition is a decisive influence, because he feels that the Isaac material that goes beyond Genesis 22 developed too late to influence the gospel accounts. The few parallels he does accept are restricted to their common use of the text of Genesis 22 and so do not pertain to a separate, later *Aqedah* tradition that reverences Isaac's willing acceptance of death. Raymond E. Brown, *The Death of the Messiah: From Gethsemane to the Grave. A Commentary on the Passion Narratives in the Four Gospels,* ed. David Noel Freedman, Anchor Bible Reference Library (New York: Doubleday, 1993), 2:1435–44. Philip Davis and Bruce Chilton argue against an early dating for the *Aqedah* tradition, and do not see evidence of a developed atoning soteriological view of Isaac's death beyond the original Genesis account before the end of the first century. However, in their argument Davis and Chilton intensify the criteria needed to recognize a strand of the *Aqedah* tradition. Having first defined the *Aqedah* as "a haggadic presentation of the vicarious atoning sacrifice of Isaac" (515), now only with a "definitive substitute" for the Temple cult "can we begin to use the term *Aqedah*" (529). They partially acknowledge the complexity and difficulty of dating these developments, since older strands may be preserved in later texts. As scholars continue to examine this issue, earlier dating for the *Aqedah* seems more probable. See also Daly, "Eucharistic Origins: From the New Testament to the Liturgies of the Golden Age," *Theological Studies* 66, no. 1 (March 2005): 3–22.

54. Philip R. Davis and Bruce D. Chilton, "The Aqedah: A Revised Tradition History," *Catholic Biblical Quarterly* 40 (1978): 516. Although he does not refer to the *Aqedah* as a possible solution, Bruce similarly observes that when the cult was cut off, the Pharisees "had to give serious thought to the rationale of the expiation

of sin in its absence. Frederick Fyvie Bruce, "Kerygma of Hebrews," *Interpretation* 23 (1969): 12.

55. Levenson, *Death and Resurrection,* 213.

56. Davies and Chilton, "The Aqedah," 529, 540. The authors stress that the link of Christ to Isaac is an implicit relation.

57. Brown, *The Death of the Messiah,* 1449.

58. Daly, *The Origins of the Christian Doctrine of Sacrifice,* chapter 3.

59. Fredriksen, *Jesus of Nazareth,* 40.

60. Chauvet, *Symbol and Sacrament,* 309.

61. See also Daly, *The Origins of the Christian Doctrine of Sacrifice,* 24.

62. Chauvet, *Symbol and Sacrament,* 240.

63. Texts that show Jesus' criticism of the cult include Acts 6:13–15, Matthew 26:61, Mark 14:58, and Mark 2:19–22. Ibid., 245.

64. Daly, *The Origins of the Christian Doctrine of Sacrifice,* 56.

65. Fredriksen, *Jesus of Nazareth,* 201, 213.

66. Jonathan Klawans, "Interpreting the Last Supper: Sacrifice, Spiritualization, and Anti-Sacrifice," *New Testament Studies* 48, no. 1 (2002). In terms of whether or not Jesus and the early communities looked upon the Last Supper as an "anti-sacrificial practice," Klawans warns against employing "spiritualizing" terminology if this means (a) taking an ahistorical view of the Last Supper, (b) judging that as a radical, anti-purity event, it could not have taken place as described, or (c) crediting Jesus with establishing an "alternative sacrificial programme" (2). Klawans emphasizes that provocative, distinctive symbolic acts such as those of Jesus and the prophets intend to provoke without meaning to thoroughly controvert, reject, or "spiritualize" the existing practices. He notes that in many studies of sacrifice, "sacrifice always comes up short, whether it is deemed to be corrupt, flawed, outmoded, or spiritually inadequate" (8) and suggests that "we should speak more neutrally of a metaphorical use of sacrificial language" (13).

67. Fredriksen, *Jesus of Nazareth,* 200.

68. Chauvet, *Symbol and Sacrament,* 240–46.

69. Edward Schillebeeckx, *Jesus: An Experiment in Christology,* trans. Hubert Hoskins (New York: Seabury Press, 1979), 311.

70. Paul Fiddes, *Past Event and Present Salvation: The Christian Idea of Atonement* (London: Darton, Longman & Todd, 1989), 44–45.

71. Schillebeeckx observes that the number of verses representing the soteriological tradition that view Jesus' death as atoning, as a "vicarious propitiatory sacrifice," is surprisingly small. He does not therefore conclude that the tradition is secondary, or derived from reflection on the Isaiah 53 tradition or the martyr tradition. Instead, he asks if the tradition must be traced back to some historical memory of Jesus' own attempt to interpret his coming death. Schillebeeckx, *Jesus,* 311.

72. Fredriksen, *Jesus of Nazareth,* 118. "For I received from the Lord what I also delivered to you, that the Lord Jesus on the night when he was betrayed took bread, and when he had given thanks, he broke it, and said, 'This is my body which is for you. Do this in remembrance of me.' In the same way also he took the cup, after supper, saying, 'This cup is the new covenant in my blood. Do this, as often as you drink it, in remembrance of me.' For as often as you eat this bread and drink the cup, you proclaim the Lord's death until he comes" (1 Cor. 11:23–36). "And as

they were eating, he took bread, and after blessing it broke it and gave it to them, and said, 'Take; this is my body.' And he took a cup, and when he had given thanks he gave it to them, and they all drank of it. And he said to them, 'This is my blood of the covenant, which is poured out for many. Truly, I say to you, I will not drink again of the fruit of the vine until that day when I drink it new in the kingdom of God' " (Mark 14:22–25).

73. David Tracy, "Metaphor and Religion: The Test Case of Religious Texts," in *On Metaphor,* ed. Sheldon Sacks (Chicago: University of Chicago Press, 1979), 95.

74. Ibid., 91.

75. Schillebeeckx, *Jesus,* 403–38.

76. Ibid., 283, 289.

77. Ibid., 294.

78. Acts 4:10, 2:22–24, 5:30–31, 10:40, Luke 13:31–33, 11:47–48, 49ff. Ibid., 275.

79. See Acts 8:26–40, and Luke 24:25–27, 48. Daly, *The Origins of the Christian Doctrine of Sacrifice,* 58.

80. The "salvation history canon" includes: Mark 8:31a, 9:12b, Luke 17:25, Mark 9:31a, 14:41c, Luke 24:7, 13–32, Galatians 3:13, Mark 2:1–3:6, 12:13–27, 14:21, 15:33. Schillebeeckx, *Jesus,* 284.

81. Ibid., 293.

82. Ibid., 292.

83. Raymund Schwager, *Jesus in the Drama of Salvation: Toward a Biblical Doctrine of Salvation,* trans. James G. Williams and Paul Haddon (New York: Crossroad, 1999), 103.

84. Schillebeeckx, *Jesus,* 294.

85. John P. Galvin, "Retelling the Story of Jesus: Christology," in *The Praxis of Christian Experience: An Introduction to the Theology of Edward Schillebeeckx,* ed. Robert J. Schreiter and Mary Catherine Hilkert (San Francisco: Harper & Row, 1989), 57.

86. Brown, *The Death of the Messiah,* 1462.

87. Ibid., 931.

88. Ibid., 901.

89. Ibid., 1435–44.

90. Ibid., 1050.

91. Ibid., 1463.

92. Ibid., 980.

93. Ibid., 931.

94. Ibid., 1012.

95. Ibid., 1104.

96. Ibid., 907.

97. Raymond E. Brown, *The Community of the Beloved Disciple* (New York: Paulist Press, 1979), 118–19.

98. Grigsby, "The Cross as an Expiatory Sacrifice in the Fourth Gospel," 52, 63.

99. Brown, *The Death of the Messiah,* 901.

100. Grigsby, "The Cross as an Expiatory Sacrifice in the Fourth Gospel," 60–62.

101. Brown, *The Community of the Beloved Disciple,* 43.

102. Ibid., 48.

103. Ibid., 116.

104. See Raymond E. Brown, *The Anchor Bible Commentary: The Gospel According to John* (Garden City, NY: Doubleday, 1966), 58–63, for three views of the Passover lamb.

105. Brown, *The Community of the Beloved Disciple*, 123.

106. Bradley H. McLean, "The Absence of an Atoning Sacrifice in Paul's Soteriology," *New Testament Studies* 38 (1992): 543.

107. Daly constitutes the canons of "dying for" and "sin offering" as follows: Jesus dies for us: 2 Corinthians 5:14–15, Romans 5:6–11, Romans 8:23, Galatians 2:20, Ephesians 5:2, 25, Colossians 1:24, 1 Timothy 2:5–6, Titus 2:13–14, 1 John 3:16. Jesus is a sin offering: 2 Corinthians 5:21, Galatians 3:13, Romans 8:3, Romans 3:24–25, 2 Corinthians 5:21. Daly, *The Origins of the Christian Doctrine of Sacrifice*, 61. Chauvet would add to this canon 2 Corinthians 9:12 and 1 Corinthians 16:1–2 regarding offerings to the Jerusalem church; see p. 254.

108. Young cautions that this sacrificial vocabulary for Christ's death and Christian life does not mean that the Temple cult was the basis for Christian worship. Rather, their early worship modeled synagogue practices. The Christian concrete experience of sacrifice would also have included first fruit offerings: presenting bread and wine in thanksgiving and charity. There would be sacrifices of communion, including the fellowship meal and the Eucharist. The full sublation of Jewish sacrificial practice into the ritual remembrance of Jesus, and the belief that Temple sacrifice was fulfilled and no longer relevant, did not occur until the Letter to the Hebrews. Young, *Sacrifice and the Death of Christ*, 50, 61–63.

109. McLean, "The Absence of an Atoning Sacrifice in Paul's Soteriology," 531.

110. Ibid., 545.

111. Ibid., 543.

112. Ibid., 534.

113. Ibid., 537.

114. Roland de Vaux, *Ancient Israel: Its Life and Institutions*, trans. John McHugh (New York: McGraw-Hill, 1961), 416.

115. Richard D. Nelson, " 'He Offered Himself': Sacrifice in Hebrews," *Interpretation* 57, no. 3 (2003): 259. See also Leviticus 4:26b and 11:44.

116. See n. 52 on p. 240 above.

117. McLean, "The Absence of an Atoning Sacrifice in Paul's Soteriology," 537.

118. Charles R. Erdman is referring to Romans 3:25; see *The Epistle of Paul to the Romans* (Philadelphia: Westminster Press, 1925), 59.

119. Complex scriptural antecedents lie behind Fitzmyer's schema. First, sacrifice effects reconciliation. Second, sacrifice effects expiation of the concrete effects of sin, which are guilt and pollution. This is not an expiation of God's wrath — the sacrifice does not act to remove God's anger at sinners. The term *hilasterion* refers to expiating sins, but is never associated in the Septuagint with God's wrath as its object. It is associated with the Day of Atonement, and the sprinkling of blood on the Ark of the Covenant. In relationship to Jesus' death, blood brings atonement as a process initiated by the Father and based on the love of Jesus. Fitzmyer warns against a juridical interpretation of this act of love and dedication. The symbolism of sacrifice is separate from a juridical metaphor of debt, though both are present in the Scriptures. The sacrificial process of atonement should not be systematized into

a theory of exchange. The third effect of sacrifice is redemptive liberation. As a slave is redeemed, we are freed from the law through union with Jesus, whose death broke the curse of the law. Again, Fitzmyer warns against emphasizing the dimension of exchange of the ransom motif. The emphasis is upon liberation. Finally, the fourth effect is justification. Fitzmyer, *Pauline Theology*, 45–51.

120. X. Leon-Dufour, *Face à la mort: Jésus et Paul* (Paris: Seuil, 1979), 182–97.

121. John A. T. Robinson, *Wrestling with Romans* (Philadelphia: Westminster Press, 1979), 46.

122. Ibid., 69.

123. Ibid., 94.

124. Ibid., 58.

125. Fitzmyer, *Pauline Theology*, 39.

126. Ibid., 69.

127. Ibid., 39.

128. Nicholas H. Taylor, "Conflicting Bases of Identity in Early Christianity: The Example of Paul," in *Handbook of Early Christianity*, ed. Jean Duhaime, Anthony J. Blasi, Paul-André Turcotte (Walnut Creek, CA: Altamira Press, 2002), 596.

129. Young, *Sacrifice and the Death of Christ*, 50.

130. Daly, *The Origins of the Christian Doctrine of Sacrifice*, 70.

131. Bruce, "Kerygma of Hebrews," 4.

132. Nelson, " 'He Offered Himself': Sacrifice in Hebrews," 254.

133. See also Bruce, "Kerygma of Hebrews," 10.

134. Ibid., 6.

135. Nelson, " 'He Offered Himself': Sacrifice in Hebrews," 255.

136. Ibid., 258.

137. Bruce, "Kerygma of Hebrews," 7. Psalm 110:1–4: "The LORD says to my Lord: 'Sit at my right hand, until I make your enemies your footstool.' The LORD sends forth from Zion your mighty scepter. Rule in the midst of your enemies! Your people will offer themselves freely on the day of your power, in holy garments; from the womb of the morning, the dew of your youth will be yours. The LORD has sworn and will not change his mind, 'You are a priest forever after the order of Melchizedek.' "

138. Ibid., 9.

139. Schillebeeckx, *Christ*, 269.

140. Nelson reads the drama of sacrifice within Hebrews as a complex, three-stage ritual including the death of the victim, the priest's entrance into the Holy Place, and the purifying use of blood. He observes that it is possible to render Hebrews 9:22 as "the shedding of blood" or as "pouring out" or "sprinkling of blood." The latter two translations emphasize casting blood around the altar, not the death of the victim per se. Nelson, " 'He Offered Himself': Sacrifice in Hebrews," 252–55. On the contrary, Wilfrid Stott argues that the writer of Hebrews intends to limit the moment of sacrifice to the moment of Christ's death. He states that the Levitical description of the Day of Atonement ritual applies the word "offer" only to the death of the bull and goat, but not to the high priest's action bringing blood into the Holy Place. There the terms used are "take" and "bring": which contain "no special sacrificial meaning." Therefore, "whatever is to be understood by 'blood' undoubtedly it referred to the work of Christ on Calvary, that is as 'blood shed.' " Stott therefore argues that

Christ's death is the offering, and the entry into the heavenly holy Place is possible only because of blood shed. Wilfrid Stott, "Conception of 'Offering' in the Epistle to the Hebrews," *New Testament Studies* 9 (1962): 64–65.

141. Bruce, "Kerygma of Hebrews," 15.

142. McLean, "The Absence of an Atoning Sacrifice in Paul's Soteriology," 552.

143. Bruce, "Kerygma of Hebrews," 16.

144. Nelson, " 'He Offered Himself': Sacrifice in Hebrews," 254.

145. Schillebeeckx, *Christ,* 252.

146. Ibid., 254.

147. Chauvet, *Symbol and Sacrament,* 249.

148. Brown, *Death,* 1107.

149. Ibid., 1106.

150. Dietrich Bonhoeffer, *The Cost of Discipleship,* trans. R. H. Fuller (New York: Macmillan, 1963), 79.

151. Chauvet, *Symbol and Sacrament,* 298, Leon-Dufour, 182–97, and Schillebeeckx, *Jesus,* 274–94.

152. Schillebeeckx, *Jesus,* 311.

153. This "new Temple" theology is stated in 1 Corinthians, 2 Corinthians, and 1 Thessalonians. It is also well developed in the Deutero-Pauline works and 1 Peter. Daly, *The Origins of the Christian Doctrine of Sacrifice,* 60–61. According to Daly (83), the central texts for describing Christian discipleship as the "liturgy of life" are Romans 12:1–2, 15:15–16, Hebrews 10:19–25, 12:18–13:1b, and 1 Peter 2.4–10. Ernest Best adds Hebrews 13:15–16, Philippians 2:17, 4:18, 2 Timothy 4:6, and Revelation 8:3. Ernest Best, "1 Peter 2:4–10: A Reconsideration," *Novum Testamentum* 11, no. 4 (1969): 280. Klawans corroborates the importance of Temple imagery and sacrificial practices for Christian community and life, 11.

154. Daly, *The Origins of the Christian Doctrine of Sacrifice,* 59–63.

155. Ibid., 65.

156. Chauvet would add 2 Corinthians 9:12 and 1 Corinthians 16:1–2 regarding offerings to the Jerusalem church. Chauvet, *Symbol and Sacrament,* 254.

157. Daly, *The Origins of the Christian Doctrine of Sacrifice,* 64.

158. Ibid.

159. Ibid., 67.

160. Best, "1 Peter 2:4–10: A Reconsideration," 273.

161. Ibid., 285.

162. Gerhard Kittel, "ιερατευμα" in *Theological Dictionary of the New Testament,* ed. Geoffrey W. Bromiley (Grand Rapids: Eerdmans, 1964–76), 249.

163. Best, "1 Peter 2:4–10: A Reconsideration," 288.

164. David Hill, " 'To Offer Spiritual Sacrifices' (1 Peter 2:5): Liturgical Formulations and Christian Paraenesis in 1 Peter," *Journal for the Study of the New Testament* 16 (1982): 57.

165. Daly, *The Origins of the Christian Doctrine of Sacrifice,* 76.

166. Young, *Sacrifice and the Death of Christ,* 95. Using terminology of later debates that contrasts the sacrifice of Christ and the disciple, the "objective" efficacy of Christ's saving work as an obedient sacrifice becomes realized "subjectively" for the Christian community when they respond and share in his sacrifice. However its objective meaning may be construed, the power of Christ's sacrifice becomes

actualized when the disciple embodies the same spirit in his or her own life. Response is made concrete in one's own self-sacrifice and sacramental participation in the life of the church. Ibid., 96. For more on the debate over models of atonement framed as the difference between the objective/subjective models of Anselm and Schleiermacher, see Mary Grey, *Feminism, Redemption and the Christian Tradition* (Mystic, CT: Twenty-Third Publications, 1990); Fiddes, *Past Event and Present Salvation;* and Gustaf Aulén, *Christus Victor: An Historical Study of the Three Main Types of the Idea of Atonement,* trans. A. G. Hebert (New York: Macmillan, 1951).

167. Daly, *The Origins of the Christian Doctrine of Sacrifice,* 73.

168. Bruce, "Kerygma of Hebrews," 10.

169. Ibid. This idea is also present in Ephesians 2:22, 1 Peter 1:2, 19, 22, and Revelation 22:3.

170. Nelson, " 'He Offered Himself': Sacrifice in Hebrews," 263.

171. Chauvet, *Symbol and Sacrament,* 251.

172. Daly, *The Origins of the Christian Doctrine of Sacrifice,* 82–83.

173. John McKenzie, "The Gospel According to Matthew," in *The Jerome Biblical Commentary,* ed. Joseph A. Fitzmyer, Raymond E. Brown, and Roland E. Murphy (Englewood Cliffs, NJ: Prentice-Hall, 1968), 77.

174. Geza Vermes, *Jesus the Jew: A Historian's Reading of the Gospels* (Philadelphia: Fortress Press, 1973), 58.

175. R. Kevin Seasoltz, "Another Look at Sacrifice," *Worship* 74 (2000): 409.

176. Otto Semmelroth, "Sacrifice I. Concept of Sacrifice; III. Sacrifice of Christ," in *Sacramentum Mundi: An Encyclopedia of Theology,* ed. Karl Rahner (New York: Herder & Herder, 1970), 389. This is also the chief explanation of sacrifice that Jon Levenson offered in "Sacrifice as the Basis of Worship: An Overlooked Commonality of Judaism and Catholicism," Annual Driscoll Lecture in Jewish-Catholic Studies, Iona College, New Rochelle, NY, March 11, 2003.

177. Semmelroth, 389.

178. Ibid., 390.

179. Karl Rahner has made this idea a pillar of his theology, expressed as the "unity of love of God and neighbor." Karl Rahner, "Reflections on the Unity of the Love of Neighbor and the Love of God," in *Theological Investigations* 6 (London: Darton, Longman & Todd, 1974), 236, 244, 247, and Karl Rahner, "Experience of Self and Experience of God," in *Theological Investigations* 13 (London: Darton, Longman & Todd, 1975), 128.

180. For a review of Girard's work, as an example of a theory that does not secularize sacrifice, and discussion of the interaction of his theory with other disciplines, see Leo D. Lefebure, "Victims, Violence and the Sacred: The Thought of René Girard," *Christian Century* (1996): 1226.

## Chapter Two / The Feminist Critique of a Distorted Ideal of Sacrifice

181. Dietrich Bonhoeffer, *The Cost of Discipleship,* trans. R. H. Fuller (New York: Macmillan, 1963), 176.

182. John Kilgallen reflects upon self-interest as part of Jesus' message in John Kilgallen, "The Wisdom of Jesus: Gospel Reflections," *Chicago Studies* 42, no. 2 (2003): 195–220.

183. Daniel Thompson has clearly outlined this theory of history as it relates to development of Christian doctrine. Daniel P. Thompson, "Schillebeeckx on the Development of Doctrine," *Theological Studies* 62 (2001): 306–8.

184. Fernand Braudel, *The Perspective of the World*, vol. 3, *Civilization and Capitalism: 15th–18th Century*, trans. Siân Reynolds (New York: Harper & Row, Publishers, 1984), 71.

185. I will be primarily considering feminist critique as it applies to sacrifice at the individual level, but note that sacrifice also has an ambivalent meaning on a social level. The negative experience of sacrifice includes political strategies that trade the well-being of a minority for perceived national benefit through genocide and scapegoating. A positive dimension of societal sacrifice can be an active awareness of social values and commitment to them on an institutional and political level. For instance, there are wartime examples such as Victory Gardens and patriotic exhortations to rationing. Examination of sacrifice on the communal level is beyond the scope of this study; however, I acknowledge the question since the principles and dynamics that govern individuals may apply also to groups.

186. See Thompson's article (n. 183 above) also for a more extensive treatment of Schillebeeckx's epistemological framework, as a series of hermeneutical circles that structure understanding within historical change.

187. Mark Muldoon, *On Ricoeur*, Wadsworth Notes (Belmont, CA: Wadsworth/Thomson Learning, 2002), 40.

188. Elizabeth Cady Stanton et al., eds., *The Women's Bible*, vol. 1 (New York: European Publishing Co., 1895), 84.

189. Grey, *Feminism, Redemption and the Christian Tradition*, 16.

190. Martin Luther, *Lectures on Genesis 2:18*, in Luther's *Works*, vol. 1, ed. Jaroslav Pelikan (St. Louis: Concordia, 1958), 111.

191. Mary Daly, *Beyond God the Father: Toward a Philosophy of Women's Liberation* (Boston: Beacon Press, 1973), 100.

192. Betty Friedan, *The Feminine Mystique* (New York: Norton, 1963).

193. Arlie Russell and Anne Machung Hochschild, *The Second Shift: Working Parents and the Revolution at Home* (New York: Viking, 1989).

194. I will focus on one article they have written because of its specificity for this topic; many theologians have expressed similar concerns. The essays published in Maryanne Stevens, *Reconstructing the Christ Symbol: Essays in Feminist Christology* (New York: Paulist Press, 1993), provide an excellent overview of feminist critiques of Christology in general and theologies of the cross in particular.

195. Joanne Carlson Brown and Rebecca Parker, "For God So Loved the World?" in *Violence against Women and Children: A Christian Theological Sourcebook,* ed. Carol J. Adams and Marie M. Fortune (New York: Continuum, 1995), 37.

196. Ibid.

197. Ibid., 39.

198. Ibid., 40–44.

199. Grey, *Feminism, Redemption and the Christian Tradition*, 16.

200. Brown, 50.

201. Ibid., 51.

202. Ibid., 57.

203. Story told by Rebecca Ann Parker in Rita Nakashima Brock and Rebecca Ann Parker, *Proverbs of Ashes: Violence, Redemptive Suffering, and the Search for What Saves Us* (Boston: Beacon Press, 2001).

204. Ibid., 53.

205. Paul Fiddes, *Past Event and Present Salvation: The Christian Idea of Atonement* (London: Darton, Longman & Todd, 1989), 66.

206. See again Daly, *The Origins of the Christian Doctrine of Sacrifice,* 32.

207. Fiddes, *Past Event and Present Salvation,* 66–77.

208. Gustaf Aulén, *Christus Victor: An Historical Study of the Three Main Types of the Idea of Atonement,* trans. A. G. Hebert (New York: Macmillan, 1951).

209. See again Joseph A. Fitzmyer, *Pauline Theology,* 51.

210. Louis-Marie Chauvet, *Symbol and Sacrament: A Sacramental Reinterpretation of Christian Existence,* trans. Patrick Madigan and Madeleine Beaumont (Collegeville, MN: Liturgical Press, 1995), 316.

211. Maurice Bellet, *Le Dieu pervers* (Paris: Editions du Cerf, 1987), 15–40.

212. Fiddes, *Past Event and Present Salvation,* 97.

213. Ibid., 101.

214. Paul Tillich, *Systematic Theology: Existence and the Christ* (Chicago: University of Chicago Press, 1951–63), 2:203.

215. Fiddes, *Past Event and Present Salvation,* 214.

216. Hans Urs von Balthasar, *Studies in Theological Style: Clerical Styles,* vol. 2, *The Glory of the Lord: A Theological Aesthetics* (Edinburgh: T. & T. Clark, 1984), 246–54.

217. Elizabeth A. Johnson, *She Who Is: The Mystery of God in Feminist Theological Discourse* (New York: Crossroad, 1997). See chapter 12.

218. Viktor Emil Frankl, *Man's Search for Meaning: An Introduction to Logotherapy* (New York: Simon & Schuster, 1963).

219. Classical Christology acknowledges that at some level Jesus had both a human and divine will; a doctrine defined at the Third Council of Constantinople. This distinction explains how Jesus' human will experiences a natural struggle with his death but overcame this divergence to accept the will of his Father, which is one with his divine will.

220. Grey, *Feminism, Redemption and the Christian Tradition,* 175.

221. Ibid.

222. JoAnne Marie Terrell, *Power in the Blood? The Cross in the African American Experience* (Maryknoll, NY: Orbis Books, 1998), 184–86.

223. Delores S. Williams, *Sisters in the Wilderness: The Challenge of Womanist God-Talk* (Maryknoll, NY: Orbis Books, 1993), 144.

224. Ibid., 149.

225. Ibid., 162.

226. Ibid., 164.

227. Ibid., 234.

228. Terrell, *Power in the Blood?* 107.

229. Ibid., 144.

230. Ibid., 107.

231. Jacquelyn Grant, *White Women's Christ and Black Women's Jesus* (Atlanta: Scholars Press, 1989), 219.

232. Terrell, *Power in the Blood?* 109.

233. Kelly Brown Douglas, *The Black Christ* (Maryknoll, NY: Orbis Books, 1994), 16.

234. Terrell, *Power in the Blood?* 112.

235. Ibid., 125.

236. Studs Terkel, *Race: How Blacks and Whites Think and Feel About the American Obsession* (New York: New Press, 1992), 21.

237. Terrell, *Power in the Blood?* 140.

238. Cheryl Townsend Gilkes, *"If It Wasn't for the Women . . . " Black Women's Experience and Womanist Culture in Church and Community* (Maryknoll, NY: Orbis Books, 2001), 187.

239. Ibid., 195.

240. Barbara Hilkert Andolsen, "Agape in Feminist Ethics," *Journal of Religious Ethics* 9 (1981): 69.

241. Ibid., 70.

242. Anders Nygren, *Agape and Eros: A Study of the Christian Idea of Love,* trans. A. G. Hebert (London: Society for Promoting Christian Knowledge, 1932), 217.

243. Reinhold Niebuhr, *The Nature and Destiny of Man,* 1: *Human Nature* (New York: Scribner's, 1941), 263.

244. Ibid., 265.

245. Andolsen, "Agape in Feminist Ethics," 70.

246. Gene Outka, *Agape: An Ethical Analysis* (New Haven, CT: Yale University Press, 1972), 221, 300.

247. Martin C. D'Arcy, *The Mind and Heart of Love, Lion and Unicorn: A Study in Eros and Agape* (New York: Meridan Books, 1956).

248. Andolsen, "Agape in Feminist Ethics," 72.

249. Ibid., 76.

250. Ibid., 79.

251. Valerie Saiving, "Human Experience: A Feminine View," *Journal of Religion* 40 (1960).

252. For example, Carol Gilligan, *In a Different Voice: Psychological Theory and Women's Development* (Cambridge, MA: Harvard University Press, 1982).

253. Saiving, "Human Experience: A Feminine View," 26.

254. Ibid., 27.

255. Ibid., 31.

256. Ibid., 38.

257. Ibid., 37.

258. Ibid., 36.

259. Ibid., 33.

260. Serene Jones diagnoses these theoretical camps as the "rock" versus the "hard place" in a very useful review of leading feminists and their stance vis-à-vis experience. See Serene Jones, "Women's Experience between a Rock and a Hard Place," in *Horizons in Feminist Theology: Identity, Traditions, and Norms,* ed. Rebecca Chopp and Sheila Greeve Davaney (Minneapolis: Fortress Press, 1997).

261. Linell Elizabeth Cady, "Identity, Feminist Theory, and Theology," in *Horizons in Feminist Theology: Identity, Traditions, and Norms,* ed. Rebecca Chopp and Sheila Greeve Davaney (Minneapolis: Fortress Press, 1997), 22–26.

262. Nygren, *Agape and Eros,* 33.

263. Andolsen, "Agape in Feminist Ethics," 70.

264. Nygren, *Agape and Eros,* 97.

265. Andolsen, "Agape in Feminist Ethics," 80.

266. Augustine, *The City of God,* XIV.7 (emphasis added).

267. Ibid., XIV.13.

268. Ibid., XIV.28.

269. Ibid., XIV.5

270. Karl Rahner, *Foundations of Christian Faith: An Introduction to the Idea of Christianity,* trans. William V. Dych (New York: Crossroad Publishing Company, 1976), 76, and Karl Rahner, "Theology of Freedom," in *Theological Investigations* 6 (London: Darton, Longman & Todd, 1974), 185, 189, 193.

271. Marjorie Hewitt Suchocki, *The Fall to Violence: Original Sin in Relational Theology* (New York: Continuum, 1995). Other scholars, notably Judith Plaskow, have made similar investigations of sin. Judith Plaskow, *Sex, Sin and Grace: Women's Experience and the Theologies of Reinhold Niebuhr and Paul Tillich* (Washington, DC: University Press of America, 1980). Plaskow's admirable study investigates the presuppositions and flaws in both Niebuhr and Paul Tillich's theology of sin in greater depth but also narrower focus than does Suchocki, which is why I have chosen to analyze Suchocki's more systematic study.

272. Suchocki, *The Fall to Violence,* 22.

273. Ibid., 18.

274. Although she brings up this sin associated with female experience, Suchocki challenges a gender identification that ascribes pride to men and hiding exclusively to women. Such generalizing presumes that gender is marked by essential characteristics and risks associating women with "nature." These are double-edged swords in feminist anthropology. Though they slay the monster of universalized, normative male experience, a new dragon appears in its place: a feminine nature that restricts women's potential while honoring it. This "natural" or material emphasis can come uncomfortably close to the patriarchal association of women with nature that reduces women to a maternal role. A norm based on "women's experience" should affirm bodily experience and the social intersubjectivity of a relational anthropology. This approach has the virtue of integrating spirit and body, instead of opposing materiality to the higher, "spiritual" qualities of intelligence and freedom long associated with maleness in the hierarchical dualism that has characterized sexism.

275. Ibid., 18.

276. Ibid., 42.

277. Ibid., 40.

278. Ibid., 43.

279. Ibid., 97.

280. Fiddes, *Past Event and Present Salvation,* 159.

281. Margaret A. Farley, "New Patterns of Relationship: Beginnings of a Moral Revolution," *Theological Studies* 36 (1975): 63.

282. Suchocki, *The Fall to Violence,* 54. The question of the interrelationship of Whiteheadian and classic Christian themes in Suchocki's work is beyond the scope of the present work. There are complex points of contact as well as similarities in their definitions of transcendence. See Alfred North Whitehead, *Process and Reality: An Essay in Cosmology,* ed. David Ray Griffin and Donald W. Sherburne (New York: The Free Press, 1978), and Leo D. Lefebure, *Toward a Contemporary Wisdom Christology: A Study of Karl Rahner and Norman Pittenger* (Lanham, MD: University Press of America, 1988), 121–38.

283. Suchocki, *The Fall to Violence,* 161.

284. Regarding her view of God's creation by influence, see ibid., 56. Leo D. Lefebure compares Whitehead's interpretation of God's presence to the world with a traditional understanding of grace in a way that highlights the subtlety of the former. Whitehead uses the term "grace" in a way very different from Christian usage. It is rather more like Pelagius's understanding of grace as the "loving presence of God permeating the natural cosmic process; Augustine's grace was an additional, gratuitous gift of God which could in no way be identified with the creative and sustaining power of God in the natural order." See Lefebure, *Wisdom Christology,* 138.

285. Suchocki, *The Fall to Violence,* 84. Suchocki also simplifies Niebuhr's view of existential anxiety, reducing it to a fear of mortality, which she dismisses.

286. Ibid., 57.

287. It is fascinating to observe that these are very similar to the qualities of Augustine's mental trinity, which are the unified functions of memory, understanding, and will. These form the apex of spiritual equality to be found in human consciousness, which he reaches at last in Book XIV of *The Trinity.* It is hard to see why spirit is not the measure of Suchocki's view of transcendence, especially if spirituality is recognized as organically grounded in the material processes of human consciousness. Augustine, *The Trinity,* vol. 5: *The Works of Saint Augustine: A Translation for the 21st Century,* ed. John E. Rotelle, trans. Edmund Hill (Brooklyn: New City Press, 1991), 382.

288. Suchocki, 67.

## Chapter Three / Interpreting Selfhood through Giving to the Other

289. Paul Ricoeur, *Oneself as Another,* trans. Kathleen Blamey (Chicago: University of Chicago Press, 1992), 354.

290. Ricoeur's work resists systemization partly because understanding never comes to a final word or definitive synthesis. Knowledge is bound by the Kantian notion of the limit concept: the totality of truth is an ideal that can be never entirely known. Muldoon, *On Ricoeur,* 2. Ricoeur continues to explore these themes over the course of his career in a variety of specific problematics, often addressing the nature of the will. His early works were intended as part of a multivolume work, *Philosophy of the Will.* These works include *Freedom and Nature: The Voluntary and Involuntary, Fallible Man,* and *The Symbolism of Evil,* the last two together comprising *Finitude and Guilt.* These are phenomenological analyses of the human will that explore the voluntary nature of human freedom, as tempered by involuntary processes of character, the unconscious, and finitude. By focusing on the will, Ricoeur critiques a view that sees human willing as part of simple objective

252

knowledge of reality. Ricoeur instead believes that incarnate existence "overflows the objectivity" of the intellect. The will is an experience in which we are submerged, not a show of the control our intelligence has over life. Muldoon, *On Ricoeur*, 12. Venema also observes the similarity between the hermeneutical circle of attestation and Augustine's motto, *credo ut intelligam*. Henry Isaac Venema, *Identifying Self-hood: Imagination, Narrative, and Hermeneutics in the Thought of Paul Ricoeur*, ed. Katherine K. Young, McGill Studies in the History of Religions (Albany: State University of New York Press, 2000), 2.

291. Ibid., 13.

292. Ricoeur's philosophical outlook reflects the rising importance of Georg W. F. Hegel, Edmund Husserl, and Martin Heidegger in his intellectual circles, moving away from Cartesian-Kantian orthodoxy. He denies the "claim of immediacy, adequation, and apodicity made by the Cartesian cogito and the Kantian 'I think.'" Lewis Edwin Hahn, ed., *The Philosophy of Paul Ricoeur*, Library of Living Philosophers (Chicago: Open Court, 1995), 4. Ricoeur's thought is based on a thorough knowledge of Husserl's phenomenology. In *Husserl: An Analysis of His Phenomenology* (1967), Ricoeur criticized Husserl's view of the transcendental and immediate self-presence of the subject. Ricoeur did not accept Husserl's position that consciousness could be separated from the natural world and empirical consciousness, a pure consciousness grounded in itself. Such a subject is a foundational ego, which asserts its own point of reference: "an egology without ontology." Paul Ricoeur, *Husserl: An Analysis of His Phenomenology*, Northwestern University Studies in Phenomenology and Existential Philosophy, trans. Edward G. Ballard and Lester E. Embree (Evanston, IL: Northwestern University Press, 1967), 194. Ricoeur remains engaged in the reflexive paradigm of French philosophy, which focuses on the possibility of self-understanding gained by the subject's ability to know and to will. However, reflexive philosophy is unable to show exactly how the cogito, the "I think," recognizes the self. Ricoeur's hermeneutics is "a radical transformation of reflexive philosophy in that any knowledge of the self is never immediate — it must be both discovered and recovered. Ricoeur felt that Husserl's analysis obscured the connection of the subject oblivious to the surrounding world. All otherness is reduced to the overarching vanity of the ego. Ricoeur instead critically adapted Heidegger, Merleau-Ponty, and the later Husserl, who recognized that consciousness is intersubjective. Meaning does not appear immediately, but must be "wrestled" from the surrounding world. In dialogue with Gabriel Marcel, Ricoeur attended to the theme of mysteries. There is a difference between a problem to be logically solved and a mystery. He also appreciated his distinction between the lived body and the body-object, and the existence of the other co-affirmed in the affirmation of my existence. These are themes that remain important in Ricoeur's thought. From Karl Jaspers, Ricoeur observes the influence of the philosophy of existence. This is the "mode of authentic existence for the individual when one moves beyond a rational scientific objectification of the self and existence. This authentic existence is characterized by freedom, infinite possibilities, loneliness and responsibilities." This freedom is challenged by boundary situations of death, suffering, guilt, chance, and conflict. There is a tragic cast to life in Jasper's view. Ricoeur admired this enduring sense of certitude and order despite tragedy. Muldoon, *On Ricoeur*, 15–18.

293. "It is in these objects, in the widest sense of the word, that the Ego must lose and find itself." Paul Ricoeur, *Freud and Philosophy: An Essay on Interpretation,* trans. Denis Savage (New Haven, CT: Yale University Press, 1970), 43. "Whether one looks back to the will to power of the Nietzschean man, to the generic being of the Marxist man, to the libido of the Freudian man, or whether one looks ahead to the transcendent home of signification which we designate here by the vague 'the sacred,' the home of meaning is not consciousness but something other than consciousness." Ibid., 55.

294. Paul Ricoeur, *From Text to Action,* trans. Kathleen McLaughlin and David Pellauer (Evanston, IL: Northwestern University Press, 1991), 15.

295. Mark I. Wallace, "From Phenomenology to Scripture? Paul Ricoeur's Hermeneutical Philosophy of Religion," *Modern Theology* 16, no. 3 (2000): 302. As a phenomenologist, Ricoeur brackets the claims of such texts to exhibit proven reality and considers them as resources for lived possibilities. As a theological thinker, Ricoeur identifies the fullest possibilities of the self as the possibilities imagined by the biblical texts, appropriated by the subject. Ricoeur deliberately attempts to bracket his personal religious convictions and biblical faith, even while he is aware that religious motivations may affect how he approaches or chooses certain problems. In the effort to separate the worlds of philosophy and theology, Ricoeur does not construct a philosophical proof or use philosophy as a substructure to faith. Faith is a risk, a risk that is verified only by the quality of the life lived upon its wager. Ibid., 303.

296. Hermeneutics in this early phase is an indirect approach to being, specifically evil, not in its fundamental structures, but as it is expressed in language. Ricoeur discovered that the phenomenology of the will must proceed through the detour of symbolic language. Philosophy and phenomenology could analyze purposive action without recourse to symbolic language, but the problem of evil evades direct language. Evil is an "involuntary conundrum at the very heart of the voluntary." The problem of language must then be addressed en route to approaching the philosophy of the will; it is not simply a topic in the philosophy of language as such. Paul Ricoeur, *The Rule of Metaphor: Multidisciplinary Studies in the Creation of Meaning in Language,* trans. Robert Czerny with Kathleen McLaughlin and John Costello (Toronto: University of Toronto Press, 1977), 316. In the later 1960s, Ricoeur shifts his focus from the symbol to the text. Ricoeur considers the dilemma of how interpreting symbols leads to existential concepts that reflect on existence. To address this dilemma, Ricoeur will redefine philosophical reflection as hermeneutics. He does so in *Freud and Philosophy: An Essay on Interpretation* (1970) and in *The Conflict of Interpretations* (1969).

297. Paul Ricoeur, *The Symbolism of Evil,* Religious Perspectives Series, ed. Ruth Nanda Anshen, trans. Emerson Buchanan (Boston: Beacon Press, 1967), 16.

298. Ibid., 348.

299. Both symbol and metaphor create and express new possibilities of meaning. The full breadth of Ricoeur's technical treatment of metaphor, symbol, and narrative is beyond the scope of this work, although a brief mention shows the similar ways they produce meaning. Ricoeur defines symbols as signings that communicate, evoke, or suggest meaning in *The Symbolism of Evil,* Religious Perspectives Series, ed. Ruth Nanda Anshen, trans. Emerson Buchanan (Boston: Beacon Press, 1967), 15. The symbol offers a double intentionality by presenting a literal and a figurative meaning.

The symbol often represents a spontaneous recognition of deeper meaning. Ricoeur calls the symbol a "word-image," a complex production of language that designates one meaning "in and through the first intentionality." See *Freud and Philosophy: An Essay on Interpretation*, trans. Denis Savage (New Haven, CT: Yale University Press, 1970), 16. A metaphor is a figure of speech. Metaphor has the power to create new meaning by the very tension it draws between two terms, a power that resides in the joining verb to be. "The metaphorical 'is' at once signifies both 'is not' and 'is like.' If this is really so, we are allowed to speak of metaphorical truth, but in an equally 'tensive' sense of the word 'truth.' " See *The Rule of Metaphor: Multidisciplinary Studies in the Creation of Meaning in Language*, trans. Robert Czerny with Kathleen McLaughlin and John Costello (Toronto: University of Toronto Press, 1977), 7. The creative meaning in the metaphor's conjunction of terms can be compared to the truth found in the tension of a paradox and the depth of a symbol.

300. Ricoeur, *Freud*, 26.

301. Ibid., 33.

302. Ibid., 36. Ricoeur also takes up the question of disclosure in all texts in contrast to revelation in Ricoeur, *Metaphor*, 321.

303. Ibid. Reflection appropriately yields existential concepts, the distillation of symbolic meaning. At the same time restorative reflection renews the elemental power of the symbol. Critical thinking pares away explanation as etiology or history from myth and restores myth to symbol. Ricoeur, *Metaphor*, 320.

304. Ricoeur, *The Symbolism of Evil*, 351.

305. Ricoeur, *Metaphor*, 318.

306. Ibid., 356.

307. The volumes of *Time and Narrative* (1983–85) are companion texts to the *Rule of Metaphor*. Both works consider the semantic innovations produced by discourse. The semantic innovation of narrative is to invent a plot whose temporal unity connects characters and events. In *Time and Narrative* Ricoeur examines the humanized time of narrative, which is neither cosmological nor subjectively psychological time. "Time becomes human time to the extent that it is organized after the manner of narrative; narrative, in turn, is meaningful to the extent that it portrays the features of temporal existence." Paul Ricoeur, *Time and Narrative*, trans. Kathleen McLaughlin and David Pellauer (Chicago: University of Chicago Press, 1985), 2:13.

308. Muldoon, *On Ricoeur*, 65.

309. *Oneself as Another* begins by analyzing the topics of language, action, and identity, and continues to ethics, morality, and practical wisdom. Chapters 1 and 2 begin with the philosophy of language as a necessary detour through language about the self. The second grouping, chapters 3 and 4, considers the philosophy of action. From how we speak about the self, Ricoeur turns to the question of who is speaking and who is acting. The third grouping presents the dialectic between two modes of personal identity. These are the modes of identity as sameness, as contrasted with selfhood. The question of personal identity takes up chapters 5 and 6. Chapters 7, 8, and 9 address the ethical and moral determinations of action.

310. Ricoeur's hermeneutics of the self attacks the claims of auto-foundationalism and certainty. "The polysemy of otherness, which I shall propose in the tenth study, will imprint upon the entire ontology of acting the seal of the diversity of sense that foils the ambition of arriving at an ultimate foundation, characteristic of the cogito

philosophy." At the same time, Ricoeur's distrust of an absolute epistemology and desire to work in an autonomous philosophical mode prevents yoking this reflection to biblical faith. Ricoeur, *Oneself as Another,* 21.

311. Ricoeur, *Oneself as Another,* 311.

312. Two principal distinctions include that between true-Being and false-Being, and between Being as substance and Being as power and act. Peter Kemp, "Another Language for the Other: From Kierkegaard to Levinas," *Philosophy and Social Criticism* 21, nos. 5–6 (1995): 45. Aristotle's notion of Being as actuality/potentiality has limitations from Ricoeur's point of view. Aristotle appears to connect substance to act and power, whereas Ricoeur is interested in exploring the distinctions between these notions. In Ricoeur's view, Aristotle's actuality does not effectively oppose an ontology of substance. By this Ricoeur means an ontology of substance that emphasizes the given, physically grounded aspects of character — the aspects Ricoeur considers to be least determinative of *ipse*-identity, identity rooted in decisions and promises. Change is relegated to Aristotle's discussion of praxis, while potentiality is directed to the fulfillment of motion. Aristotle's concept of praxis does enlarge the concept of action beyond the limits of analytical philosophy. However, as Ricoeur expresses it, there are "signs of resistance" in *Metaphysics* to reappropriating act and power for an ontology of selfhood. Also, Aristotle's idea of action and power seems to imply "a source of movement or change, which is another thing than the thing moved." The relation of power and act as originating in the agent is not considered. See *Metaphysics,* E. 2. Ricoeur, *Oneself as Another,* 304.

313. Charles Reagan, "Personal Identity," in *Ricoeur as Another: The Ethics of Subjectivity,* ed. Richard A. Cohen and James L. Marsh (Albany: State University of New York Press, 2002), 13.

314. Ricoeur's attention to the acting subject also directs his use of Heidegger's thought. In Heidegger's ontology, selfhood is in a relation of dependence upon its mode of being, which is Dasein. Selfhood exists as the dependence of "a modality of self-apprehension and as a mode of being in the world." Selfhood thus depends upon Dasein, and care mediates between selfhood and Dasein. Ricoeur considers the ontological dimension of action as an equivalent to Heidegger's notion of care. "Only a being that is the self is in the world...the being of the self presupposes the totality of world that is the horizon of its thinking, acting, feeling — in short, of its care." As Kemp showed, it is important for Ricoeur that the self is intimately connected with the world. The world in fact hermeneutically circumscribes Ricoeur's quest for the self, via the detour by way of things. "There is no world without a self who finds itself and acts it; there is no self without a world that is practicable in some fashion." It is by acting that one is grounded in the world. The acting self presupposes the whole world, and so presupposes the horizon of its care. Ricoeur, *Oneself as Another,* 309.

315. Kemp, "Another Language for the Other," 49.

316. Ricoeur, *Oneself as Another,* 297.

317. Ricoeur breaks down the approach to action into three discourses, whose purposes are to describe, narrate, or judge. This is the "polysemy of action": description, narration, and prescription (Muldoon, *On Ricoeur,* 12). Anglo-American analytical philosophy and the human sciences describe action. The role of analysis is to specify what can be said about action. Analysis provides rules of discourse for

speaking about the subject. For example, P. F. Strawson's linguistic analysis demonstrates the way language refers to persons or things. Persons are bodies, but also souls, yet are considered as one thing. A person can receive both physical and psychological predicates, but not two series of predicates, applied as if to two subjects (one the physical person, the other the psychological person). The linguistic analysis of speech acts, as exemplified by J. L. Austin, illustrates the active accomplishment of speech such as promising. Ricoeur is intrigued by the intersection of language and action represented by speech acts. This type of speech also demonstrates the presence of the other who is addressed. Speech means conversation among persons. Despite these insights, analysis has its limits. Linguistic analysis risks a referential narrowness that mistrusts the extralinguistic order. In the extreme, analysis may merely cycle through a chain of language games. Analytical philosophy may overlook the "who" in its minute attention to "how." By focusing on things and events, philosophy of action somehow evades profound attention to the agent. The agent who has a motive for action is overlooked in the attention to the act itself. It is necessary to proceed from identifying the reference of language to the acting subject herself. Reagan, "Personal Identity," 12. Ricoeur explains why he uses analytic philosophy in *Rule of Metaphor*, 317: this theory provides "a way both of renewing phenomenology and of replying to the excesses of structuralism."

318. Reagan, "Personal Identity," 14. Ricoeur's reflection on character in *Oneself as Another* is preceded by his treatment of the topic in *Freedom and Nature* and *Fallible Man*.

319. Muldoon, *On Ricoeur*, 88.

320. Reagan, "Personal Identity," 28.

321. Ricoeur, *Oneself as Another*, 64. Feminist critique warns against separating the "body" from the "self," and identifying a deeper, "more true" mode of self apart from the body, localized in "conscience" or "spirit." While his analysis necessarily distinguishes different dimensions of passivity, Ricoeur is not recommending a form of mind-body dualism but instead showing how all experience is mediated by the bodily location of the self in its encounter with the world.

322. Ibid., 318.

323. Ricoeur, *Oneself as Another*, 192.

324. Ibid., 327.

325. Ibid., 320.

326. Ibid., 354.

327. Paul Ricoeur, "From Metaphysics to Moral Philosophy," *Philosophy Today* 40 (1986): 453–55, quoted in Wallace, "From Phenomenology to Scripture? Paul Ricoeur's Hermeneutical Philosophy of Religion," 307.

328. The Augustinian themes of willing and self-awareness that recur in Ricoeur's reflection resonate with and instruct the interpretation of Christian sacrifice. Augustine viewed the will as the central mechanism of human action without which there can be neither virtue nor vice, and so the will is the determining structure of human personality and holiness, which is the goal of Christian sacrifice. However, simply because one has acted deliberately one has not necessarily acted virtuously. The ambiguity of willing means that strongly pursued, deliberate sacrifices may be part of a schema of evil. It is not simply by being passive that sacrifices can be vicious. However, the particular temptation of Christian sacrifice glorifies the posture of passivity,

of the victim, of the long-suffering one, and so it is this weakness in the idealization of sacrifice on which I focus. By pursuing the phantom of false sacrifice, I hope to come closer to appreciating the nature of active, genuine sacrifice.

329. Ricoeur, *Oneself as Another,* 294–96.

330. Ibid., 329.

331. Reagan, "Personal Identity," 17. Reagan's parenthetical citation refers to *Oneself as Another.*

332. Ricoeur, *Oneself as Another,* 179.

333. Paul Ricoeur, "The Problem of the Foundation of Moral Philosophy," *Philosophy Today* (1978): 178.

334. Ricoeur, *Oneself as Another,* 192.

335. Patrick L. Bourgeois, "Ricoeur and Levinas: Solicitude in Reciprocity and Solitude in Existence," in *Ricoeur as Another: The Ethics of Subjectivity,* ed. Richard A. Cohen and James L. Marsh (Albany: State University of New York Press, 2002), 119. Another refutation of the absolute external origin of command is affect, feelings, and sympathy. See page 120. On page 125, note 33, Bourgeois discusses the importance of sympathy for Levinas — not as constitutive of intersubjective relation, but part of the decency of everyday life.

336. Ricoeur, *Oneself as Another,* 193.

337. Reagan, "Personal Identity," 24.

338. Helen M. Buss, "Antigone, Psyche, and the Ethics of Female Selfhood: A Feminist Conversation with Paul Ricoeur's Theories of Self-Making in *Oneself as Another,*" in *Paul Ricoeur and Contemporary Moral Thought,* ed. John Wall, William Schweiker, and W. David Hall (New York: Routledge, 2002), 71. Buss contends that Ricoeur prematurely aborts the potential for feminist reflection in his reflection upon the tragic case of Antigone, shifting the focus from Antigone's particular dilemma as a woman to the universal fact of conflicting duties. Nor does the example he selects of Antigone's terrible choices effectively illustrate the challenge of selfhood: Antigone's private life is hidden. Buss proposes to examine instead the myth of Psyche.

339. Ibid., 76. Because self-negation is already worked into patriarchy, there needs to be a model of coming to selfhood that is not sacrificial or heterogeneous; a journey of self- and social-development marked not by loss but joy. Buss interprets the myth of Psyche as a journey of growing agency rewarded with the birth of her daughter. This is a mutual progression, not a zero-sum game.

340. Emmanuel Levinas, *Ethics and Infinity: Conversations with Philippe Nemo,* trans. Richard A. Cohen (Pittsburgh: Duquesne University Press, 1985), 12.

341. Ibid., 77–85.

342. Ricoeur, *Oneself as Another,* 337.

343. Ibid., 331. The notion of otherness has a similar double distinction as that within the idea of the Same (the distinction between the Same as *idem* and the Same as *ipse*).

344. Such an extension of respect is an "analogical transfer," a concept borrowed from Husserl. Ricoeur emphasizes that the other is recognized first as a subject who is not reducible to a projection of mine. Interacting with the other does indeed confirm my sense of identity. Reciprocally, my own subjectivity provides an analogous recognition of the other's subjectivity. This is Husserl's analogical transfer, which Ricoeur finds richly productive as a means to exceed phenomenology's restricted

258                                                                      *Notes*

ability to make statements about the other. Phenomenology traditionally represents the experience of one's own flesh. However, through analogy, the other need not be an anonymous stranger, but can be "my counterpart, that is, someone who, like me, says 'I.'" *Oneself as Another,* 335. At the same time, the other is discovered to exist in the paradoxical mode of givenness. The givenness of the other is authentic, but separate from one's own original, given experience. The dissymmetry of the other never attains the quality of one's original experience. Nevertheless, an analogical transfer enables one to recognize the subjectivity of the other. Peter Kemp identifies Ricoeur's criticism of Levinas as the search for a mediating position between the radical stances of Heidegger and Levinas. Heidegger and Levinas stand at opposing poles: "the former analyzing the attestation of self, conscience (*Gewissen*) without the other's injunction, and the latter claiming the injunction by the other without attestation of the self-affection of conscience." Kemp, "From Kierkegaard to Levinas," 54. Ricoeur believes Heidegger's weak ethical sensitivity must be corrected. Patrick L. Bourgeois agrees that Ricoeur diverges from Husserl's and Heidegger's focus on the isolated self, toward Levinas's other-orientation. "Neither Husserl's nor Heidegger's accounts [of the analogical transfer] get to the necessary point of addressing the other's movement towards me, and that is precisely why they need the movement of Levinas's analysis" (Bourgeois, "Ricoeur and Levinas," 120). But although Ricoeur strongly supports this movement, he insists that moral response requires conscientious subjectivity. The analogical transfer originates in the subject toward the other; one's moral direction is not wholly received from the other. Ricoeur mediates between an independent movement originating from the self for the other, and the external, separated movement of the other toward me. For Levinas, the analogical transfer is still a totalizing representation, the mechanism of the Same which absorbs the other into the self-centered self. Adriaan Peperzak, *To the Other: An Introduction to the Philosophy of Emmanuel Levinas,* Purdue Series in the History of Philosophy, ed. Joseph J. Kockelmans, Arion Kelkel, Adriaan Peperzak, Calvin O. Schrag, and Thomas Seebohm (West Lafayette, IN: Purdue University Press, 1993), 52.

345. This contrasts with Nygren's rejection of self-love.

346. Ricoeur, *Oneself as Another,* 340. As an exterior command, without engaging the subject's commitment, being-assigned occurs without foundation. It becomes arbitrary. This assignment of responsibility imprisons and persecutes, even to the point of substitution. Reading *Otherwise Than Being,* Ricoeur observes Levinas's language becoming more extreme. "'Obsession of the Other,' 'persecuted by the Other,' and highly, and especially, 'substitution of the I for the Other.' Here, the work reaches its paroxysm: 'under accusation by everyone, the responsibility for everyone goes to the point of substitution. The subject is the hostage' (112)." *Oneself as Another,* 338.

347. I was going to say the self is lost, but that is exactly what the gospel calls us to do. Reflecting on being lost suggests that to be lost is still to exist, but to find oneself in a place other than where one expected to be. It does not necessarily mean to vanish altogether.

348. Wallace, "From Phenomenology to Scripture? Paul Ricoeur's Hermeneutical Philosophy of Religion," 309.

349. Ricoeur, *Oneself as Another,* 339.

350. Bourgeois, "Ricoeur and Levinas," 113.

351. Ibid., 310.

352. I am drawing parallels between the theological language used in previous chapters, and the philosophical terminology to be employed here. Though Paul Ricoeur does not invoke the language of sin and of religious sacrifice, he addresses the case of a person who is compelled to act, the problem feminists addressed previously. I am also taking the philosophical description of realized selfhood to represent a parallel idea, or one that functions similarly in the philosophical analysis of the aims of action, as the gospel vision of "finding oneself," which is an anticipatory experience of salvation. Likewise, the terminology of self-love employed by the feminist theologians is expressed by the term "self-regard." The ideas and the interrelationship are parallel.

353. According to Richard A. Cohen, Ricoeur both differs from and misunderstands Levinas on certain points. Ricoeur charges Levinas with the "fundamental error . . . to attempt, per impossible, to think what Hegel called 'external relation,'" when in truth such an alleged relation is no relation at all, an "irrelation" (199), as Ricoeur calls it. Although Levinas seems to be in the good company of Kant and Plato on this point, for Ricoeur, as for Hegel, genuine philosophy must be limited to "internal" or "dialectical" relations, that is to say, relations whose terms do not in any irreducible sense exceed their relationality. Richard A. Cohen, "Moral Selfhood: A Levinasian Response to Ricoeur on Levinas," in *Ricoeur as Another: The Ethics of Subjectivity,* ed. Richard A. Cohen and James L. Marsh (Albany: State University of New York Press, 2002), 130. Cohen further indicates Ricoeur and Levinas's diverging paths out of the philosophical heritage by demonstrating their particular critique of Heidegger (as did Kemp). Both find Heidegger's view of self and conscience to be morally deficient. Whereas Ricoeur attempts to reconstruct conscience as the inner voice of the other (selfhood is being-enjoined), Levinas rejects the entire philosophical construction in favor of a radical ethical base (136).

354. More critically, Cohen points out that Ricoeur overlooks Levinas's attention to the self's capacity for reception in Part IV of *Totality and Infinity.* Ibid., 138. This seems to be an important oversight. However, Cohen's description of Levinas's view of receptivity in that work is cast in the model of the child's relation to its parents and family. This only underscores the immature and vulnerable position of the child-self in relation to the commanding parent-other. Peter Kemp also believes Ricoeur draws on the later *Otherwise Than Being* and overlooks Levinas's more moderate expression of the intersubjective self in *Totality and Infinity.* Levinas's more extreme presentation of the "stubbornly closed, locked up, separate ego" is found in the more radical text *Otherwise Than Being.* Even so, Kemp also feels there is the possibility of finding a nuanced view in *Otherwise Than Being,* if the vulnerability Levinas acknowledges there is taken as a form of attestation to relationality. Kemp, "From Kierkegaard to Levinas," 54–57.

355. Ricoeur, *Oneself as Another,* 336.

356. Paul Ricoeur, "Emmanuel Lévinas, penseur de témoignage," in *Répondre d'autrui, Emmanuel Lévinas,* ed. Jean-Christophe Aeschlimann, 38 (Neuchâtel: De la Baconnière, 1989), quoted in Kemp, "From Kierkegaard to Levinas," 55.

357. Wallace, "From Phenomenology to Scripture? Paul Ricoeur's Hermeneutical Philosophy of Religion," 302. Wallace observes on page 311 that Levinas attends chiefly to the command discourse of the Bible, whereas Ricoeur engages a polyphonic

range of scriptural discourse, in which God does not only command. Perhaps Levinas's focus on prescriptive teaching in Scripture justifies Wallace's insight in part, but the law is also regularly concerned with one's own rights. Furthermore, salvation history's tales of rescue are central to the Hebrew Scriptures.

358. In his 1978 article "The Problem of the Foundation of Moral Philosophy," Ricoeur examines moral action as an exchange between self and other whose source and goal is the experience of freedom. Ethics depends on my experience of freedom as the analogy for the other. I must affirm my freedom in order to value and will freedom for others. Likewise, so will my despair and bondage make it impossible for me to hope for the other. Paul Ricoeur, "The Problem of the Foundation of Moral Philosophy," *Philosophy Today* (1978): 179.

359. This term originates with Alasdair MacIntyre. John Wall, "Moral Meaning: Beyond the Good and the Right," in *Paul Ricoeur and Contemporary Moral Thought,* ed. William Schweiker, John Wall, and W. David Hall (New York: Routledge, 2002), 51.

360. Ricoeur, *Oneself as Another,* 172.

361. Ibid., 331. A teleological orientation toward society requires critique, because society exercises power and force which may corrupt its view of the good. The Kantian themes of universal law and respect for the human being as an end correct the misuse of power. The deontological test restrains otherness in its violent power to instrumentalize another. The universal corrects what may be a privatized and aggressive vision of a group in power. Thus deontology corrects a corrupted teleology. Nevertheless, the deontological approach must rely itself on a teleological conception of the good. For example, fair distribution must account for the goodness of what is to be fairly distributed. See also Martha C. Nussbaum, "Ricoeur on Tragedy: Teleology, Deontology, and *Phronesis,*" in *Paul Ricoeur and Contemporary Moral Thought,* ed. William Schweiker, John Wall, and W. David Hall (New York: Routledge, 2002), 271.

362. *Oneself as Another,* 215. While the norm is an appropriately self-critical and anti-ideological curb, it is not harshly restrictive. Respect for others reflects the inclination and affection of free persons, and so coheres with solicitude and personal feeling, rather than moral formalism. Formalism develops alongside prohibition. The norm introduces the negative element of deviance, or a desire that conflicts with obligation. The norm thus divides preference from prohibition with what Ricoeur calls the "scission of the norm." The norm casts the scission of the preferable as a shadow and judge over the desirable. The aspect of scission in norms becomes explicit in the imperative. The separation of judgment from desire and its command emerges from an inner duality apparent in conscience, in which one part commands another. The imposition and externality of imperative becomes concrete in social institutions. The ultimate formal stage of law cannot be identified with its genesis in the movement of freedom. Kant sanctifies the scission, overwhelming the movement of freedom with the weight of universal law. Ricoeur strongly opposes the elevation of abstract law as an ideal reflected in the harmony of the heavens. "But is not this symbolization the fruit of an abstraction? Not just of an abstraction that eliminates desire, but of an abstraction that strikes the entire dynamism, that across the ideas of institutions, norms, values, and imperative, nourishes the anemic imperative of the moral law, analogous to that of nature, and that continues to bind that law to

freedom, thereby allowing us to also speak of a law of freedom." Ricoeur, "Moral Philosophy," 188.

363. Ibid., 172.

364. Ibid., 185.

365. Ibid., 243.

366. Martha C. Nussbaum shows how Ricoeur uses the topic of tragic conflict to explore the limits and interaction between deontology and teleology. Nussbaum employs the tale of Arjuna agonizing between the battle lines from the Indian epic *Mahabharata*, facing friends on both sides. What makes his choice specifically tragic, in her view, is not that he had a difficult choice to make. The tragic element of his dilemma is that all of the possible choices are bad. Nussbaum, "Ricoeur on Tragedy: Teleology, Deontology, and *Phronesis*," 266. Persons with a more limited perspective may persist in asserting only their own narrow claims, or avoid a hard decision altogether. Nussbaum illustrates this problem with her reading of Sophocles' *Antigone*. Creon and Antigone considered only their own narrow domains: the family, or the city. They do not recognize the necessary interdependence of the city and the family upon each other's well-being. "Each has an impoverished conception not only of value in general but also of his or her own cherished sphere of value.... Because neither sees the tragedy inherent in the situation, because neither so much as poses the tragic question, both are in these two distinct ways impoverished political actors" (268). The wiser choice is not to affect a simplistic resolution, but to broaden one's perspective. Tragedy generates meaning by illuminating the multiple values in life. "The contingencies of life make it almost inevitable that some disharmony will materialize among our many commitments. The only alternative to the permanent possibility of tragedy would appear to be a life so impoverished in value that it neglects many things that human beings should not neglect. And of course such a life does not really avoid tragedy: it just fails to see the tragedy involved in its own neglect of genuine values" (269).

367. Wall, "Moral Meaning: Beyond the Good and the Right," 58.

368. Ibid., 59.

369. Ibid., 61.

370. Nussbaum, "Ricoeur on Tragedy: Teleology, Deontology, and *Phronesis*," 270.

371. Mark Muldoon, *On Ricoeur*, Wadsworth Notes (Belmont, CA: Wadsworth/Thomson Learning, 2002), 23.

372. Paul Ricoeur, *Freedom and Nature: The Voluntary and the Involuntary*, Northwestern University Studies in Phenomenology and Existential Philosophy, ed. John Wild, trans. Erazim V. Kohák (Evanston, IL: Northwestern University Press, 1966), 346.

373. The Annunciation is another paradigmatic example of consenting to a risk and accepting personal sacrifice. Elizabeth A. Johnson points to the portrayal of the danger of Mary's pregnancy in the Gospel of Matthew. An unmarried, pregnant woman faced great risks: divorce, expulsion, or stoning. The conception and birth occurred under the shadow of the cross. Mary had a choice, and she gives her consent — but she is not forced. Nor could she then foresee all the future consequences of her assent. Elizabeth A. Johnson, *Truly Our Sister: A Theology of Mary in the Communion of Saints* (New York: Continuum, 2003), 254, 238.

374. Ricoeur, "Moral Philosophy," 179.

375. Ibid., 181.

376. Reagan, "Personal Identity," 23.

377. Ricoeur, *Oneself as Another,* 351.

378. Mark I. Wallace, "From Phenomenology to Scripture? Paul Ricoeur's Hermeneutical Philosophy of Religion," *Modern Theology* 16, no. 3 (2000): 304.

379. Ibid., 308.

380. Charles Taylor, *Sources of the Self: The Making of the Modern Identity* (Cambridge: Harvard University Press, 1989), 111.

381. Ibid., 131.

382. Having reached this conclusion, Augustine reverses it in the next book, as the transcendence of worship draws the inner gaze to the more supreme object, God. In book XIV.15 Augustine extends his analysis of self-presence as memory, understanding, and will to consider the more transcendent attention of the soul when it ponders not itself, but God. He calls this act of contemplation, the "worship trinity," saying that the "trinity of the mind is not really the image of God because the mind remembers and understands and loves itself, but because it is also able to remember and understand and love him by whom it was made. And when it does this it becomes wise." Augustine, *The Trinity,* 383.

383. Paul Ricoeur, "The Problem of the Foundation of Moral Philosophy," *Philosophy Today* (1978): 190.

384. Glenn Whitehouse, "Ricoeur on Religious Selfhood: A Response to Mark Wallace," *Modern Theology* 16, no. 3 (2000): 320.

385. Paul Ricoeur, "Love and Justice," in *Figuring the Sacred: Religion, Narrative, and Imagination,* ed. Mark I. Wallace (Minneapolis: Fortress Press, 1995), 325.

386. Ricoeur, "Golden Rule," 299.

387. Ricoeur is responding to Kant's one-sided focus on the symbolism of sin. Paul Ricoeur, "Ethical and Theological Considerations on the Golden Rule," in *Figuring the Sacred: Religion, Narrative, and Imagination,* ed. Mark I. Wallace (Minneapolis: Fortress Press, 1995), 297.

388. The logic of exchange is not total; Ricoeur observes that ethnologists account for ancient expressions of an economy of the gift that emerged in festivity, generosity, and abundance. Paul Ricoeur, "The Logic of Jesus, the Logic of God," in *Figuring the Sacred: Religion, Narrative, and Imagination,* ed. Mark I. Wallace (Minneapolis: Fortress Press, 1995), 282.

389. Ibid.

390. Ibid., 281.

391. Ricoeur, "Love and Justice," 325.

392. Ibid., 318.

393. The praise of love in hymn and metaphor is not mere ornamentation. Ricoeur identifies the error of Nygren to be an impoverished understanding of the real analogy in eros between the affective feeling of love and the metaphors it engages. "The trope expresses what we might call the substantive tropology of love: that is, both the real analogy between feeling and the power of eros to signify agape and to put it into words." Ibid., 321.

394. Ricoeur, "Golden Rule," 297.

395. Ricoeur, "Love and Justice," 326.

396. Ricoeur sees no possible basis for justice and penal law in the love command. These rules must remain in tension. "The golden rule is set in this way, in a *concrete* fashion, at the heart of an incessant conflict between self-interest and self-sacrifice." Ricoeur, "Golden Rule," 297.

397. Ricoeur, "Love and Justice," 327.

398. Ricoeur, "Golden Rule," 302.

399. Whitehouse, "Ricoeur on Religious Selfhood: A Response to Mark Wallace," 319.

400. Wallace, "From Phenomenology to Scripture? Paul Ricoeur's Hermeneutical Philosophy of Religion," 303.

## Chapter Four / Sacrifice in a Creation Catechism

401. Edward Schillebeeckx, "Prologue," in *The Praxis of the Reign of God: An Introduction to the Theology of Edward Schillebeeckx*, ed. Mary Catherine Hilkert and Robert J. Schreiter (New York: Fordham University Press, 2002), xvii.

402. According to John Bowden, Schillebeeckx's method is best described as cumulative: "perspective is added to perspective until we have considered the subject from every possible angle." Schillebeeckx circles around his topic, piling on commentaries from various relevant aspects. The reader may lose the initial direction or purpose in the process. Discussions can become quite long. However, Schillebeeckx intends to cover the material as fully as possible, without being misunderstood. This is a danger he perhaps makes more likely by trying to forestall it. John Bowden, *Edward Schillebeeckx: In Search of the Kingdom of God* (New York: Crossroad, 1983), 16. Philip Kennedy more bluntly acknowledges that Schillebeeckx can be difficult to understand. See Philip Kennedy, *Schillebeeckx,* Outstanding Christian Thinkers, ed. Brian Davies (Collegeville, MN: Liturgical Press, 1993), 3.

403. Schillebeeckx, *Reader,* 10, 13.

404. Kennedy, *Schillebeeckx,* 33.

405. Ibid., 27.

406. Ibid., 29.

407. Ibid., 8, 37–43.

408. Bowden, *Edward Schillebeeckx,* 35.

409. The effort to reinterpret the faith for contemporary times drove Schillebeeckx to a new engagement with philosophies that no longer look for the meaning of things in themselves, but that seek that meaning in the intersubjective relationship of things in association with other things. His earlier work engaged phenomenology (the relationship between the subjective interpreter and the objective world). The "philosophies of relation" that Schillebeeckx takes up in later writings include hermeneutics (the relation between the text and interpreter), philosophy of ordinary language, critical theory (the study of the social relationship between the subject and her historical environment), and Emmanuel Levinas's philosophy of the ethical relationship between persons. Schillebeeckx's study of hermeneutics encompassed the philosophical hermeneutics of Hans-Georg Gadamer and Paul Ricoeur, philosophies of language, Gerhard Ebeling and Ernst Fuchs, and critical theory, particularly Jürgen Habermas. The philosophy of language emphasized to Schillebeeckx how meaning is filtered by language structures. Critical theory brought social and political questions

to the forefront and further undermined any attempt for a purely theoretical hermeneutics. Student rebellions and travel through Latin America opened his eyes to the
importance of the critical theory of the Frankfurt school. Hermeneutics must be liberative and political and must be driven by praxis that opposes oppressive structures.
A critical apprehension of suffering can then dialectically inform our understanding.
Kennedy, 50.

410. Ibid.

411. Bowden analyzes the differences between the *Christ the Sacrament of the
Encounter with God* and Schillebeeckx's later work in four ways. Schillebeeckx's
earlier work is less scriptural, more churchy, and shows limited attention to the
questions of a modern audience. Finally, Bowden makes the interesting observation
that this work is more tranquil without the tension of contrast experiences, probing
attention to the wider world, and the need for witness which is sometimes refractory.
Ibid., 53.

412. Kennedy, *Schillebeeckx*, 101.

413. Schillebeeckx, "Christian Identity," 27.

414. Giovanni Pico della Mirandola, *De dignitate hominis*, E. Garin (Florence
1942), quoted in Edward Schillebeeckx, *Church: The Human Story of God*, trans.
John Bowden (New York: Crossroad, 1990), 1. Use of non-inclusive language follows
Schillebeeckx for consistency.

415. Edward Schillebeeckx, *I Am a Happy Theologian: Conversations with
Francesco Strazzari* (New York: Crossroad, 1994), 47. The most concentrated ex-
pressions of Schillebeeckx's doctrine of creation are found in chapter 16 of *God
among Us*, "I Believe In God, Creator of Heaven and Earth"; chapter 6 of *Interim
Report*, "Kingdom of God: Creation of Salvation"; and chapter 5 of *Church: The
Human Story of God*.

416. Philip Kennedy, "God and Creation," in *The Praxis of the Reign of God: An
Introduction to the Theology of Edward Schillebeeckx*, ed. Mary Catherine Hilkert
and Robert J. Schreiter (New York: Fordham University Press, 2002), 41.

417. Kennedy, *Schillebeeckx*, 10.

418. William J. Hill, "A Theology in Transition," in *The Praxis of the Reign of
God: An Introduction to the Theology of Edward Schillebeeckx*, ed. Mary Catherine
Hilkert and Robert J. Schreiter (New York: Fordham University Press, 2002), 4.

419. Kennedy, *Schillebeeckx*, 36.

420. Edward Schillebeeckx, *For the Sake of the Gospel* (New York: Crossroad,
1990), 58.

421. Edward Schillebeeckx, *Interim Report on the Books Jesus and Christ*, trans.
John Bowden (New York: Crossroad, 1981), 116.

422. Kennedy, "God and Creation," 47.

423. Schillebeeckx, *Interim Report*, 116.

424. Ibid., 114.

425. Kennedy, "God and Creation," 49.

426. Edward Schillebeeckx, "Critical Theories and Christian Political Commitment," in *Political Commitment and Christian Community*, ed. Alois Muller and
Norbert Greinacher, *Concilium* (New York: Herder and Herder, 1973), 49.

427. Schillebeeckx, *Church: The Human Story of God*, 231.

428. Edward Schillebeeckx, *Christ: The Experience of Jesus as Lord,* trans. John Bowden (New York: Crossroad, 1981), 728.

429. Schillebeeckx characteristically conceives all themes as organically inter-related, not easily separated or presented as if in a clear line of deduction. However, it is interesting to note that the strong relationship between creation and God's will to be Creator of humanity places a discussion of anthropology more naturally along-side creation than with Christology. This observation anticipates my integration of sacrifice as a reflection of creation as well as of Christ in the last chapter.

430. Schillebeeckx, *Interim Report,* 115.

431. Ibid., 232.

432. Kennedy, "God and Creation," 53.

433. Schillebeeckx, *Interim Report,* 111.

434. Janet M. Callewaert, "Salvation from God in Jesus the Christ: Soteriology," in *The Praxis of Christian Experience: An Introduction to the Theology of Edward Schillebeeckx,* ed. Robert J. Schreiter and Mary Catherine Hilkert (San Francisco: Harper & Row, Publishers, 1989), 69.

435. Edward Schillebeeckx, *Jesus: An Experiment in Christology,* trans. Hubert Hoskins (New York: Seabury Press, 1979), 72, 47.

436. Ibid., 210.

437. Ibid., 201.

438. Ibid., 226.

439. Ibid., 104.

440. Ibid., 142.

441. Ibid., 159.

442. Edward Schillebeeckx, "Jesus' Story of God," in *God among Us: The Gospel Proclaimed* (New York: Crossroad, 1983), 28.

443. Schillebeeckx, *Jesus,* 180.

444. Ibid., 194.

445. Schillebeeckx uses the criterion of Jesus' preaching and praxis to ascertain his view of the law. Jesus does not reject ceremonial practice, but insists that such practice be consistent with ethical concern for the neighbor. The conflict between a strict, scrupulous attention to Mosaic law versus a Graeco-Jewish universalism cen-tered on the Decalogue in preference to "man-made" laws is a debate that predates Jesus. It is unclear whether or not Jesus would have been influenced by universalizing Hellenistic attitudes in Galilee. Even if he was not, his open attitude toward the law is not novel and is an inner-Jewish option. Schillebeeckx, *Jesus,* 230–31. The two great commandments provide another criterion for judging the law in the light of Jesus' attitude. In Schillebeeckx's view, Jesus endorses the combination of the two great commandments, but does not invent it. This ethical ideal is a universalistic development of Greek-speaking Jews who have combined Deuteronomy 6:4–5 and Leviticus 19:18.

446. Ibid., 235.

447. Ibid., 254–55.

448. "Whether Jesus did or did not utter in person the logion about 'loving one's enemies' is of secondary importance here; the chief thing is that this was his way of life in practice, a result of his proclaiming (even in parables) the approaching rule of God." Ibid., 237.

449. Ibid., 241.

450. Ibid., 256.

451. Callewaert, "Salvation from God in Jesus the Christ: Soteriology," 72.

452. Janet M. O'Meara, "Salvation: Living Communion with God," in *The Praxis of the Reign of God: An Introduction to the Theology of Edward Schillebeeckx*, ed. Robert J. Schreiter and Mary Catherine Hilkert (New York: Fordham University Press, 2001), 113.

453. Bowden, *Edward Schillebeeckx*, 98.

454. Schillebeeckx, *Christ*, 638–39.

455. Schillebeeckx, *Jesus*, 638, 610.

456. Ibid., 610, 623. Salvation is encountered sacramentally in Jesus and the church. Schillebeeckx does not restrict salvation to church members; he speaks of the awareness of humanity, its coming together, and search for justice as a transcendent experience. Nevertheless, he focuses upon the Christian tradition and its ongoing relevance.

457. Schillebeeckx, *Church*, 157.

458. Schillebeeckx, *Interim Report*, 105.

459. Schillebeeckx, *Jesus*, 25.

460. Edward Schillebeeckx, "Critical Theories and Christian Political Commitment," in *Political Commitment and Christian Community* (New York: Herder and Herder, 1973), 57.

461. Hill, "A Theology in Transition," 7.

462. Schillebeeckx, *Jesus*, 615.

463. Edward Schillebeeckx, "Christian 'to the Death' (Matt.16.21; Jer. 20:7–9)," in *God among Us*, 200.

464. Edward Schillebeeckx, "God as a Loud Cry (Mark 15.37; Matt.27.50)," in *I Believe in God, Creator of Heaven and Earth* (New York: Crossroad, 1983), 74.

465. John P. Galvin, "The Story of Jesus as the Story of God," in *The Praxis of the Reign of God: An Introduction to the Theology of Edward Schillebeeckx*, ed. Mary Catherine Hilkert and Robert J. Schreiter (New York: Fordham University Press, 2002), 86.

466. Schillebeeckx, *Jesus*, 301–3.

467. Bowden, *Schillebeeckx*, 63.

468. Schillebeeckx, *Christ*, 729.

469. Ibid., 730.

470. Edward Schillebeeckx, "Christian Identity and Human Integrity," in *Is Being Human a Criterion of Being Christian?* ed. Jean-Pierre Jossua and Claude Geffré (New York: Seabury Press, 1982), 31.

471. Galvin, "The Story of Jesus as the Story of God," 88.

472. His preaching announces the reign of God, which is God's intent for humanity, and he insists that people look to the future and prepare for the full presence of God's reign. When Jesus is faced with the rejection of his message and mode of life and his own possible death, the persecution and martyrdom of Israel's prophets provide him with an interpretive key. Bradford E. Hinze, "Eschatology and Ethics," in *The Praxis of the Reign of God: An Introduction to the Theology of Edward Schillebeeckx*, ed. Mary Catherine Hilkert and Robert J. Schreiter (New York: Fordham University Press, 2002), 171.

473. Schillebeeckx, *Jesus,* 311.

474. Ibid., 212.

475. Ibid., 305.

476. Ibid., 319.

477. Schillebeeckx, "Christian 'to the Death,' " 202.

478. Schillebeeckx, *Jesus,* 610.

479. Schillebeeckx, *Christ,* 698. Our perennial need for story, and especially dramatic tales of sacrifice and endurance, is strikingly apparent in the most celebrated films of 2004: *The Passion of the Christ* and Tolkien's *Lord of the Rings* trilogy.

480. Galvin, "The Story of Jesus as the Story of God," 82.

481. Schillebeeckx, *Christ,* 699.

482. Edward Schillebeeckx, "I Believe in God, Creator of Heaven and Earth," in *God among Us,* 99.

483. Schillebeeckx, "Prologue," x.

484. Schillebeeckx, *Church,* 5.

485. Mary Catherine Hilkert, "Experience and Revelation," in *The Praxis of the Reign of God: An Introduction to the Theology of Edward Schillebeeckx,* ed. Mary Catherine Hilkert and Robert J. Schreiter (New York: Fordham University Press, 2002), 62.

486. Schillebeeckx, *Church,* 6.

487. Mary Catherine Hilkert, "Discovery of the Living God: Revelation and Experience," in *The Praxis of Christian Experience: An Introduction to the Theology of Edward Schillebeeckx,* ed. Robert J. Schreiter and Mary Catherine Hilkert (San Francisco: Harper & Row, Publishers, 1989), 35.

488. Kennedy, *Schillebeeckx,* 129.

489. Schillebeeckx, *Christ,* 513.

490. Schillebeeckx, *Jesus,* 614–20.

491. Edward Schillebeeckx, "God, Society and Human Salvation," in *Faith and Society* (Gembloux, Belgium: Editions Duculot, 1978), 88.

492. William P. George observes that suffering criticizes and also combines the religious and ethical forms of knowledge. "It seems to follow that suffering also criticizes and yet binds together religion and ethics. Suffering, in other words, would appear to be at the very heart of, if not the key to Schillebeeckx's understanding of ethics, which, of course, he does not want to divorce from religion in general and Christian faith in particular." William P. George, "The Praxis of the Kingdom of God: Ethics in Schillebeeckx's *Jesus* and *Christ,*" *Horizons* 12 (1985): 52.

493. Elizabeth Kennedy Tillar, "Suffering for Others in the Theology of Edward Schillebeeckx," Ph.D. dissertation, Fordham University, 1999, 320.

494. Schillebeeckx, *Jesus,* 621.

495. Even if only through a curse: Schillebeeckx recounts the despair he felt when hearing of the assassination of Archbishop Oscar Romero and finding that cursing can be a form of prayer. Bowden, *Edward Schillebeeckx,* 95.

496. Schillebeeckx, *Jesus,* 310.

497. Schillebeeckx, *Christ,* 699.

498. Edward Schillebeeckx, "Christian 'to the Death,' " 202.

499. Schillebeeckx, *Christ,* 725.

500. Schillebeeckx, *Jesus,* 228.

501. O'Meara, "Salvation: Living Communion with God," 101.

502. Ibid., 236.

503. Ibid., 222.

504. Ibid., 229.

505. Ibid.

506. Ibid., 91.

507. Ibid., 566.

508. In this document, as in many other sections of New Testament literature, there is no exhortation to resistance against oppressive political and social conditions. Christians are not challenged to overthrow governments that persecute them or resist social stratification between rich, poor, and slaves. Christians sought to avoid a revolutionary or political reputation for two reasons. Religiously, as long as the end was expected imminently, there was no point in reforming social structures that would soon pass away. Practically, as long as the church tried to endure among hostile governments, a pacifist and accommodating stance was prudent. For Schillebeeckx, this represents the divided attitude of New Testament Christianity vis-à-vis the world and the church. *Christ*, 569–72.

509. Schillebeeckx, *Jesus*, 625.

510. Schillebeeckx, "Christian 'to the Death,' " 201.

511. Ibid.

512. William P. George, "The Praxis of the Kingdom of God: Ethics in Schillebeeckx's *Jesus* and *Christ*," *Horizons* 12 (1985): 51.

513. Schillebeeckx, *Jesus*, 616.

514. Schillebeeckx, *Christ*, 532.

515. O'Meara, "Salvation: Living Communion with God," 111.

516. Schillebeeckx, *Christ*, 497.

517. Schillebeeckx cites Levinas as a representation of the practical and ethical side of religion. This can be contrasted to the theoretical, symbolic, ascetic, or mystical. Both symbolic and orthopractical expressions of God are essential. The ethical expression gains priority because it gives "density reality" to symbolic-religious language. In *Essays on Judaism*, 61, Schillebeeckx compares this to Rahner's emphasis on love of neighbor as the source of the mystical knowledge of God. "Revelation can be understood as the manifestation of the transcendent meaning in our historical arising, together with the responsive affirmation of this manifestation."

518. Schillebeeckx, *Church*, 96.

519. Schillebeeckx, *Jesus*, 226.

520. Schillebeeckx, *Church*, 419. The gift of the Spirit and the sending of the disciples complete Jesus' resurrection. "So it is the Spirit which provides the connection between the historical Jesus of Nazareth and the contemporary life of faith of the Johannine community; the Paraclete provides the connection between the past and the present; he brings up to date the revelation which is accomplished in Jesus. The contemporary church is the place in which the saving work that God has begun in Christ is continued by the Spirit." *Christ*, 535.

521. Schillebeeckx, *Christ*, 464.

522. Ibid., 470–74.

523. Grace makes one a new creature, created in Christ, with a new outlook, and new life. One's destiny and identity are changed as a result of the response to

Jesus. "Finally, by grace we receive a new name (Rev. 2:17; see 3:12); that is, only at the eschaton will we see what is the deepest identity of our being renewed by grace. It will even become manifest as identity, being ascribed glorified corporeality...a public expression of perfect Christian identity." Ibid., 531.

524. Schillebeeckx, *Christ,* 600.
525. Schillebeeckx, "I Believe in God," 100.
526. Schillebeeckx, *Christ,* 737.
527. Ibid., 495.
528. Schillebeeckx, *Interim Report,* 122.
529. Ibid.
530. Schillebeeckx, *Church,* 233.
531. Schillebeeckx, *Christ,* 497.
532. O'Meara, "Salvation: Living Communion with God," 112.

## Chapter Five / Sacrifice in the Image of God

533. Schillebeeckx, *Christ,* 263.
534. David Tracy, "Metaphor and Religion," 95.
535. For example, Paul Fiddes emphasized the creative and redemptive purpose of atonement, expressed in sacrificial language. To the early church, sin offerings and spiritual offerings were readily understood. However, he also acknowledges that the idea of a sin offering, and particularly the offering of a victim, is strange to most contemporary Westerners today. Paul Fiddes, *Past Event and Present Salvation: The Christian Idea of Atonement* (London: Darton, Longman & Todd, 1989), 66.
536. Martin Luther, *Lectures on Genesis 2:18,* in Luther's *Works,* Vol. 1, ed. Jaroslav Pelikan (St. Louis: Concordia, 1958), 111.
537. Williams, *Sisters in the Wilderness,* 234.
538. Schillebeeckx, *Church,* 183.
539. Schillebeeckx, *Christ,* 464.
540. Schillebeeckx, "Christian 'to the Death,'" 200.
541. Schillebeeckx, "Prologue," x.
542. Schillebeeckx, *Church,* 4.
543. See Sarah Coakley, "Theological Meanings and Gender Connotations," in *The Work of Love: Creation as Kenosis,* ed. John Polkinghorne (Grand Rapids: Eerdmans, 2001), 202, for a summary of the views of many theologians on this theme, including Arthur Peacocke, Ian Barbour, Paul Fiddes, Jürgen Moltmann, Holmes Rolston III, and Hans Urs von Balthasar.
544. One such controversial treatment is Jürgen Moltmann's *God in Creation: A New Theology of Creation and the Spirit of God,* trans. Margaret Kohl (Minneapolis: Fortress Press, 1985).
545. John Haught, *God after Darwin: A Theology of Evolution* (Boulder, CO: Westview Press, 2000), 111.
546. Coakley, "Theological Meanings and Gender Connotations," 192.
547. Arthur Peacocke, *Theology for a Scientific Age: Being and Becoming — Natural, Divine and Human* (Minneapolis: Fortress Press, 1993), 121.
548. Ibid., 123.
549. Ibid., 124.
550. Ibid., 307–8.

551. Ibid., 309.

552. Ibid., 329–33.

553. John Haught, *God after Darwin: A Theology of Evolution* (Boulder, CO: Westview Press, 2000), 49.

554. Ibid., 112.

555. Ibid., 114.

556. Paul Ricoeur, "The Problem of the Foundation of Moral Philosophy," *Philosophy Today* (1978): 190.

557. R. Kevin Seasoltz, "Another Look at Sacrifice," *Worship* 74 (2000): 401.

558. Ibid., 407.

559. David N. Power, "Sacrament: An Economy of Gift," *Louvain Studies* 23 (1998): 157.

560. Sarah Coakley, "Kenosis and Subversion: On the Representation of 'Vulnerability' in Christian Feminist Writing," in *Swallowing a Fishbone? Feminist Theologians Debate Christianity,* ed. Daphne Hampson (London: Society for Promoting Christian Knowledge, 1996), 107.

561. Power, "Sacrament: An Economy of Gift," 156.

562. David Tracy, "Religion and Human Rights in the Public Realm," *Daedalus* 112 (1983): 248.

563. Hilkert, "Cry Beloved Image," 200.

564. Ibid., 202.

565. Schillebeeckx, *Church,* 4.

566. David Tracy, "Do Christians Any Longer Feel the World as God's Creation?" (keynote address, *The Person, the Poor and the Common Good,* a conference co-sponsored by the United States Conference of Catholic Bishops and the University of St. Thomas, St. Paul, Minnesota, October 29–31, 2004), 2.

567. David Tracy, *The Analogical Imagination: Christian Theology and the Culture of Pluralism* (New York: Crossroad, 1981), 199.

568. Tracy, "God's Creation?" 4.

569. Ibid., 8–9.

570. Ibid., 5.

571. Ibid., 12.

572. Ibid., 10.

573. Ibid., 12.

574. Tracy, *The Analogical Imagination,* 395.

575. Tracy, "God's Creation?" 9.

# BIBLIOGRAPHY

Abe, Masao. "Kenotic God and Dynamic Shunyata." In *The Emptying God: A Buddhist-Jewish-Christian Conversation,* ed. Christopher Ives and John B. Cobb. Maryknoll, NY: Orbis, 1990.

Andolsen, Barbara Hilkert. "Agape in Feminist Ethics." *Journal of Religious Ethics* 9 (1981): 69–83.

Augustine. *The City of God.* Trans. Marcus Dods. New York: Modern Library, 1993.

———. *The Trinity.* Trans. Edmund Hill. Vol. 5. *The Works of Saint Augustine: A Translation for the 21st Century,* ed. John E. Rotelle. Brooklyn: New City Press, 1991.

Aulén, Gustaf. *Christus Victor: An Historical Study of the Three Main Types of the Idea of Atonement.* Trans. A. G. Hebert. New York: Macmillan, 1951.

———. *The Drama and the Symbols: A Book of Images of God and the Problems They Raise.* Trans. Sydney Linton. Philadelphia: Fortress Press, 1970.

Behm, Johannes. "Sacrifice." In *Theological Dictionary of the New Testament,* ed. Geoffrey W. Bromiley, 3, 180–90. Grand Rapids: Eerdmans, 1964–76.

Bellet, Maurice. *Le Dieu pervers.* Paris: Editions du Cerf, 1987.

Benda, Vladimir. "World Catechism and the Conciliar Process for Justice, Peace and the Preservation of Creation." In *Concilium,* ed. Edward Schillebeeckx: Edinburgh: T. & T. Clark, 1989.

Best, Ernest. "1 Peter 2:4–10: A Reconsideration." *Novum Testamentum* 11, no. 4 (1969): 270–93.

Boff, Leonardo. *Ecology and Liberation: A New Paradigm.* Trans. Phillip Berryman. Maryknoll, NY: Orbis Books, 1997.

Bonhoeffer, Dietrich. *The Cost of Discipleship.* Trans. R. H. Fuller. New York: Macmillan, 1963.

Bourgeois, Patrick L. "Ricoeur and Levinas: Solicitude in Reciprocity and Solitude in Existence." In *Ricoeur as Another: The Ethics of Subjectivity,* ed. Richard A. Cohen and James L. Marsh, 109–26. Albany: State University of New York Press, 2002.

Bowden, John. *Edward Schillebeeckx: In Search of the Kingdom of God.* New York: Crossroad, 1983.

Braudel, Fernand. *The Perspective of the World.* Trans. Siân Reynolds. Vol. 3. *Civilization and Capitalism: 15th-18th Century.* New York: Harper & Row, 1984.

Brock, Rita Nakashima. "Losing Your Innocence but Not Your Hope." In *Reconstructing the Christ Symbol: Essays in Feminist Christology,* ed. Maryanne Stevens, 30–53. New York: Paulist Press, 1993.

271

Brock, Rita Nakashima, and Rebecca Ann Parker. *Proverbs of Ashes: Violence, Redemptive Suffering, and the Search for What Saves Us.* Boston: Beacon Press, 2001.

Bronner, Stephen Eric, and Douglas MacKay Kellner, eds. *Critical Theory and Society: A Reader.* New York: Routledge, 1989.

Brown, Joanne Carlson, and Rebecca Parker. "For God So Loved the World?" In *Violence against Women and Children: A Christian Theological Sourcebook,* ed. Carol J. Adams and Marie M. Fortune, 36–59. New York: Continuum, 1995.

Brown, Raymond E. *The Gospel According to John.* Anchor Bible Commentary. Garden City, NY: Doubleday & Company, 1966.

———. *The Community of the Beloved Disciple.* New York: Paulist Press, 1979.

———. *The Death of the Messiah: From Gethsemane to the Grave. A Commentary on the Passion Narratives in the Four Gospels.* Vol. 2. Anchor Bible Reference Library. Ed. David Noel Freedman. New York: Doubleday, 1993.

Bruce, Frederick Fyvie. "Kerygma of Hebrews." *Interpretation* 23 (1969): 3–19.

Burggraeve, Roger. "Responsibility for a New Heaven and a New Earth." In *No Heaven without Earth,* ed. Edward Schillebeeckx, 107–18. Philadelphia: Trinity Press International, 1991.

Buss, Helen M. "Antigone, Psyche, and the Ethics of Female Selfhood: A Feminist Conversation with Paul Ricoeur's Theories of Self-Making in *Oneself as Another.*" In *Paul Ricoeur and Contemporary Moral Thought,* ed. John Wall, William Schweiker, and W. David Hall, 64–79. New York: Routledge, 2002.

Cady, Linell Elizabeth. "Identity, Feminist Theory, and Theology." In *Horizons in Feminist Theology: Identity, Traditions, and Norms,* ed. Rebecca Chopp and Sheila Greeve Davaney, 17–32. Minneapolis: Fortress Press, 1997.

Callewaert, Janet M. "Salvation from God in Jesus the Christ: Soteriology." In *The Praxis of Christian Experience: An Introduction to the Theology of Edward Schillebeeckx,* ed. Robert J. Schreiter and Mary Catherine Hilkert, 68–85. San Francisco: Harper & Row, 1989.

Carr, Anne E. *Transforming Grace: Christian Tradition and Women's Experience.* New York: Continuum, 1996.

Chauvet, Louise-Marie. *Symbol and Sacrament: A Sacramental Reinterpretation of Christian Existence.* Trans. Patrick Madigan and Madeleine Beaumont. Collegeville, MN: Liturgical Press, 1995.

Chopp, Rebecca S., and Sheila Greeve Devaney, eds. *Horizons in Feminist Theology: Identity, Tradition, and Norms.* Minneapolis: Fortress Press, 1997.

Clifford, Anne M., CSJ. "Foundations for a Catholic Ecological Theology of God." In *And God Saw That It Was Good: Catholic Theology and the Environment,* ed. Walter Grazer, 19–46. Washington, DC: United States Catholic Conference, 1996.

Coakley, Sarah. "Creaturehood before God: Male and Female." *Theology* 93 (1990): 343–54.

———. "The Eschatological Body: Gender, Transformation, and God." *Modern Theology* 16, no. 1 (2000): 61–73.

———. "Kenosis and Subversion: On the Representation of 'Vulnerability' in Christian Feminist Writing." In *Swallowing a Fishbone? Feminist Theologians Debate Christianity,* ed. Daphne Hampson, 82–111. London: Society for Promoting Christian Knowledge, 1996.

———. "Theological Meanings and Gender Connotations." In *The Work of Love: Creation as Kenosis,* ed. John Polkinghorne, 192–210. Grand Rapids: Eerdmans, 2001.

Cohen, Richard A. "Moral Selfhood: A Levinasian Response to Ricoeur on Levinas." In *Ricoeur as Another: The Ethics of Subjectivity,* ed. Richard A. Cohen and James L. Marsh, 127–60. Albany: State University of New York Press, 2002.

Crossan, John Dominic. *In Parables: The Challenge of the Historical Jesus.* New York: Harper & Row, 1973.

Cullis-Suzuki, Severn. "The Young Can't Wait." *Time* 160, no. 9 (2002): A56.

Daly, Mary. *Beyond God the Father: Toward a Philosophy of Women's Liberation.* Boston: Beacon Press, 1973.

Daly, Robert J. *The Origins of the Christian Doctrine of Sacrifice.* Philadelphia: Fortress Press, 1978.

D'Arcy, Martin C. *The Mind and Heart of Love, Lion and Unicorn: A Study in Eros and Agape.* New York: Meridan Books, 1956.

Davies, Philip R., and Bruce D. Chilton. "The *Aqedah:* A Revised Tradition History." *Catholic Biblical Quarterly* 40 (1978): 514–46.

Derrida, Jacques. "Response to 'Loose Canons: Augustine and Derrida on Their Selves.'" In *God, the Gift, and Postmodernism,* ed. John D. Caputo and Michael J. Scanlon, 98–111. Bloomington: Indiana University Press, 1999.

Derrida, Jacques, and Jean-Luc Marion. "On the Gift: A Discussion between Jacques Derrida and Jean-Luc Marion, Moderated by Richard Kearney." In *God, the Gift, and Postmodernism,* ed. John D. Caputo and Michael J. Scanlon, 54–78. Bloomington: Indiana University Press, 1999.

de Vaux, Roland. *Ancient Israel: Its Life and Institutions.* Trans. John McHugh. New York: McGraw-Hill, 1961.

Dodaro, Robert. "Loose Canons: Augustine and Derrida on Their Selves." In *God, the Gift, and Postmodernism,* ed. John D. Caputo and Michael J. Scanlon, 79–97. Bloomington: Indiana University Press, 1999.

Douglas, Kelly Brown. *The Black Christ.* Maryknoll, NY: Orbis Books, 1994.

Dunnill, John. "Methodological Rivalries: Theology and Social Science in Girardian Interpretations of the New Testament." *Journal for the Study of the New Testament* 62 (1996): 105–19.

Erdman, Charles R. *The Epistle of Paul to the Romans.* Philadelphia: Westminster Press, 1925.

Farley, Margaret A. "New Patterns of Relationship: Beginnings of a Moral Revolution." *Theological Studies* 36 (1975): 627–46.

———. "Sources of Sexual Inequality in the History of Christian Thought." *Journal of Religion* 56, no. 2 (1976): 162–76.

Fiddes, Paul. *The Creative Suffering of God.* Oxford: Clarendon Press, 1988.

———. *Past Event and Present Salvation: The Christian Idea of Atonement.* London: Darton, Longman & Todd, 1989.

Fitzmyer, Joseph A. *Pauline Theology: A Brief Sketch.* Englewood Cliffs, NJ: Prentice-Hall, 1967.

Frankl, Viktor Emil. *Man's Search for Meaning: An Introduction to Logotherapy.* New York: Simon & Schuster, 1963.

Fredriksen, Paula. *Jesus of Nazareth, King of the Jews: A Jewish Life and the Emergence of Christianity.* New York: Alfred A. Knopf, 1999.

Friedan, Betty. *The Feminine Mystique.* New York: Norton, 1963.

Galvin, John P. "Retelling the Story of Jesus: Christology." In *The Praxis of Christian Experience: An Introduction to the Theology of Edward Schillebeeckx,* ed. Robert J. Schreiter and Mary Catherine Hilkert, 52–67. San Francisco: Harper & Row, 1989.

———. "The Story of Jesus as the Story of God." In *The Praxis of the Reign of God: An Introduction to the Theology of Edward Schillebeeckx,* ed. Mary Catherine Hilkert and Robert J. Schreiter, 79–96. New York: Fordham University Press, 2002.

George, William P. "The Praxis of the Kingdom of God: Ethics in Schillebeeckx's *Jesus* and *Christ.*" *Horizons* 12 (1985): 44–69.

Gibbs, Robert. "Enigmatic Authority: Levinas and the Phenomenonal Effacement." *Modern Theology* 16, no. 3 (2000): 325–34.

Gilkes, Cheryl Townsend. *"If It Wasn't for the Women . . ."* Black Women's Experience and Womanist Culture in Church and Community. Maryknoll, NY: Orbis Books, 2001.

Gilligan, Carol. *In a Different Voice: Psychological Theory and Women's Development.* Cambridge, MA: Harvard University Press, 1982.

Girard, René. *Job the Victim of His People.* Trans. Yvonne Freccero. Stanford, CA: Stanford University Press, 1987.

———. *I See Satan Fall Like Lightning.* Trans. James G. Williams. Maryknoll, NY: Orbis Books, 2001.

———. *Violence and the Sacred.* Trans. Patrick Gregory. Baltimore: Johns Hopkins University Press, 1977.

Goergen, Donald J. "Presence to God, Presence to the World: Spirituality." In *The Praxis of Christian Experience: An Introduction to the Theology of Edward Schillebeeckx,* ed. Robert J. Schreiter and Mary Catherine Hilkert, 86–100. San Francisco: Harper & Row, 1989.

Grant, Jacquelyn. " 'Come to My Help, Lord, for I'm in Trouble': Womanist Jesus and the Mutual Struggle for Liberation." In *Reconstructing the Christ Symbol: Essays in Feminist Christology,* ed. Maryanne Stevens, 54–71. New York: Paulist Press, 1993.

———. *White Women's Christ and Black Women's Jesus.* Atlanta: Scholars Press, 1989.

Grey, Mary. *Feminism, Redemption and the Christian Tradition.* Mystic, CT: Twenty-Third Publications, 1990.

Grigsby, Bruce H. "The Cross as an Expiatory Sacrifice in the Fourth Gospel." *Journal for the Study of the New Testament* 15 (1982): 51–80.

Grundmann, Walter. "Sin." In *Theological Dictionary of the New Testament,* ed. Geoffrey W. Bromiley, 1, 293–316. Grand Rapids: Eerdmans, 1964–76.

Gunton, Colin. "*Christus Victor* Revisited: A Study in Metaphor and the Transformation of Meaning." *Journal of Theological Studies* 36, no. 1 (1985): 129–45.

Gutiérrez, Gustavo. *On Job: God-Talk and the Suffering of the Innocent.* Trans. Matthew J. O'Connell. Maryknoll, NY: Orbis Books, 1987.

Hahn, Lewis Edwin, ed. *The Philosophy of Paul Ricoeur.* Library of Living Philosophers. Chicago: Open Court, 1995.

Haught, John. *God after Darwin: A Theology of Evolution.* Boulder, CO: Westview Press, 2000.

Heidegger, Martin. *Being and Time.* Trans. John Macquarrie and Edward Robinson. Oxford: Basil Blackwell, 1978.

Henninger, Joseph. "Sacrifice." In *The Encyclopedia of Religion,* ed. Mircea Eliade. New York: Macmillan, 1987.

Hermann, Ingo. "Expiation." In *Theological Dictionary of the New Testament,* ed. Geoffrey W. Bromiley, 3, 302–10. Grand Rapids: Eerdmans, 1964–76.

Heschel, Abraham J. *The Prophets.* New York: Jewish Publication Society of America, 1962.

———. "The Sabbath: Its Meaning for Modern Man." In *The Earth Is the Lord's and the Sabbath,* 2–136. New York: Harper & Row, 1950.

Hilkert, Mary Catherine. "Cry Beloved Image: Rethinking the Image of God." In *In the Embrace of God: Feminist Approaches to Theological Anthropology,* ed. Ann O'Hara Graff, 190–205. Maryknoll, NY: Orbis, 1995.

———. "Discovery of the Living God: Revelation and Experience." In *The Praxis of Christian Experience: An Introduction to the Theology of Edward Schillebeeckx,* ed. Robert J. Schreiter and Mary Catherine Hilkert, 35–51. San Francisco: Harper & Row, 1989.

———. "Experience and Revelation." In *The Praxis of the Reign of God: An Introduction to the Theology of Edward Schillebeeckx,* ed. Mary Catherine Hilkert and Robert J. Schreiter, 59–78. New York: Fordham University Press, 2002.

———. "*Imago Dei:* Does the Symbol Have a Future?" *The Santa Clara Lectures* 8, no. 3 (2001).

Hill, David. "'To Offer Spiritual Sacrifices' (1 Peter 2:5): Liturgical Formulations and Christian Paraenesis in 1 Peter." *Journal for the Study of the New Testament* 16 (1982): 45–63.

Hill, William J. "Human Happiness as God's Honor: Background to a Theology in Transition." In *The Praxis of Christian Experience: An Introduction to the Theology of Edward Schillebeeckx,* ed. Robert J. Schreiter and Mary Catherine Hilkert, 1–17. San Francisco: Harper & Row, 1989.

———. "A Theology in Transition." In *The Praxis of the Reign of God: An Introduction to the Theology of Edward Schillebeeckx,* ed. Mary Catherine Hilkert and Robert J. Schreiter, 1–18. New York: Fordham University Press, 2002.

Hinze, Bradford E. "Eschatology and Ethics." In *The Praxis of the Reign of God: An Introduction to the Theology of Edward Schillebeeckx,* ed. Mary Catherine Hilkert and Robert J. Schreiter, 167–84. New York: Fordham University Press, 2002.

———. "A Prophetic Vision: Eschatology and Ethics." In *The Praxis of Christian Experience: An Introduction to the Theology of Edward Schillebeeckx,* ed. Robert J. Schreiter and Mary Catherine Hilkert, 131–46. San Francisco: Harper & Row, 1989.

Hochschild, Arlie Russell, and Anne Machung. *The Second Shift: Working Parents and the Revolution at Home.* New York: Viking, 1989.

Hubert, Henri, and Marcel Mauss. *Sacrifice: Its Nature and Function.* Chicago: University of Chicago Press, 1964. Translation of "Essai sur la nature et la fonction du sacrifice," *L'Année Sociologique* 2 (1899).

Irwin, Kevin W. "Sacramentality and the Theology of Creation: A Recovered Paradigm for Sacramental Theology." *Louvain Studies* 23 (1998): 159–79.

Jacko, Dorothy A. "Schillebeeckx's Creation-Based Theology as Basis for Ecological Spirituality." In *An Ecology of the Spirit: Religious Reflection and Environmental Consciousness,* ed. Michael Barnes, 147–60. Lanham, MD: University Press of America, 1994.

John Paul II. "The Ecological Crisis: A Common Responsibility. Message of His Holiness Pope John Paul II for the Celebration of the World Day of Peace, January 1, 1990." In *And God Saw That It Was Good: Catholic Theology and the Environment,* ed. Walter Grazer and Drew Christiansen, 215–22. Washington, DC: United States Catholic Conference, 1996.

Johnson, Elizabeth A. "Does God Play Dice? Divine Providence and Chance." *Theological Studies* 57 (1996): 3–18.

———. *She Who Is: The Mystery of God in Feminist Theological Discourse.* New York: Crossroad, 1997.

———. *Truly Our Sister: A Theology of Mary in the Communion of Saints.* New York: Continuum, 2003.

Johnson, Patricia Altenbernd. *On Gadamer.* Wadsworth Philosophers Series. Belmont, CA: Wadsworth, 2000.

Jones, Serene. "Women's Experience between a Rock and a Hard Place." In *Horizons in Feminist Theology: Identity, Traditions, and Norms,* ed. Rebecca Chopp and Sheila Greeve Davaney, 33–53. Minneapolis: Fortress Press, 1997.

Jungmann, Josef A. *The Early Liturgy to the Time of Gregory the Great.* Trans. Francis A. Brunner. Notre Dame, IN: University of Notre Dame Press, 1959.

Kant, Immanuel. *Groundwork of the Metaphysic of Morals.* Trans. H. J. Paton. New York: Harper Torchbooks, 1964.

Keenan, Marjorie. *From Stockholm to Johannesburg: An Historical Overview of the Concern of the Holy See for the Environment, 1972–2002.* Vatican City: Pontifical Council for Justice and Peace, 2002.

Keller, Catherine. "Scoop up the Water and the Moon Is in Your Hands: On Feminist Theology and Dynamic Self-Emptying." In *The Emptying God: A Buddhist-Jewish-Christian Conversation,* ed. Christopher Ives and John B. Cobb, 102–15. Maryknoll, NY: Orbis, 1990.

Kemp, Peter. "Another Language for the Other: From Kierkegaard to Levinas." *Philosophy and Social Criticism* 21, nos. 5–6 (1995): 41–61.

———. "Narrative Ethics and Moral Law in Ricoeur." In *Paul Ricoeur and Contemporary Moral Thought,* ed. William Schweiker, John Wall, and W. David Hall, 32–46. New York: Routledge, 2002.

Kempis, Thomas à. *The Imitation of Christ.* Trans. Richard Whitford, ed. Harold C. Gardiner. New York: Doubleday, 1955.

Kennedy, Philip. "God and Creation." In *The Praxis of the Reign of God: An Introduction to the Theology of Edward Schillebeeckx,* ed. Mary Catherine Hilkert and Robert J. Schreiter, 37–58. New York: Fordham University Press, 2002.

———. *Schillebeeckx.* Outstanding Christian Thinkers. Ed. Brian Davies. Collegeville, MN: Liturgical Press, 1993.

Kilgallen, John. "The Wisdom of Jesus: Gospel Reflections." *Chicago Studies* 42, no. 2 (2003): 195–220.

Kittel, Gerhard. "Priesthood." In *Theological Dictionary of the New Testament,* ed. Geoffrey W. Bromiley, 4, 249–51. Grand Rapids: Eerdmans, 1964–76.

Klawans, Jonathan. "Interpreting the Last Supper: Sacrifice, Spiritualization, and Anti-Sacrifice." *New Testament Studies* 48, no. 1 (2002): 1–17.

"The Kutadanta Sutta." In *The Long Discourses of the Buddha: A Translation of the Digha Nikaya,* 133–41. Boston: Wisdom Publications, 1995.

Lathrop, Gordon W. "Justin, Eucharist, and 'Sacrifice': A Case of Metaphor." *Worship* 64 (1990): 30–48.

Lefebure, Leo D. *Toward a Contemporary Wisdom Christology: A Study of Karl Rahner and Norman Pittenger.* Lanham, MD: University Press of America, 1988.

———. "Victims, Violence and the Sacred: The Thought of René Girard." *Christian Century* (1996): 1226–29.

Leon-Dufour, X. *Face hà la mort: Jésus et Paul.* Paris: Seuil, 1979.

Levenson, Jon Douglas. *The Death and Resurrection of the Beloved Son: The Transformation of Child Sacrifice in Judaism and Christianity.* New Haven, CT: Yale University Press, 1993.

———. "Sacrifice as the Basis of Worship: An Overlooked Commonality of Judaism and Catholicism." *Annual Driscoll Lecture in Jewish-Catholic Studies.* Iona College, New Rochelle, NY. March 11, 2003.

Levinas, Emmanuel. *Ethics and Infinity: Conversations with Philippe Nemo.* Trans. Richard A. Cohen. Pittsburgh: Duquesne University Press, 1985.

Lowe, Walter James. "Review, *Freud and Philosophy: An Essay on Interpretation.*" *Religious Studies Review* 4, no. 4 (1978): 246–54.

Malan, D. J. "The Implications of Schillebeeckx's Theology of Liberation for Anthropology and Creation." *Skrif en Kerk* 14, no. 2 (1993): 249–62.

McGinn, Bernard. *The Flowering of Mysticism: Men and Women in the New Mysticism (1200–1350).* Vol. 3: *The Presence of God: A History of Western Christian Mysticism.* New York: Crossroad, 1998.

McKenzie, John. "The Gospel According to Matthew." In *The Jerome Biblical Commentary,* ed. Joseph A. Fitzmyer, Raymond E. Brown, and Roland E. Murphy, 62–114. Englewood Cliffs, NJ: Prentice-Hall, 1968.

McLean, Bradley H. "The Absence of an Atoning Sacrifice in Paul's Soteriology." *New Testament Studies* 38 (1992): 531–53.

Menken, Martinus J. J. "The Source of the Quotation from Isaiah 53:4 in Matthew 8:17." *Novum Testamentum* 39 (1997): 313–27.

Mersch, Emile. *The Whole Christ: The Historical Development of the Doctrine of the Mystical Body in Scripture and Tradition.* Religion and Culture Series. Trans. John R. Kelly. Ed. Joseph Husslein. Milwaukee: Bruce Publishing Company, 1938.

Moltmann, Jürgen. *God in Creation: A New Theology of Creation and the Spirit of God.* Trans. Margaret Kohl. Minneapolis: Fortress Press, 1985.

Muldoon, Mark. *On Ricoeur.* Wadsworth Notes. Belmont, CA: Wadsworth/Thomson Learning, 2002.

Morny, Joy. "Levinas: Alterity, the Feminine, and Women — a Meditation." *Studies in Religion/Sciences Religieuses* 22, no. 4 (1993): 463–85.

Nelson, Richard D. " 'He Offered Himself': Sacrifice in Hebrews." *Interpretation* 57, no. 3 (2003): 251–65.

Niebuhr, Reinhold. *The Nature and Destiny of Man.* Vol. 1. *Human Nature.* (New York: Scribner's, 1941

Nussbaum, Martha C. "Ricoeur on Tragedy: Teleology, Deontology, and *Phronesis.*" In *Paul Ricoeur and Contemporary Moral Thought,* ed. William Schweiker, John Wall, and W. David Hall, 264–78. New York: Routledge, 2002.

Nygren, Anders. *Agape and Eros: A Study of the Christian Idea of Love.* Trans. A. G. Hebert. London: Society for Promoting Christian Knowledge, 1932.

Ochs, Peter. "From Phenomenology to Scripture: A General Response." *Modern Theology* 16, no. 3 (2000): 341–45.

O'Donovan, Oliver. *The Problem of Self-Love in St. Augustine.* New Haven, CT: Yale University Press, 1980.

Omanson, Roger L. "A Superior Covenant: Hebrews 8:1–10:18." *Review and Expositor* 82 (1985): 361–73.

O'Meara, Janet M. "Salvation: Living Communion with God." In *The Praxis of the Reign of God: An Introduction to the Theology of Edward Schillebeeckx,* ed. Mary Catherine Hilkert and Robert J. Schreiter, 97–116. New York: Fordham University Press, 2001.

Outka, Gene. *Agape: An Ethical Analysis.* New Haven, CT: Yale University Press, 1972.

Peacocke, Arthur. *Theology for a Scientific Age: Being and Becoming — Natural, Divine and Human.* Minneapolis: Fortress Press, 1993.

Peperzak, Adriaan. *To the Other: An Introduction to the Philosophy of Emmanuel Levinas.* Purdue Series in the History of Philosophy, ed. Joseph J. Kockelmans, Arion Kelkel, Adriaan Peperzak, Calvin O. Schrag, and Thomas Seebohm. West Lafayette, IN: Purdue University Press, 1993.

Perrin, Norman. *Jesus and the Language of the Kingdom: Symbol and Metaphor in New Testament Interpretation.* Philadelphia: Fortress Press, 1976.

————. *The Kingdom of God in the Teaching of Jesus.* Philadelphia: Westminster, 1963.

Plaskow, Judith. *Sex, Sin and Grace: Women's Experience and the Theologies of Reinhold Niebuhr and Paul Tillich.* Washington, DC: University Press of America, 1980.

Portier, William J. "Interpretation and Method." In *The Praxis of Christian Experience: An Introduction to the Theology of Edward Schillebeeckx,* ed. Robert J. Schreiter and Mary Catherine Hilkert, 18–34. San Francisco: Harper & Row, 1989.

Power, David N. "Sacrament: An Economy of Gift." *Louvain Studies* 23 (1998): 143–58.

Rahner, Karl. "Experience of Self and Experience of God." In *Theological Investigations* 13:122–32. London: Darton, Longman & Todd, 1975.

————. *Foundations of Christian Faith: An Introduction to the Idea of Christianity.* Trans. William V. Dych. New York: Crossroad, 1976.

————. "Reflections on the Unity of the Love of Neighbor and the Love of God." In *Theological Investigations* 6:231–49. London: Darton, Longman & Todd, 1974.

————. "Theology of Freedom." In *Theological Investigations* 6:178–96. London: Darton, Longman & Todd, 1974.

Rankka, Kristine M. *Women and the Value of Suffering: An Aw(E)Ful Rowing toward God.* Collegeville, MN: Liturgical Press, 1998.

Reagan, Charles. "Personal Identity." In *Ricoeur as Another: The Ethics of Subjectivity,* ed. Richard A. Cohen and James L. Marsh, 3–32. Albany: State University of New York Press, 2002.

Ricoeur, Paul. "The Conflict of Interpretations: Debate with Hans-Georg Gadamer." In *A Ricoeur Reader: Reflection and Imagination,* ed. Mario J. Valdés, 216–41. Toronto: University of Toronto Press, 1991.

————. "Ethical and Theological Considerations on the Golden Rule." In *Figuring the Sacred: Religion, Narrative, and Imagination,* ed. Mark I. Wallace, 293–302. Minneapolis: Fortress Press, 1995.

————. *Fallible Man. Philosophy of the Will Part II: Finitude and Guilt.* Chicago: Henry Regnery Company, 1965.

————. *Freedom and Nature: The Voluntary and the Involuntary.* Northwestern University Studies in Phenomenology and Existential Philosophy. Trans. Erazim V. Kohák. Ed. John Wild. Northwestern University Press, 1966.

————. *Freud and Philosophy: An Essay on Interpretation.* Trans. Denis Savage. New Haven, CT: Yale University Press, 1970.

————. "From Metaphysics to Moral Philosophy." *Philosophy Today* 40 (1986): 453–55.

———. *From Text to Action.* Trans. Kathleen McLaughlin and David Pellauer. Evanston, IL: Northwestern University Press, 1991.

———. *Hermeneutics and the Human Sciences: Essays on Language, Action, and Interpretation.* Trans. John B. Thompson. London: Cambridge University Press, 1981.

———. "The Hermeneutics of Testimony." In *Essays on Biblical Interpretation,* ed. Lewis S. Mudge, 119–54. Philadelphia: Fortress Press, 1980.

———. *Husserl: An Analysis of His Phenomenology.* Northwestern University Studies in Phenomenology and Existential Philosophy. Trans. Edward G. Ballard and Lester E. Embree. Evanston, IL: Northwestern University Press, 1967.

———. "The Logic of Jesus, the Logic of God." In *Figuring the Sacred: Religion, Narrative, and Imagination,* ed. Mark I. Wallace, 279–83. Minneapolis: Fortress Press, 1995.

———. "Love and Justice." In *Figuring the Sacred: Religion, Narrative, and Imagination,* ed. Mark I. Wallace, 315–30. Minneapolis: Fortress Press, 1995.

———. *Oneself as Another.* Trans. Kathleen Blamey. Chicago: University of Chicago Press, 1992.

———. "The Problem of the Foundation of Moral Philosophy." *Philosophy Today* (1978): 175–92.

———. *The Rule of Metaphor: Multidisciplinary Studies in the Creation of Meaning in Language.* Trans. Robert Czerny with Kathleen McLaughlin and John Costello. Toronto: University of Toronto Press, 1977.

———. "The Summoned Subject in the School of the Narratives of the Prophetic Vocation." In *Figuring the Sacred: Religion, Narrative, and Imagination,* ed. Mark I. Wallace, 262–78. Minneapolis: Fortress Press, 1995.

———. *The Symbolism of Evil.* Religious Perspectives Series. Trans. Emerson Buchanan. Ed. Ruth Nanda Anshen. Boston: Beacon Press, 1967.

———. *Time and Narrative.* Vol. 2. Trans. Kathleen McLaughlin and David Pellauer. Chicago and London: University of Chicago Press, 1985.

———. " 'Whoever Loses Their Life for My Sake Will Find It.' " In *Figuring the Sacred: Religion, Narrative, and Imagination,* ed. Mark I. Wallace, 284–89. Minneapolis: Fortress Press, 1995.

Robinson, John A. T. *Wrestling with Romans.* Philadelphia: Westminster Press, 1979.

Rosemont, Henry, Jr. "Whither the World's Religions in the Twenty-First Century?" *Religion East and West: Journal of the Institute for World Religions,* no. 1 (2001): 1–16.

Ruether, Rosemary Radford. *Sexism and God-Talk: Toward a Feminist Theology.* Boston: Beacon Press, 1983.

———. "Feminist Hermeneutics, Scriptural Authority, and Religious Experience: The Case of the *Imago Dei* and Gender Equality." In *Paradigm Change in Theology: A Symposium for the Future,* ed. Hans Küng and David Tracy, 95–106. New York: Crossroad, 1989.

Sakenfeld, Katharine Doob. "Feminist Perspectives on Bible and Theology: An Introduction to Selected Issues and Literature." *Interpretation* 42 (1988): 5–18.

Saiving, Valerie. "Human Experience: A Feminine View." *Journal of Religion* 40 (1960).

Scheffczyk, Leo. "Sacrifice II. Substitution (Representation)." In *Sacramentum Mundi: An Encyclopedia of Theology,* ed. Karl Rahner, 5, 391–92. New York: Herder & Herder, 1970.

Schillebeeckx, Edward. *Christ: The Experience of Jesus as Lord.* Trans. John Bowden. New York: Crossroad, 1981.

———. "Christian Identity and Human Integrity." In *Is Being Human a Criterion of Being Christian?* ed. Jean-Pierre Jossua and Claude Geffré, 23–31. New York: Seabury Press, 1982.

———. "Christian 'to the Death' (Matt. 16:21; Jer. 20:7–9)." In *God among Us: The Gospel Proclaimed,* 199–203. New York: Crossroad, 1983.

———. *Church: The Human Story of God.* Trans. John Bowden. New York: Crossroad, 1990.

———. "Critical Theories and Christian Political Commitment." In *Political Commitment and Christian Community,* ed. Alois Muller and Norbert Greinacher, 48–61. New York: Herder and Herder, 1973.

———. *For the Sake of the Gospel.* New York: Crossroad, 1990.

———. "God as a Loud Cry (Mark 15:37; Matt. 27:50)." In *I Believe in God, Creator of Heaven and Earth,* 73–77. New York: Crossroad, 1983.

———. "God, Society and Human Salvation." In *Faith and Society,* 87–99. Gembloux, Belgium: Editions Duculot, 1978.

———. *I Am a Happy Theologian: Conversations with Francesco Strazzari.* New York: Crossroad, 1994.

———. "I Believe in God, Creator of Heaven and Earth." In *God among Us: The Gospel Proclaimed,* 91–102. New York: Crossroad, 1983.

———. "I Believe in the Man Jesus: The Christ, the Only Beloved Son, Our Lord." In *I Believe in God, Creator of Heaven and Earth,* 103–15. New York: Crossroad, 1983.

———. *Interim Report on the Books Jesus and Christ.* Trans. John Bowden. New York: Crossroad, 1981.

———. *Jesus: An Experiment in Christology.* Trans. Hubert Hoskins. New York: Seabury Press, 1979.

———. "Jesus' Story of God." In *God among Us: The Gospel Proclaimed,* 27–32. New York: Crossroad, 1983.

———. "Prologue." In *The Praxis of the Reign of God: An Introduction to the Theology of Edward Schillebeeckx,* ed. Mary Catherine Hilkert and Robert J. Schreiter, ix–xix. New York: Fordham University Press, 2002.

———. "Questions on Christian Salvation of and for Man." In *Toward Vatican III: The Work That Needs to Be Done,* ed. David Tracy with Hans Küng and Johann B. Metz, 27–44. New York: Seabury Press, 1978.

———. "The Religious and the Human Ecumene." In *The Future of Liberation Theology: Essays in Honor of Gustavo Gutiérrez,* ed. Marc H. Ellis and Otto Maduro, 177–88. Maryknoll, NY: Orbis, 1989.

———. *Revelation and Theology, 2: The Concept of Truth and Theological Renewal.* London: Sheed & Ward, 1968.

———. "You Cannot Arbitrarily Make Something of the Gospel." In *Twenty Years of Concilium: Retrospect and Prospect,* ed. Edward Schillebeeckx and Anton Weiler Paul Brand, 15–19. New York: Seabury Press, 1983.

Schreiter, Robert J. "Edward Schillebeeckx: His Continuing Significance." In *The Praxis of Christian Experience: An Introduction to the Theology of Edward Schillebeeckx,* ed. Robert J. Schreiter and Mary Catherine Hilkert, 147–55. San Francisco: Harper & Row, 1989.

Schwager, Raymund. *Jesus in the Drama of Salvation: Toward a Biblical Doctrine of Salvation.* Trans. James G. Williams and Paul Haddon. New York: Crossroad, 1999.

Schweiker, William. "Starry Heavens and Moral Worth: Hope and Responsibility in the Structure of Theological Ethics." In *Paul Ricoeur and Contemporary Moral*

*Thought,* ed. William Schweiker, John Wall, and W. David Hall, 117–42. New York: Routledge, 2002.

Seasoltz, R. Kevin. "Another Look at Sacrifice." *Worship* 74 (2000): 386–413.

Semmelroth, Otto. "Sacrifice I. Concept of Sacrifice; III. Sacrifice of Christ." In *Sacramentum Mundi: An Encyclopedia of Theology,* ed. Karl Rahner, 5, 388–94. New York: Herder & Herder, 1970.

Soelle, Dorothee. *The Strength of the Weak.* Trans. Robert and Rita Kimber. Philadelphia: Westminster Press, 1984.

Stanton, Elizabeth Cady et al., eds. *The Women's Bible.* Vol. 1. New York: European Publishing Co., 1895.

Stevens, Maryanne. *Reconstructing the Christ Symbol: Essays in Feminist Christology.* New York: Paulist Press, 1993.

Stott, Wilfrid. "Conception of 'Offering' in the Epistle to the Hebrews." *New Testament Studies* 9 (1962): 62–67.

Strathmann, Hermann. "Service." In *Theological Dictionary of the New Testament,* ed. Geoffrey W. Bromiley, 4, 61–65. Grand Rapids: Eerdmans, 1964–76.

Suchocki, Marjorie Hewitt. *The Fall to Violence: Original Sin.* New York: Continuum, 1995.

Surber, Jean Paul. "Ricoeur and the Dialectics of Interpretation." *Iliff Review* 35 (1978): 13–26.

Taylor, Charles. *Sources of the Self: The Making of the Modern Identity.* Cambridge, MA: Harvard University Press, 1989.

Taylor, Nicholas H. "Conflicting Bases of Identity in Early Christianity: The Example of Paul." In *Handbook of Early Christianity,* ed. Jean Duhaime, Anthony J. Blasi, Paul-André Turcotte, 577–97. Walnut Creek, CA: Altamira Press, 2002.

Terkel, Studs. *Race: How Blacks and Whites Think and Feel about the American Obsession.* New York: New Press, 1992.

Terrell, JoAnne Marie. *Power in the Blood? The Cross in the African American Experience.* Maryknoll, NY: Orbis Books, 1998.

Thompson, Daniel P. "The Church as Sacrament: Schillebeeckx's Contributions to the Construction of a Critical Ecclesiology." *Religious Studies and Theology* 17, no. 33 (1998): 45.

———. "Schillebeeckx on the Development of Doctrine." *Theological Studies* 62 (2001): 303–21.

Thompson, Daniel Speed. *The Language of Dissent: Edward Schillebeeckx on the Crisis of Authority in the Catholic Church.* Notre Dame, IN: Notre Dame University Press, 2003.

Tillar, Elizabeth Kennedy. "Suffering for Others in the Theology of Edward Schillebeeckx." New York: Fordham University, 1999.

Tillich, Paul. *Systematic Theology: Existence and the Christ.* Vol. 2. Chicago: University of Chicago Press, 1951–63.

Tolbert, Philip. "Actualizing the Gospel: Three Lectures by Edward Schillebeeckx." *Epiphany* 3, no. 4 (1983): 86–88.

Tracy, David. *The Analogical Imagination: Christian Theology and the Culture of Pluralism.* New York: Crossroad, 1981.

———. "Do Christians Any Longer Feel the World as God's Creation?" Keynote address, *The Person, the Poor and the Common Good.* Scholars' Conference sponsored by the United States Conference of Catholic Bishops. University of St. Thomas, St. Paul, Minnesota, October 2004.

————. "Metaphor and Religion: The Test Case of Religious Texts." In *On Metaphor,* ed. Sheldon Sacks, 89–105. Chicago: University of Chicago Press, 1979.

————. *On Naming the Present: Reflections on God, Hermeneutics, and Church.* Maryknoll, NY: Orbis, 1994.

————. "Religion and Human Rights in the Public Realm." *Daedalus* 112 (1983): 248.

Trible, Phyllis. *God and the Rhetoric of Sexuality.* Overtures to Biblical Theology. Ed. Walter Brueggemann and John R. Donahue. Philadelphia: Fortress Press, 1978.

Turner, Victor. "Sacrifice as Quintessential Process: Prophylaxis or Abandonment?" In *Blazing the Trail: Way Marks in the Exploration of Symbols,* ed. Edith Turner, 89–112. Tucson: University of Arizona Press, 1992.

Vandervelde, George. "Creation and Cross in the Christology of Edward Schillebeeckx: A Protestant Appraisal." *Journal of Ecumenical Studies* 20 (1983): 257–71.

Venema, Henry Isaac. *Identifying Selfhood: Imagination, Narrative, and Hermeneutics in the Thought of Paul Ricoeur.* McGill Studies in the History of Religions. Ed. Katherine K. Young. Albany: State University of New York Press, 2000.

Vermes, Geza. *Jesus the Jew: A Historian's Reading of the Gospels.* Philadelphia: Fortress Press, 1973.

von Balthasar, Hans Urs. *Studies in Theological Style: Clerical Styles.* Vol. 2. *The Glory of the Lord: A Theological Aesthetics.* Edinburgh: T. & T. Clark, 1984.

Wall, John. "Moral Meaning: Beyond the Good and the Right." In *Paul Ricoeur and Contemporary Moral Thought,* ed. William Schweiker, John Wall, and W. David Hall, 47–63. New York: Routledge, 2002.

Wallace, Mark I. "From Phenomenology to Scripture? Paul Ricoeur's Hermeneutical Philosophy of Religion." *Modern Theology* 16, no. 3 (2000): 301–13.

Whitehead, Alfred North. *Process and Reality: An Essay in Cosmology,* ed. David Ray Griffin and Donald W. Sherburne. New York: Free Press, 1978.

Whitehouse, Glenn. "Ricoeur on Religious Selfhood: A Response to Mark Wallace." *Modern Theology* 16, no. 3 (2000): 315–23.

Williams, Delores S. *Sisters in the Wilderness: The Challenge of Womanist God-Talk.* Maryknoll, NY: Orbis Books, 1993.

Young, Frances M. *Sacrifice and the Death of Christ.* London: SPCK, 1975.

————. "New Wine in Old Wineskins, XIV: Sacrifice." *Expository Times* 86 (1975): 305–9.

# Index

Abelard, 83
Adam, Karl, 158
agape
  Andolsen critiquing narrow views of,
    97–101
  enlarging the scope of, 105–9
  idealization of, as self-sacrifice, 98
  rooted in the Trinity, 99–100
*Agape: An Ethical Analysis* (Outka), 99
*Agape and Eros* (Nygren), 98
alleluia Christianity, 174, 189, 213
anachronisms, complicating assessment of
    sacrificial theological language, 85–87
analogical transfer, 257–58n334
Andolsen, Barbara Hilkert, 10, 97–101, 104,
    105, 106, 118, 210
*Annales* school, 74
Annunciation, 261n373
Anselm, 83, 88
anthropodicy, 165
Antigone, 257n338
anxiety, due to nature/spirit duality, 110
*Aqedah*, 30–32
Aquinas, 161–62
Aristotle, 126, 255n312
atonement
  critique of theologies, promoting self-
    sacrifice, 81–85
  distinct from propitiation, 20
  doctrine of, outweighed by God's
    outpouring love, 105
  as God's self-giving, 114–15
  linked to sacrificial love, 98
  not interchangeable with sacrifice, 85–86
  sacrificial process of, 243–44n119
atonement theology, uniting action of God
    and Jesus, 91
atonement theories
  alternate assessments of passivity and
    suffering in, 87–91
  critiques of, 85–91, 211
  womanist theologians' confronting, 93–94

atoning death canon, 39–40
Augustine, 111
  distinguishing love of self and love of God,
    107
  figure of the inner teacher, 147
  on inner and outer sacrifice, 5–6
  on the language of sacrifice, 5
  love determined by orientation in
    relationship to God, 107
  on proper relationship to God, 107–8
  on self-love, 6–7
Aulén, Gustav, 87
Austin, J. L., 256n
auto-foundationalism, 254–55n310

Bellet, Maurice, 88
Benedict XVI, 9
Bible, non-liberative strand in, 93
Binding of Isaac (*Aqedah*), 30–32
blood, related to atonement, 19, 20
bloodless sacrifice, 14
blood sacrifice, 18–20
Bonhoeffer, Dietrich, 9, 116
  on cost of discipleship, 56
  on union with Christ requiring work and
    obedience, 71
Bourgeois, Patrick L., 138
Bowden, John, 159, 176, 177
Braudel, Fernand, 74, 75
Brown, Joanne Carlson, 10, 81–91, 191, 210
Brown, Raymond, 41–42, 43, 54
Bruce, Frederick Fyvie, 51, 52
Buss, Helen, 134, 144

Cady, Linell Elizabeth, 104
change
  characteristics of, 74–76
  requiring re-enactment of doctrines and
    ideas in new times, 77
character, 127
Chauvet, Louis-Marie, 28–29, 33, 34, 49,
    54, 88

Chenu, Marie-Dominique, 158–59
child sacrifice, 17
Chilton, Bruce D., 31
Christ
  ground of hope for creation's fulfillment,
    155–56
  identity of, linked with identity of the
    disciple, 1
  as model of self-giving, expressed with
    Jewish sacrificial imagery, 76–77
  power of sacrifice, 245–46n166
  self-gift and self-emptying of, sharing in,
    222
  union with, requiring work and obedience,
    71
*Christ* (Schillebeeckx), 170, 172
Christian community, blessing of, 62
Christian discipleship, reality of suffering in,
    189–90
Christianity
  acculturating women to accept abuse, 82
  needing to eliminate the idea of the
    atonement, 85
Christian life
  as cultic service, 58
  describing as sacrificial, 10
  sacrifice as fundamental to, 13
Christian natural theology, 115–16
Christians
  acceptance of suffering, 198
  Christology of early communities, 43
  early worship of, modeling synagogue
    practices, 243n108
  as the new Temple, 57–58, 61
Christian sacrifice. *See also* sacrifice
  defined in relation to God and community,
    199
  God's creativity as theological ground for,
    216–18
  as offering of self to show love of God and
    neighbor, 231
  outwardly expressed by loving the
    neighbor, 68
Christian theology, symbols of sacrifice in, 4
Christology, as confirmation of God's
    commitment to creation's final salvation,
    167
*Christus Victor* (Aulén), 87
*Christus Victor* tradition, 82–83
church, as mediator of Christians' relation to
    Jesus' life, 171–72
*Church: The Human Story of God*
    (Schillebeeckx), 160

Coakley, Sarah, 218, 222–23
Cohen, Richard A., 259n353
Cone, James, 92
Congar, Yves, 158
conjunctural history, 75
conscience
  as depth dimension of self-other awareness,
    131
  mediating tension of summons and
    response between self and other,
    135–39
  preserving the existence of the self, 138
  as the voice of God, 147
consciousness, doubting, 124
consent, 143
contemplative prayer, 223
continuance principle, 65
*Cost of Discipleship* (Bonhoeffer), 71
creation
  acts of violence against, 111
  as central theme for Schillebeeckx, 155–58,
    161–62
  endowing with freedom, riskiness of, 219
  finding value in and through God, 117
  involving self-limitation, 218–19
  as revelation of who God is, 161–62
  sin against, 116–17
  symbol of, 148–50, 224
creation catechism, 155, 214
creation faith, 199–206
creative sacrifice, 230
creativity, human attempts at, 231
critical negativity, 196
critical suffering, 196
cross
  as definitive sign of God's solidarity with
    humanity, 180
  interpretations of, not based on sacrifice or
    cult, 47–48
  as surrogacy, critiqued by womanists,
    92–97
  ultimate contrast of, 173–82
cult, Jesus' view of, 33–34
cultic practice, as root of sacrifice, 4

Daly, Mary, 7, 80
Daly, Robert, 16, 18, 31, 45, 50, 52, 222
  on preaching, 58
  on sacrifices having ethical meaning, 63
D'Arcy, Martin, 99
Dasein, 255n314
Davies, Philip R., 31
death, as service for others, 194

debt images, combined with justice
  metaphors, 87–88
dedication, as core meaning for Christian
  sacrifice, 66, 193, 209
density reality, 268n517
De Petter, Dominic, 158
de Vaux, Roland, 46
discernment, 137, 145
disciples
  experience of Jesus, 209
  not expecting a crucified messiah, 37
  shared experience of salvation in Jesus,
    168
  suffering of, 189–95
  three core elements of living as, 58
discipleship
  destructive theology of, 90–91
  linked with sacrifice, 195–96
disclosure experiences, 196
divine creativity, 226
  kenotic nature of, 12
divine generosity, logic of, 149–50
divine impassibility, reconsidered, 84
Douglas, Kelly Brown, 95
Durkheim, Émile, 238n28

economy of the gift, 149–51, 155
empathy, 112
ephemeral history, 75
ethical duty, 229
ethical identity, philosophical and religious
  views of, 198
ethical proclamation, 229
ethical sensibility, proclamatory, 229

*Fall to Violence, The: Original Sin in
  Relational Theology* (Suchocki), 109
Farley, Margaret, 115
fasting, as form of sacrifice, 28
felt synthesis, of cosmos and person, 228–29
female nature, universal, 104
*Feminine Mystique* (Friedan), 80
feminist anthropology, 250n274
feminist theology
  addressing risk of self-loss inherent in
    sacrifice, 10–11
  experience as key source in, 104
  questioning violent and arbitrary nature of
    atonement model, 83–84
  on the rhetoric of sacrifice, 210–11
Fiddes, Paul, 35, 85, 87, 88, 114–15,
  269n535
fidelity, cost of, 143

finite creatures, interdependence of, 214–15
finitude, 129, 215
  believers' and non-believers' approaches
    to, 164–65
  belonging to the goodness of creation, 164
  as a created good, 155, 164
  reconciliation to, 202–5
  sacrifices resulting from, 165–66
First John, presenting Christian community
  as the new Temple, 61
First Peter, important source for descriptions
  of Christian discipleship, 59–61
firstfruits offerings, 18
Fitzmyer, Joseph A., 47–49, 87–88
forgiveness, opposite of sin, 109
Frankl, Viktor, 89
Fredriksen, Paula, 32, 34, 35, 239n44
Freud, Sigmund, 123–24
*Freud and Philosophy: An Essay on
  Interpretation* (Ricoeur), 123–24
Friedan, Betty, 80
future, sovereignty over, reserved to God,
  204

Galvin, John, 40, 175–76, 178, 181
Gandhi, Mahatma, 9
George, William P., 267n492
gift economy, 222
Gilkes, Cheryl Townsend, 96–97
Gilson, Etienne, 158
Girard, René, 18, 238n22
God. *See also* God, creativity of
  acting in history, 171
  becoming the image of, 224–25, 229–31
  calling disciple to unconditional service,
    197
  entrusting creation to the autonomy of
    finite creatures, 155, 165–66
  found in the intimacy of self-presence, 147
  as origin of love, 116–17
  outpouring love of, larger than doctrine of
    the atonement, 105
  positive affirmations about, 162
  present in Jesus Christ, 167, 171
  present to human suffering and sacrifice,
    155–56, 166
  as pure existence, 161
  rejecting suffering, 184
  revealed by suffering, 186–87
  self-giving of, as source of new life, 216
  self-limitation of, 220
  willing human salvation in spite of threats
    in history, 170–71

God, creativity of
  compared with human self-giving, 217
  involving self-concealment, 221
  as sacrificial or kenotic, 218
  as theological ground of Christian sacrifice,
    216–18
golden rule, 146, 150–52
gospel, ethical function of, 148
Gospels, editorial emphases in views of Jesus'
    death, 40–44
grace
  effects of, 199–202
  as experience of liberation from concrete
    evils, 185
  as life in fullness, 203
  new being and, 199–202
Grant, Jacquelyn, 94–95
Grey, Mary, 79–80, 91
Grigsby, Bruce H., 30–31, 42–43, 52

harm, human capacity for, 111
*hatta't* (sin offering, reparation offering),
    45–46
Haught, John, 218, 220–21
Hebrew monotheism, critique of sacrifice in,
    24, 26–27
Hebrews, Letter to the
  on heavenly sanctuary, 62
  sacrificial imagery in, 50–54
Heidegger, Martin, 126–27, 139
Henninger, Joseph, 18
hermeneutics of sacrifice, 94–95, 129, 230
  establishing the centrality of the aim for,
    141–42
  practical criteria for, 144–45
  requiring a religious view of salvation,
    suffering, and finitude, 154
hermeneutics of suspicion, 78, 122, 208
Heschel, Abraham, 24–25
hiding, sin of, 112–14
*hilasterion*, 243n119
Hilkert, Mary Catherine, 184, 224–25
history, as continuity punctuated by fractures,
    74–75
Hubert, Henri, 18, 20–21, 22
human existence, intersubjectivity of, 120
human nature, interpreted by suffering, 186
Husserl, Edmund, 252n292

identity
  creation of, via response to otherness,
    131–41
  *idem*-identity, 127, 128

identity (*continued*)
  *ipse*-identity, 127–28
  sense of, reliant on others' support of one's
    individuality, 201
identity formation, different between the
    sexes, 102
Ignatius of Antioch, 143
imagination, 113
*imago Christi*, 217
*imago Dei*, 217, 224, 226
incarnational spiritualization of sacrifice,
    222
inner sacrifice, 26–27
interdependence, theological dimensions of,
    154
interpretation
  complexity of, 123–24
  as element within experience, 187–89
  as source of peace, 117
  theoretical view of, 187–88
Irenaeus, 163
Israel, renewed concern with expiation, after
    the exile, 30–31

Jaspers, Karl, 252n292
Jesus. *See also* Jesus, death of; Jesus, life of
  combining roles of Royal Messiah and
    Priestly Messiah, 51
  criticizing the sacrificial system, 33
  disciples' experience of, 209
  early followers of, transitioning between
    Jewish and Christian approaches to
    sacrifice, 29–33
  as explicit revelation of God's sacrificial
    love, 220
  guarantor of God's relationship of creation,
    167
  idea of wholeness, as basis for meaning of
    salvation, 168
  identified as priest, 51
  identified as sacrificial offering, 15
  inviting humanity to recognize God's no to
    suffering, 169–70
  living out a divine plan for salvation, 39
  method of living as a means of proclaiming
    the reign of God, 169
  as parable of God's care for humanity,
    168–69
  parallels with Isaac, 30–32
  as passive victim of the crucifixion, 84
  passivity of, rejected, 87
  pre-gospel traditions addressing, as
    sacrifice, 38–40

Jesus (*continued*)
  priesthood of, expressing a philanthropic Christology, 53
  as prophet in Deuteronomic pattern, 38
  rejecting exclusivity, 34
  represented as one who bears suffering of humankind, 188
  as sacrifice, multiple scriptural interpretations of, 36–57
  salvific nature of suffering questioned, 81–83
  saving work of, including forgiveness, 210
  self-gift as basic meaning of life, 66
  as self-limitation of God, 219–20
  suffering of, opacity of, 181–82
  unexpectedness for disciples of crucified messiah, 37
  view of the cult, 33–34
  view of his death in relation to the cult, 34–36
Jesus, death of
  changing possibility and function of sacrifice in the Christian church, 63–64
  expiating sin, 32
  gaining meaning from opposition to his message, 174
  interpreted in continuity with Hebrew tradition, 209
  interpreting in continuity with his life, 178–79
  interpreting together with his life, 56–57
  non-sacrificial interpretations of, 56
  as reason to affirm him as savior, 39–40
  as service, 179–81
  as sin offering, 45
  three ways of organizing interpretations of, 176–77
Jesus, life of
  describing as sacrificial, 10
  interpreted in continuity with Hebrew tradition, 209
  providing meaning to his death, 64
*Jesus: An Experiment in Christology* (Schillebeeckx), 160, 181
John, Gospel of, presenting Christian community as the new Temple, 61
John Paul II, 9
Johnson, Elizabeth A., 89
Jones, Serene, 249n260
Julian of Norwich, 117
justice, interrelated with sacrifice, 24–25

Kant, Immanuel, 198
Käsemann, Ernst, 34
Kemp, Peter, 258n
Kennedy, Philip, 160, 161, 162
kenosis, divine, 216–17
kenotic theologies, 218–25
King, Martin Luther, Jr., 9
Klawans, Jonathan, 34
Kutadanta Sutta, 14

Last Supper, significance of, 34–35
Lefebure, Leo D., 251n284
Léon-Dufour, X., 47–48, 56
Levenson, Jon, 27, 31, 52
Levinas, Emmanuel, 134, 135, 137–41, 191, 197
levitical impurity, 239n44
*lex talionis*, 149, 151
liberation theology, 84, 160
losing one's life to save it, 3, 56, 129, 173, 212, 230
love
  crowning Christian virtue, 111
  definition of as self-giving, challenged, 101
  opposite to sin, 102
love of all, embraced in the unity of Christ, 114
love command, 146, 150–52
Luther, Martin, 80

manifestation, 227–28
Marcel, Gabriel, 252n292
martyrdom, as paradigmatic Christian model of consent, 143
Marx, Karl, 123–24
Mauss, Marcel, 18, 20–21, 22
McKenzie, John, 65
McLean, Bradley H., 45–47, 52
Melchizedek tradition, 51–52
memory, 113
merit, transferred, 89
mimetic rivalry, 238n22
Mobley, Mamie, 96
Moltmann, Jürgen, 162
moral impurity, 239n44
moral influence theory, 84
Mother Teresa, 9
Muldoon, Mark, 143
mutuality, 212
  as full expression of Christian ideal, 100
  not restricted to love, 106
  ontology of, 137
mysticism, 196

narrative, role of, 125
natural theology, 115–16
natural transcendence, sin in light of, 112
Ndembu community, 239n30
negative contrast experiences, 183–87
negativity, productiveness of, 186
neighbor, love of, 5
    related to self-love, 6–7
Nelson, Richard D., 46, 50, 51
Niebuhr, Reinhold, 98, 100–101, 102, 107,
    113, 118
    distinguishing between nature and spirit,
    110
    on sensuality, 116
Nietzsche, Friedrich, 123–24
Nussbaum, Martha C., 142, 186, 261n366
Nygren, Andres, 98, 100, 101, 102, 105–6,
    107, 108, 118, 138

obedience
    as chief virtue of Christ's death, 48
    linking Jesus' sacrifice and discipleship, 61
O'Donovan, Oliver, 3
O'Meara, Janet, 196
*Oneself as Another* (Ricoeur), 120, 121,
    125–27, 138, 146
original sin, rejecting pride as, 109–15
other
    call to justice from, 135
    Heidegger's exclusion of, 126–27
    interaction with, creating self-esteem and
        solicitude, 132
    primacy of, 136–37
otherness, 128–30
    multiple dimensions of, 121
    related to sacrifice and identity, 128–29
*Otherwise Than Being or Beyond Essence*
    (Levinas), 135
Outka, Gene, 99

paradox, leading to greater truth, 123
Parker, Rebecca, 10, 81–91, 191
Parliament of World's Religions (1993), 9
participation, religious sense of, 229
participatory sensibility, 228–29
passion narratives, 40–44
passive receptivity, 196
passivity, 128–32
    different types of, 89–90
Passover, symbols of, connected with Jesus'
    death, 44–45

Paul
    alternating between theologies of history,
    49
    use of sacrificial images to refer to Jesus'
    death, 44–49
    viewing Christians as the new Temple,
    57–58
peace, interrelation as source of, 117
Peacocke, Arthur, 218–20
phenomenological hermeneutics, 120
    and the hermeneutics of self-interpretation,
    121–31
phenomenology, 258n
Philo, criticizing the sacrificial system, 33
philosophies of relation, 263n409
Plaskow, Judith, 116
Power, David, 222
pride
    as dominant mode of sin, 109
    rejecting, as original sin, 109–15
    sin exaggerated as, 101–9
process thought, 109, 115
proclamation, 227–28
promise, as example of self-extension that
    creates identity, 134, 215
promising, 142
prophetic proclamation, 229
prophet-martyr contrast scheme, 38
propitiation, distinct from atonement, 20

Qumran community, criticizing the sacrificial
    system, 33–34
Qumran tradition, associating new Temple
    with spiritual sacrifice, 60

radical mystery, religious experience of, 227
Rahner, Karl, 108
Reagan, Charles, 128, 134
reality, revealed in terms of potentialities,
    121
redemption, revisionist theology of, 91
redemptive liberation, 244n
reign of God
    anticipated in Jesus, 167–68, 169
    church witnessing to, 171–72
    priority of, 197–99
    sacrifice oriented toward, 197
religion, polarity of, 226–27
religious identity, sacrifice and, 15–36
religious models, viewing in context, 77
religious symbols, guiding the formation of
    identity, 122
renunciatory sacrifice, 23

resurrection, God judging suffering and affirming Jesus' life through, 180

revelation, found in misery and oppression, 184

Ricoeur, Paul, 1, 11, 78–79, 97, 115, 175, 192

  on becoming a self by responding to the other, 136–37

  calling for second Copernican revolution, 124–25

  compared to Levinas, 139–41

  debate with Levinas on total priority of the other, 135

  definition of ethics, 140

  emphasizing symbolism of dependence and creation, 148–49

  on ethical function of the gospel, 148

  on excessive priority of the other, 197

  on failed agency and lost authenticity, 210

  freedom affirming one's being, 140

  on freedom of conscience, 134

  grounding for the journey of self-interpretation, 121

  hermeneutic approach to intersubjectivity and identity, 119

  hermeneutics of suspicion, 208

  identifying fundamental command of the other as a plea for love, 145

  on interdependence, 215

  on interpreting one's ethical identity, 212–13

  interpreting the self via the other, 127–31

  movement of other toward the self, 136

  passivity of one's body, 165

  philosophical anthropology of, 120

  placing the voice of conscience in the voice of God, 146–47

  putting oneself at the service of the kingdom of God, 197–98

  reflection on the imitation of Christ, 146

  relating sacrifice to self-realization, 132

  response to Heidegger's approach to Being, 126–27

  on self-dispossession, 134

  selfhood as indirect interpretation, 196

  on striving for moral norms, 141

  studying interpretation, 123–24

  technical treatment of metaphor, symbol, and narrative, 253–54n299

  theory of experience, 194

  on tragic awareness, 142, 186, 229

  viewing selfhood as being summoned to responsibility, 137–38

ritual prophylactic sacrifice, 22–23, 212

ritual sacrifice, 17

Robinson, John A. T., 48, 52, 208

root metaphors, used to express a religion's central truths, 36–37

sacramental understanding, 96

sacrifice. *See also* Christian sacrifice

  affirmed as natural extension of love, 2

  alternate terms for, 2–3

  ambiguity of, 2–3

  ancient cultic practices of, 17–23

  balancing with the self, 210–12

  becoming victim of another's, 238n22

  as choice that expresses compassion and relationship to others, 209

  Christian definition of, 14

  Christian ideal of, 3–4

  contributing to religious identity, 23

  correlated with constricted freedom, 103

  cost of, 144–45

  creating self-realization, 132–33

  creative, as God is creative, 206

  danger in language of, 13

  determining appropriate time for, 101

  determining what it means to Jesus and his hearers, 77

  diverse forms of, 18–19

  etymological origins of, 18

  evolution of concept, 76

  existential definition of, 14–15

  as existential response and dedication, 67–70

  as expression of dedication, 20–21, 193

  as expression of production creation faith, 157

  in extreme cases, as seal on identity, 192–93

  feminist critique of, 78

  as form of worship, 15–16

  fostering right relations in the community, 25

  functions of, 18

  fundamental to Christian life, 13

  general definition of, 14

  as gift from God, 38

  as gift of self, 4

  God's acceptance of, not guaranteed, 25–26

  Hebrew model of, 23

  Hebrew renewal of, 24–29

  implying acceptance of hardship and suffering, 182

sacrifice (*continued*)
  incarnational spiritualization of, 16
  as indirect route to salvation, 196
  inevitability of, 155–56
  influence of early ideas about, 30
  inner and outer, 5, 26–27
  intended to change moral status of
    sacrificer, 18
  internal, 22
  interpreting social factors that intensify a
    distorted view of, 78–81
  Jesus' message of, subject to
    misinterpretation, 118
  language of, evolving over time, 24
  linked with discipleship, 195–96
  linked with identity, for believers in
    Christ, 1
  as liturgy of life, 57–63
  loss of original vibrant cultural context,
    76–77
  as mainstay of religious-force barter
    system, 21
  meaning of, for today's Christians, 14
  as means for relating to the divine, 17
  meeting with misgivings, 2
  metaphor of, defining core meaning,
    63–67
  metaphorical/spiritual reading of, 35
  as mode of worship, 4
  needed for well-being of the planet, 9
  need for mutuality of, 100
  negative experience of, 247n185
  obedience as essential element of, 29
  oriented toward reign of God, 197
  outer, 5
  paradox of, 8
  as pervasive theme in Christianity, 4–5
  philosophical critique of, 27–29
  practice of, counteracted by call for justice,
    27
  preserving the insight of, 8–9
  presupposing being gifted by God, 68
  as profound experience of humanity's
    not-yet realized wholeness, 204
  purpose of, 20–21
  purposeful, 188
  reinterpretation of, 26–27
  related to identity, 15
  religious identity and, 15–36
  renewing the symbol of, 226–31
  requiring discernment, 71
  as response to God, gift offering, and
    means of communion, 86

sacrifice (*continued*)
  risks of, 7–8
  shaping Christian discipleship, 14
  shifting status of, 35–36
  spiritualization of, in Judaism, 28–29, 30,
    33
  spiritualized orientation toward,
    influencing Christian approach, 27
  as spiritual obedience, 62–63
  symbol of, in relation to Christian identity
    and action, 226
  symbolism of, used to describe one who
    follows Jesus, 13
  terminated for Jews with destruction of the
    Temple, 27
  theology of, 59–60, 64
  theories of, 17–21
  tragic element of, 142–43
  transforming identity through, 21–23
  viewed from conjunctural history
    perspective, 76
  as way of God, 222
  women's history of, marked by sexism, 78
  as worship made incarnate through love of
    neighbor, 16
sacrifice of abandonment, 22–23, 212
sacrifice of prophylactics, 22–23, 212
*Sacrifice: Its Nature and Function* (Hubert
  and Mauss), 20–21
sacrificial creativity, 230–31
sacrificial discipleship
  as affirmation of Christian identity, 203
  Trinitarian definition of, 205–6
sacrificial identity, linked with new
  relationship to God, 200
sacrificial images, fluidity of, 209
sacrificial language, historical developments
  in, 74–78
sacrificial sacramental economy, participation
  in, 221–24
sacrificial symbolism, complexity of, in New
  Testament writers, 54–56
sacrificial symbols, 208
sacrifier, distinct from sacrificer, 21
Saiving, Valerie, 101–9, 111, 116, 118, 130,
  210
salvation
  as cosmic hope, 200–201
  expectation of affected by current world-
    views and interpretation of human
    nature, 170
  as an experience of Jesus, 171

salvation (*continued*)
  as fullness of human life, 201–2
  offered, despite human rejection and the
    cross, 205
  principles that structure the experience of,
    170–73
  related to a person's experience of Jesus,
    170
  tension with liberation, 172
salvation history canon, 39
Sartre, Jean-Paul, 161
satisfaction theory, 83
Schillebeeckx, Edward, 12
  acknowledging risk of violence to self, 210
  approach to recognizing meaning, 194
  on capturing authentic meaning of a
    message, 77
  categories for distinctive experience of
    grace, 201, 203
  Christian salvation relating to a person's
    experience of Jesus, 170
  on Christology, 167
  on communion between human and divine,
    200
  continuance principle, 65
  core elements for, 157–58
  creation as central theme for, 155–58,
    161–62
  on cultural documents as expression of
    community faith, 208–9
  development of his thinking, 158–61
  developing model of human nature in
    relation to cosmos, 201
  emphasis on grace as mystical and political,
    203
  emphasis on social and global conditions
    of suffering, 212
  on experience, objective and subjective
    sides of, 187
  focusing on gladness and celebration in
    Jesus' relations with his disciples, 168
  on God's presence to creation, 166
  on God wanting human happiness and
    salvation, 163–67
  on Hebrews, 50–51, 53–54
  on human history and progress, 162–63
  identifying early frameworks for
    interpreting Jesus' death, 37, 38–40
  identifying suffering image of God, 225
  interest of, in contemplation, 172
  on interpreting one's ethical identity,
    212–13
  on intersubjectivity of life, 215

Schillebeeckx, Edward (*continued*)
  on Jesus' death, 179
  on Jesus' suffering, 175–78, 181–82
  juxtaposition of salvation (wholeness) and
    suffering, 155–56, 166–67
  on Last Supper as final extension of
    fellowship, 35
  non-sacrificial interpretations of Jesus'
    death, 56
  on other as privileged place for the
    experience of God, 197
  on paradox of self-sacrifice and self-
    realization, 175
  on principles that structure the experience
    of Christian salvation, 170–73
  realigning orientation of sacrificial action
    to God, 198
  resisting understanding of Jesus' suffering
    as salvific in itself, 156
  on sacrifice as charism of Christian identity,
    213–14
  on salvation as fullness of human life,
    201–2
  on the gospel parables, 168–69, 229
  salvation including earthly well-being, 155
  soteriological formulae as self-contained
    tradition, 40
  on suffering, 183–95
  on suffering being overvalued, 192–93
  on suffering revealing God, 186–87
  three ways of organizing interpretations of
    Jesus' death, 176
Schwager, Raymond, 40
science, supplanting faith, 184–85
scission of the norm, 260–61n362
Seasoltz, R. Kevin, 66–67, 222
self
  balancing with sacrifice, 210–12
  constituted reflexively through other,
    132–41
  determined by contrast with sameness, 127
  dimensions of, 201
  engaging in three relationships with
    otherness, 129
  ethical relationship with the other, 120
  interpreting, via the other, 127–31, 212–14
  offering of, as supreme sacrifice, 63
  ontology of, 125–31
self-abnegation, as sinful, 109
self-actualization, of everyone by everyone
    else, 144
self-constancy, 142

self-denial, 7
  women's predisposition to, 101
self-esteem
  containing expression of desire for
    company of others, 133
  primacy of, 135
selfhood, treated as hermeneutical topic,
  11
self-imputation, having exterior origin,
  135
self-interpretation, intersecting with
  scriptural interpretation, 146
self-knowledge, as interpretation, 125
self-love
  affirmation of, 211–12
  characterized as unchristian, 98
  as Christian virtue, 109
  distrust of, 98–99
  expression of seeking the soul's true
    fulfillment, 6
  grounding love of others, 96–97
  paradox of, 3–4
  related to love of neighbor, 6–7
  retrieving, 99–101
self-other relationship, as relationship of
  equals, 11
self-realization
  canon of, 64–65
  discovered in the process of surrender,
    132
  productive tension with self-sacrifice,
    117–18, 212
self-realizing sacrifice, 231
self-regard, 259n352
self-sacrifice
  balanced with self-realization, 97, 108–9
  distortion of, 79–80
  idealization of, as paradigm of Christian
    love, 98
  involving inner paradox, 3
  judging the value of, 12
  male recommendations of, for women,
    79–80
  as means of self-realization, 72–73, 81
  as necessary part of Christian identity, 1
  productive tension with self-realization,
    117–18, 192–93, 212
  united with self-realization, 1
  as way to God, 222
self-sacrificing love, 66–67
self-understanding, Ricoeur's insight on,
  119
Semmelroth, Otto, 67–68, 69

service
  call to, expressed with Christological
    emphasis on the cross, 190
  under the proviso of the reign of God,
    195–99
serving
  as ethical paradigm framing the Last
    Supper and the passion, 180
sexism, intensifying an imbalanced
  understanding of sacrifice, 78–79
Shaw, Anna Howard, 100
sin
  against creation, 116–17
  different for men and women, 102
  as evasion of responsibility, 111
  as failure to transcend limits, 110–11
  imbalanced view of, resulting from placing
    pride as dominant mode, 109
  in light of natural transcendence, 112–15
  for men, as aggressive response to anxiety,
    102, 103
  opposite of forgiveness, 109
  opposite to love, 102
  as rebellion against God, 111
  as violation of empathy, memory, or
    imagination, 113
sin offerings, 20, 85–86
solicitude, drawing on self-esteem, 133–34
spirituality, mystical and political, 196
spiritual offerings, 85–86
spiritual worship, 58
spiritual/reasonable sacrifice, 58–60
Stanton, Elizabeth Cady, 7, 79
Stott, Wilfrid, 244–45n140
Strawson, P. F., 256n
structural history, 75
Suchocki, Marjorie Hewitt, 10, 96, 109–18,
  130, 194, 210, 223
suffering
  caused by human sin, 165
  chosen sacrificial actions serving as seal on
    one's willed identity, 183
  cognitive effect of, 186
  of the disciple, 189–95
  God regarding with favor, 191–92
  having meaning, as purposeful sacrifice,
    188
  human, opacity of, 193–95
  implicit ethical demand of, 186
  innocent, acceptability of, 190–91
  interpreting, in light of Jesus' sacrifice, 174
  marking Christian identity through
    imitation of Christ, 182

suffering (*continued*)
 meaning of, centered in dedication to a
  chosen value, 192, 193
 for others, 191, 194
 Schillebeeckx's resistance to, 175
 tolerance of, 73
 as unifying experience, 183–84
"Suffering God" theologies, 84, 89
suffering servant imagery, 32, 64–65
summoned self, 146–48
surrogacy, cross as, critiqued by womanists,
 92–97
suspicion, use of, to discipline interpretation,
 123–24
sweet savour, 27
*Symbolism of Evil* (Ricoeur), 122–23
symbols
 hermeneutics of, 122–25
 need for mutual hospitality of, with
  criticism, 124
 power of, 122–23
 as resource for self-interpretation, 124
systematic philosophy, failure of, to absorb
 the hermeneutics of myth, 123

Taylor, Charles, 147
Terrell, JoAnne Marie, 92, 94–96
theopaschite theologies, 89
Till, Emmett, 96
Tillich, Paul, 88, 110
*Time and Narrative* (Ricoeur), 125, 254n307
*todah*, 28–29, 41
Torah, proof of God's love, 169
*Totality and Infinity: An Essay on Exteriority*
 (Levinas), 135
Tracy, David, 209, 224, 225
 comparing chaos and creation at the
  human level, 231
 on the polarity of religion, 226–28
tragedy, generative potential of, 186

tragic awareness, 142
transcendence
 horizontal view of, 113–14
 possibilities for, 117
*Trinity, The* (Augustine), 147–48
Turner, Victor, 18, 212
 approaching sacrifice as a social practice,
  22
 two models of sacrifice, 22–23
 using Christian language to label models
  of sacrifice, 22–23

Venema, Henry Isaac, 252n
vicarious martyr tradition, 40
von Balthasar, Hans Urs, 88–89

Walker, Alice, 96–97
Wallace, Mark I., 122, 140, 146
Whitehead, Alfred North, 115
wholeness
 as goal of Christian living, 97
 paradoxical type of, 198–99
 quest for, having religious dimension, 173
Williams, Delores, 92–93, 94, 95–96
willing, act of, associated with valuing and
 choosing the good, 132
womanist Christology, 94–95
womanist theology, critiquing the cross as
 surrogacy, 92–97
women
 punished because of identification with
  Eve, 79–80
 strengths of, correlating with natural
  weaknesses, 102–3
 tendency of, toward self-abnegation,
  104–5
worship, 5
 sacrifice related to, 15–16

Young, Frances, 15–16, 20, 21, 45, 61

# Of Related Interest

**Elizabeth A. Johnson**
**CONSIDER JESUS**
*Waves of Renewal*
*in Contemporary Christology*

The best introduction to Jesus available in English. Perfect for adult education classes, individuals, and study groups.

"Thoughtful readers will find profound theological insights into the person and mission of Jesus Christ.... To read *Consider Jesus* is to experience popular theology at its very best." — *Sisters Today*

0-8245-1161-1, paperback

Check your local bookstore for availability.
To order directly from the publisher,
please call 1-800-707-0670 for Customer Service
or visit our Web site at *www.cpcbooks.com*.
For catalog orders, please send your request to the address below.

THE CROSSROAD PUBLISHING COMPANY
16 Penn Plaza, Suite 1550
New York, NY 10001

crossroad